D1599975

The Hieroglyph of Tradition

The Hieroglyph of Tradition

Freud, Benjamin, Gadamer, Novalis, Kant

Angelika Rauch

Madison • Teaneck
Fairleigh Dickinson University Press
London: Associated University Presses

FLORIDA GULF COAST
UNIVERSITY LIBRARY

© 2000 by Associated University Presses, Inc.

All rights reserved. Authorization to photocopy items for internal or personal use, or the internal or personal use of specific clients, is granted by the copyright owner, provided that a base fee of $10.00, plus eight cents per page, per copy is paid directly to the Copyright Clearance Center, 222 Rosewood Drive, Danvers, Massachusetts 01923. [0 8386–3846–5/00 $10.00 + 8¢ pp, pc.]

Associated University Presses
440 Forsgate Drive
Cranbury, NJ 08512

Associated University Presses
16 Barter Street
London WC1A 2AH, England

Associated University Presses
P.O. Box 338, Port Credit
Mississauga, Ontario
Canada L5G 4L8

The paper used in this publication meets the requirements of the American National Standard for Permanence of Paper for Printed Library Materials Z39.488—1984.

Library of Congress Cataloging-in-Publication Data

Rauch, Angelika, 1956–
    The hieroglyph of tradition : Freud, Benjamin, Gadamer, Novalis, Kant / Angelika Rauch.
        p. cm.
    Includes bibliographical references and index.
    ISBN 0–8386–3846–5 (alk. paper)
    1. Tradition (Philosophy) 2. History—Philosophy. I. Title.

B105.T7 .R38 2000
148—dc21

                                                                        99–086009

PRINTED IN THE UNITED STATES OF AMERICA

To
Herman Rapaport
and
Hanno Rauch Rapaport

Contents

Introduction

THIS BOOK ATTEMPTS A CRITIQUE OF THE CONCEPT OF HISTORY BY juxtaposing it to a carefully argued theory of tradition. Rather than investigating tradition as a collection of things, this book tries to explain tradition as a communicative process of transmitting experience and meaning. By arguing that histories of human experience are necessary for the creation of meaning, this book shows that we cannot do without tradition if we want to use language for understanding both others and ourselves.

In recent years, attacks on canonical works in the humanities by sociologically oriented critiques have made the word tradition objectionable. Such criticism considers *tradition* to be nothing more than socially elitist and politically reactionary. Critics of tradition assume that traditions deny a constructivist or nominalist philosophy that these critics themselves embrace. This is the conviction that ideas and values are in essence relativistic social or linguistic constructions that are politically motivated by those whose interests are backed by social and political power. In other words, the notion of tradition has been equated to intellectual hegemony (so-called "gatekeeping") and ideology (false consciousness). Such criticism of tradition has necessarily turned a blind eye to what is irresistible and ineradicable in tradition, namely, the transmission and transformation of meaning in language. Precisely because meanings of words do, in fact, change, the interpretations of cultural ideas also change. Unlike history, tradition is not an inventory of represented facts; it is never monolithic or absolute but a process in which events are continuously translated and retranslated into idioms of language and figures of speech. Tradition is responsible for metaphorical, symbolic, and allegorical uses of language. Such figural uses of language have a human history that is not recorded in history books, for this type of history is one of feelings and imagination.

Despite these recent attacks on tradition, however, there has been increasing awareness in Europe, at least, of a "crisis of transmission," namely, the substitution of information for education in the sense of personal formation or *Bildung*. At the heart of this crisis is a concern that tradition is being replaced by what in France is called "l'informatique," the technology of electronically dispensing historical or statistical facts without regard for any sort of critical or hermeneutical background that would require the development of an integrated historical memory. The issue that presently concerns European educators is not simple recollection, but historical cognition, the ability to critically analyze information through the careful development of various mental abilities, among them, reason, imagination, and judgment. Given the fragmented immediacy of an informatic electronic apparatus like the personal computer, there is concern that informatics, which shortcuts the thinking process, has much more general appeal to the public than education, which requires concentrated cognitive development. Worrysome is that informatics will increasingly replace education, "l'instruction," something that Europeans are noticing with alarm in first world countries. In essence, tradition is alien to informatics in that tradition is a hermeneutical understanding of history that requires reflecting on one's own experience. Informatics merely layers data in such a way that an index or logic tree becomes the dominant interpretive correlative. What has become evident to European intellectuals like Alain Finkelkraut is that students who are informatic in orientation are incapable of thinking through historical materials in logical and imaginative ways, since for them these materials are atomized bits of information—what in America are called "factoids"—that cannot be synthesized or brought into meaningful, cultural, or social relation.

Both "l'informatique" and constructivist cultural criticism—as inspired by Bill Gates and Michel Foucault, respectively—strategically forget that there are real social subjects with particular psychologies who are not reducible to technical manipulation. One has to recognize the existence of subjects with personal psychologies who necessarily imagine themselves and organize their lives in terms of there being a tradition or sociohistorical context or situation that transcends the limits of the individual. Indeed, what I will demonstrate at great length is that tradition is an essential part of how one experiences the world, since without tradition experience lacks those orientations to the past that enables one to be adequately situated. Tradition, in other words, is a necessary part of cognition and a vital part in managing, interpreting, and applying information to our lives.

In my attempt to rethink the concept or, rather, the cognitive process of tradition, I turn to Immanuel Kant who, in my reading of his *Critique of Judgment*, had already demonstrated that tradition required both conscious and unconscious individual experiences that are inherently in dialogue with the past and its relation to the present. Mental faculties, historico-philosophically defined as imagination, genius, judgment, and wit, must be active in such a way that the individual is brought into a complex experiential relation with the past that breaks with simple linear temporality and the mechanical repeating of official histories or, as Jean-François Lyotard calls them, master narratives. Indeed, it is within a certain history of aesthetics, one that privileges affect and desire over instrumental reason or Platonic forms, that Kant is of importance as someone who initiates a philosophy of experience by examining what humans feel and think in the realm of the beautiful. Kant was the first to determine the importance of feeling in our ability to judge that something is unique. However, the feeling of pleasure is never new; it is a repetition of a forgotten, pleasurable past. Therefore I treat aesthetic experience as the prototype of experience as such, because its analysis demonstrates how the past signifies for the present.

Hermeneutically inclined thinkers such as Freud, Benjamin, Gadamer, and the Romantic philosopher, Novalis, virtually unknown in the Anglo-American philosophical tradition, explore how language, the body, sensation, experience, subjectivity, desire, affect, and rhetorical figures relate to ways in which individuals come to an interpretive understanding of their own relationship to the past. Indeed, by coming to terms with tradition as the transmission or transference of human experience, we are more likely to achieve an understanding of how emotion affects our individual and collective psychological experience of the past, something that cannot be achieved by turning to historical conceptions that avoid individual experience. My position is that the only vehicle for this kind of transmission is language and the intense mental operations that reading demands. But not just the awareness of a cognitive self is at stake, the self's capacity and motivation to relate to others seems equally jeopardized by the decline of literacy. As the TV critic David Marc observes in Bonfire of the Humanities: "Reading a book opens the conduit from page to eye to body. The ink alphabet signs are transformed into meanings and images that penetrate the body as irony, fear, anger, and so on, stimulating the emotional capacities for *empathy and sympathy.* The body is seduced and entertained as the mind is instructed."[1] Although Marc grants and advocates both the synaesthetic pleasure of multimedia experience and the socially emancipatory effects of mass-media dominance and access to information, he questions whether the system of culture made possible by mass communications technology can fulfill the physically based emotional needs of the atomized consumer. "The chronic epidemic of clinical depression, the rising rates of murder, suicide, and random violence . . . the appearance of whole new psychosomatic ailments . . . are evidence of a population that has been disconnected from the roots of its organic capacity to remember: to recall, to re-experience, to recuperate, to recreate itself."[2] Skipping around in virtual reality represents a search for something to remember, with an indifference to what one should forget.

Tradition is also crucial in that it gives us the inner resources with which to contemplate our life histories in the context of ethics. At least my understanding of tradition implies an ethical dimension that familiar conceptions of history lack. Here I am sympathetic to the kind of analysis done by Charles Taylor in *The Ethics of Authenticity*. Taylor argues that modern and postmodern societies place a high value on self-fulfillment; hence, such secular societies encourage us to seek a fulfilling pleasure that is experienced as authentic. For Taylor authenticity is an ethical concept since it responds to the historical collective activities of men and women. I infer from this that authenticity is a fundamental ethical concept basic to converting the mere externality of historical facticity into tradition: the past as psychologically internalized and hence truly experienced. Following Hegel, Taylor argues that we are dependent upon others—that is, society—to set standards, if for no other reason than that consciousness requires these others (or, as some say, an Other) to acknowledge and recognize its successes and failures. Since others in official and unofficial capacities represent the laws for behavior and desirable identities, we are bound to other people by virtue of what they represent for us. What we take to be the law is the practice of others. If we object to that law or standard, we have to confront it in others, since, in any case, we hardly lead a solipsistic existence and are necessarily involved in communal and hence ethical lives. Since we always encounter the other in agreement or disagreement, pleasure or displeasure, our being takes shape in ethically affective life histories.

With the dissolution or abandonment of traditional communities in countries like the United States, the importance of the "significant other" is vitiated both in the sense of a guiding law and the authentic involvement of actual persons. Only by way of a tradition can the Other establish a frame of reference or horizon of signification that is meaningful for the individual. Hence, the loss of community—the living in immediate relation to a significant other—threatens the possibility of meaningful existence, an existence whereby meaning is a creative process that involves the other as a standard to work with and against. No longer reckoning with an authentic other, who no longer models, incites, responds or criticizes, the subject is out of bounds with respect to consciousness of what determines him. Of course, there is still an other of some sort—say, a virtual other such as a movie star or advertisement model—but this other merely pretends to be an authentic self and substitutes for this self in the form of an imaginary consciousness that more often than not reproduces state or corporate ideology.

Of interest to my theory of tradition—experience as preserved, transmitted, and transformed in language—is that, in contrast, Taylor sees ideology as a form of illiteracy, something that anticipates recent debates over "l'informatique." According to Taylor, those under the spell of ideology are not literate because they are unable to understand anything that is not prefabricated. In connection with Taylor's concern for history, illiteracy means, above all, the disappearance of those reading and writing skills in our culture that enable us to express ourselves in our own words. The importance of writing would lie not merely in the replication of thoughts, but in the creation of new and original meanings. When we use language consciously, we are not parroting but working and reworking a repertoire of possible thoughts and expressions already formulated by others. We *actively* relate in writing and reading to these other human beings. Our relation thus takes the form of dialogue; we respond to what others have said in language while, at the same time, expanding the horizon of what is sayable. Without such an active response, we shun our responsibility for what is happening, that is, for history as a happening.

In the current aftermath of the critique of the sign (semiotics and deconstruction), Gadamer's theory of hermeneutics, which explains how we respond to cultural signs and their history, supplies a necessary humanist correction to not only cultural illiteracy in Taylor's sense, but to various deconstructionist and postmodern critiques that aestheticize a dehumanized, fragmented culture. The rejection or lack of hermeneutical understanding prevents us from assuming not only responsibility but also historical agency, given that as critics we use language to comment on, shape, and change ideas about life. Obviously, such work in and with language is always chiefly a matter of communication, what in modernity often substitutes for the myth of a lost community.

In the history of cultures, the fundamental desire for communication and community has been articulated in the search for an ideal state of living together. It is primarily this search for a social utopia that connects us historically with previous generations. *Tradition* is the manifest form of this search for happiness and is an ongoing process of interpreting human experience in light of this eternally shared desire of harmony between self and other. Within this historically shared desire, *history* is not the object of the search, but, on the contrary, its temporary arrest in the production of meaning that feels true for the here and now. This is a historical truth, limited by the historical experience of people. The temporality of meaning guarantees the possibility of change, though historical change requires a lesson learned from the past—the meaning of the past. Change is not possible without remembrance and working through, and tradition supports the habitus of remembering which revives the meaning of history for its revision in the present. The struggle for meaning is never over, but the future, as Walter Benjamin has said, is an experience of time "in which every second represents the small doorway through which the messiah might enter."[3]

My text is divided into four parts. Part one introduces the idea that tradition rather than history is the process by means of which experience is transmitted, transformed, and translated into language. Only through tradition do we really come to know the past as something that can be personally felt. I turn to the role of language in the awareness and interpretation of experience and consider Hayden White's demonstration of how the rhetorical, even fictional representation of history in textual forms, can be juxtaposed with Jacques Lacan's analysis of desire. I show that our sense of history is constructed by affective textual representations and not the acquisition of factual knowledge which is, in essence, inert. These affective representations have a transformative effect on our minds because they implicate our own biography within the context of a cultural history that is the product of language. The question of what motivates the cultural production of signs as a replacement for an inaccessible but longed for experience of the past points the way toward future chapters on aesthetic representation and a psychological cleavage between *Vorstellung* and *Darstellung*.

Part two represents a revision of German Idealism in order to philosophically ground how tradition is a constitutive part of cognition. In this part I examine Kant's *Critique of Judgment* for a precise definition of *Vorstellung* and its centrality in aesthetic experience. This is crucial, since in Kant *Vorstellung* takes to the side of tradition, while *Darstellung* takes to the side of history. I argue that Kant grounds aesthetic judgments in the feeling of pleasure which answers a desire for pleasure and the memory of bliss and that hence the problematic nature of a "transcendental" imagination free of bodily affects is exposed and attacked within an argument for a historical imagination tinted by feeling and unconscious memories. I also advance an excursus into the history of "wit," since wit can be demonstrated to be a faculty of unconscious association in Kant whose creative capacity is essentially based on what Kant has referred to as "mother wit," the natural talent (of taste) that can find meaningful connections between dissimi-

lar things. This justifies my attempt to link the aesthetic with the historical—first as a biological (drive) disposition in the individual and second in
social (self/other relations) fantasies that sustain cultural experience. From
this vantage point, the eighteenth century's discourse on perfection and
beauty is opened up for a psychoanalytic interpretation of art and subjectivity that shows Kant's leaning to tradition, as I have defined it, rather than
to history per se. Finally, I position Kant in terms of a relation between
genius and spirit. Genius is the faculty that turns a person's fantasies into
linguistic representations. Kant's model of the mind inverts itself when the
productions of unconscious fantasy turn out to be the actual social support of artistic genius through the communal agreement on taste. What is
crucial and new in my analysis of Kant is less a correspondence between
the faculty of genius (the artist) and the capacity for taste (the recipient)
than the fact that this mutual resonance occurs through the medium of
language. Therefore what is handed down to us from the past in works
of art are not fixed images or symbols of ideas but affects which still res-
onate in our own experience and which we have to grasp with images of
our own.

Part three interprets the fragmented philosophical work of the German
Romantic thinker Novalis, who is generally only known through his
poetry. I chose to write on Novalis because he carries further Kant's analysis of aesthetics. I consider how the ideas of Novalis on genius, *Geist*, and
language approach Freud's findings, if not to say, Benjamin's thoughts on
language and memory. Although Novalis elaborates the same aesthetic
concepts as Kant, a conceptual break exists between the two thinkers. It is
within this break that I believe many of Benjamin's ideas take place. Also,
my treatment of Novalis foreshadows my later argument of how Gadamerian hermeneutics and its concern with tradition might still be relevant in
today's era of *post-histoire*. This coincides with my reading of Benjamin
which emphasizes his synthesis of history and psychoanalysis within the
context of a theoretical formulation of tradition. Lastly, I will argue that, if
early Romanticism (1785–1805) is commonly seen as a German idealism
that has detached itself from the material world, Novalis demonstrates a
shift toward materialism through his emphasis on language and the materiality of the sign. Novalis, in fact, prefigures Benjamin's theory of allegory,
which will be the main theme of part four.

Supplying a connection between Benjamin and Novalis clarifies the
methodological significance of the hieroglyph: that signs have to be read as
an assemblage of meaning, not decoded as organic symbols, as German
Idealism would have it. The hieroglyph is a metaphor for the remnants of
experience that need to be read, put together, instead of interpreted. In the

hieroglyph both Novalis and Benjamin express the idea that experience underlies the signifying structure of language.

Finally, I build on the legacy of Novalis for 20th-century hermeneutics and, in particular, Gadamerian hermeneutics. If Gadamer is lacking the psychoanalytic component that Novalis at least foreshadows, Gadamer centralizes the idea of the subject's need to consciously acquire a horizon of meaning and gain a sense of historicity by engaging a literary tradition. In place of subjectivity and a well-developed theory of language, Gadamer offers a theory of "pre-judgments" that can push a hermeneutic model of text and mind or history and culture much further, once a structuralist analysis is applied to his critique of the logos. I do this by using Lacan's material reading of the signifier because it supplies Gadamer's hermeneutics with the missing psychoanalytic dimension of language. That is, language already interprets our unacknowledged desires and repressed experiences.

The appeal to Lacan underscores my interest in the psychoanalytical situation as a necessary dialogue that takes into account both the historicity of experience and the variability of language, its inadvertent figurality in the expression of affective contents. The psychological process at work in the interpretation of feelings, thoughts, and memories as triggered by language was already anticipated in the philosophical work of Wilhelm Dilthey, who is a major precursor of contemporary hermeneutics. However, unlike those who came after him, Dilthey had idealized consciousness and self-reflexivity. Edmund Husserl, Martin Heidegger, and Hans Georg Gadamer were all highly critical of Dilthey's so-called "psychologism," and Gadamer took the step of revising Dilthey by means of a linguistic turn in which Gadamer stressed the historicity of language and cognition. Gadamer's hermeneutics counteracted Dilthey's idealism, but it did so at the cost of suppressing the affective character of experience that is germane to language. Moreover, Gadamer's linguistic turn failed to address the possibility of an unconscious dimension to hermeneutics, let alone questions of desire and fantasy in language and experience. This objection has been fundamental to various French thinkers influenced by phenemonology, among them, Paul Ricoeur, Maurice Merleau-Ponty, and Jacques Lacan. Yet, whereas such French thinkers have transposed hermeneutics into a Cartesian philosophical key, I have remained faithful to a tradition that has its roots in German Idealism. It is here that I introduce a psychoanalytical frame of reference in order to better assess the epistemological foundations of hermeneutics. In addition to mounting a critique of Gadamerian hermeneutics, a psychoanalytical frame of reference enables me to address what I see as the inchoate project in Walter Benjamin's critique of history and language, namely a theory of tradition that emphasizes the cognitive value of the material history of affective experience. Similarly, my analyses of Kant and Novalis show that there is a rigorous philosophical groundwork for discussing unconscious affective hermeneutical issues independently of Freud and that retroactively a Freudian understanding of psychoanalysis also enables us to see some of the strengths and weaknesses in both Kant and Novalis's epistemologies.

Part four is devoted exclusively to Walter Benjamin and follows from previous discussions of how figurality and rhetorical structures of language affect us emotionally. I try to bring the body-oriented meaning effects of literary tradition down to the common denominator of allegorical reading strategies that can retrieve a forgotten past. Since allegory in Benjamin recycles the fragments or "ruins" of historical meanings, I present the structure of the hieroglyph as an allegorical configuration of signifiers within an enigmatic master-sign (or totalizing emblem). This enigmatic mega-sign refers to the initial unreadability of (artistic) texts that no longer imitate nature but refigure cultural history.

I elaborate on Benjamin's association of the hieroglyph with the "death mask of history." Insofar as the hieroglyph corresponds to word clusters or figures in a specific text, I propose that Benjamin turned to allegory in order to represent a historical moment in which hieroglyphs are relevant to a retrospection in which we become aware of language as a literature at once idiomatic and figural. Moreover, Benjamin used allegory because of the psychological effect that it had, especially as a motive for developing our historical sensibility as readers.

Lastly, I maintain that language projects the passions and the sufferings of previous generations into the subject's realm of experience. These passions inform the coinage of linguistic tropes and metaphors which create the horizon of our ideas about life. Here I link Jacques Derrida's exposure of ideas as originally constructed images in language with Benjamin's examination of the *Trauerspiel* for a dead physis that speaks the body in the allegorical requisites on the baroque stage. Besides Benjamin and Novalis, Derrida, too, considers the hieroglyph (symbol for his attempt to write the "history of writing") as the origin whence meaning and sense emanates. The melancholia typical of allegorical scenes that deconstruct hieroglyphs stems from the symbolical status of metaphors that has dissociated us, over time, from the mortality of our own bodies. Benjamin, however, shows that the alienated creaturely body finally appears on the stage of consciousness as part of an unknown collective world or, as I will suggest, an historical unconscious in language. Hence I conclude that ideas are derived from bodily experiences and feelings that structure our unconscious memory through the *mnemic* work of a linguistic tradition.

The Hieroglyph of Tradition

Part I

History or Tradition?

1

Tradition: Search for the Lost Object

> There is neither an entity nor a sacred hypostasis of community—there
> is the "unleashing of passions," the sharing of singular beings, and the
> communication of finitude. In passing to its limit, finitude passes "from"
> the one "to" the other: this passage makes up sharing [*Mit-teilen*].
> —(Jean-Luc Nancy, *The Inoperative Community*)

EVEN IF HISTORY AND TRADITION BOTH SHARE A SEARCH FOR LOST
objects and for time past, they are not interchangeable terms. History is
generally understood as an account of events that lie in the past—known
only through the record they have left behind. Such events have no meaning
unless we give them significance by interpreting the evidence. That is, without attaching significance to the event through narrative or other forms of
symbolization, we could not register the event as such, and hence could not
appropriate it into our repertoire of knowing the world. Indeed, it is precisely this repertoire of knowledge that I will be calling tradition. After all,
this kind of knowledge is not a positivistic accumulation of facts, but is inherently hermeneutical, by which I mean that it is based on the interpretive
significance of a cultural history that has meaning for us as individuals. But
what motivates individuals to want to know the past and interpret history?
I take this question to be the same as "why do we continuously try to make
sense of our experiences, our lives"? I will try to link this question of the
desire for meaning by exploring the tools we use, both consciously and
unconsciously, to create meaning from the past.

From the hermeneutical perspective, as Hans-Georg Gadamer has developed it, the past is experienced as a quasi-entity because of the meaning
it has in the present. Yet this meaning differs in status and quality from
finite knowledge, that is, from the significance of specific events which constitute knowledge in the scientific sense. For tradition manifests itself not as
knowledge, but as legacy or inheritance and is therefore transferential in

a psychoanalytic sense. As such, it contributes to the way in which we feel about what we know and to the way in which we translate experience into meaning. Hence, tradition is related to a search process with the aim of finding out the significance of events past.

Since the desire for meaning formation emerges from a desire toward integrating the other into the self, experience is motivated by a myth of self-sameness that is carried on in a culture and its historical representations. By virtue of this myth, culture is not the same as tradition but rather its stage of enactment. Inasmuch as the identity of the self is defined in relation to an other, it is also always a product of tradition, which is to say a product motivated by the desire for meaning. But given such a concept of identity, the difference between tradition and history becomes one of an open-ended formation. Tradition regulates the movement of desire, whereas history brings this movement to an end in a representation of the other as self. History in its manifestation of representations cannot deal with a different idea of the Other, namely, that which underlies the formation of representations. This Other I will address as the force of desire.

If history as past event is the unrecoverable object of a search whose process I have related to tradition, why the search at all? The answer may not be a rational one; and by the same token, the search may not be conscious. For at issue is always a necessary desire for the lost object, or precedent, that motivates the search. But what constitutes desire as a psychological phenomenon as such? And, by extension, what role does tradition play on a psychological level for us as individuals? As we know, desire stems from an awareness of a lack and results in a feeling of dissatisfaction with the status quo. But unlike a need that can be filled, desire transcends material and physical needs that, when conscious, can be acted upon. Desire therefore refers to a metaphysical state of bliss which is negatively expressed in a feeling of longing. "Long-ing" addresses a distance, the far-away property of this state. Its distance pertains to a temporal distance between the present and the past in which this blissful state was experienced, an experience that is remembered in the feeling of longing.

Psychoanalysis has shown, within its psychogenetic model of the individual, that the experience of bliss refers to the early stage of childhood when the subject existed in union with the mother. Psychodynamically, this blissful experience of wholeness becomes the lost object of desire. Freud derives these virtually first experiences of satisfaction from the child's physical needs which, due to the child's helplessness, can only be satisfied by the mother, an external other. This first experience, Freud says, is essential for the development of the psychological processes of perception and memory.[1] The memory, which in this case is pleasurable experience, unconsciously imbues the representations of perceived objects. Freud thus proposes the concept of "perceptual identities" (*Wahrnehmungsidentität*). These are not true representations of the objects, but are merely linked to them metonymically by triggering an experience of satisfaction that is not contingent on the object itself but on its cathexis with the libido. Thus the perceptual identities contain the potential to become signs for a satisfactory experience. Freud characterizes this as an association of memory with a new object representation and hence as cathexis of the primary process. Yet these associations have to be kept in check by repression—the task of the secondary process—so as to create identity in the psychical order, and especially with regard to verbal representations.[2]

In its complete identification with the mother, the subject enjoys a feeling of wholeness that, in later stages of differentiation between self and (m)other, is remembered only by a feeling of incompleteness and unspecified lack, or lack-in-being. Since the original union with an other, and thus the first identity via identification with the other, is lost, the subject is "driven" to compensate for its lack-in-being by seeking replacement objects for pleasurable identification. While this search is an ongoing process, the goal of regaining the original experience, and of finding one's origin, is perpetually delayed in a detour through surrogate objects, situations or acts which constitute a history in the form of noticeable and significant instances.

Freud derived the concept of perceptual identity from an analysis of the individual's history, connecting it with the analysis of the person's psychological construction of present reality. In the psychoanalytical approach to experience and meaning formation, these connections between individual history and psyche came to constitute the psychological basis of transforming perceptions into experiences in the sense of meaning events. The problem lurking in this approach concerns the role of cultural history in the construction of meaning. Specifically, the question might be formulated as "what determines the significance of Freud's concern with childhood states for cultural history?" If childhood experiences reach their maturity in the adult's construction of his or her reality, what is the influence of the cultural past for that construction? It seems to me that this question cannot be answered within the sole confines of psychoanalysis unless one accepts a phylogenetic and hence evolutionary model of history. Freud, himself, while torn between a biological and cultural model, seems to have been ambivalent about such a phylogenetic conclusion, an ambivalence that, in my mind, he never resolved.[3]

In dealing with this question, insight was achieved by Walter Benjamin who tried to think psychoanalysis and history together by shifting their relationship onto the linguisitc level as *the* cultural representative of history. The use of language in transforming events into meanings injects cultural history into the structure of experience. In experience the connection between language and cultural history creates the signifying framework for personal histories. Hence I take Benjamin's category of experience as the link in the synthesis of psychoanalytic explanation and historical significance. If the early experience of a lack-of-being unconsciously exerts its significance for the conscious judgment of later experiences, namely, that they do not yet regain the desired unity of self and other, then this desire necessarily must be evident in language through the representation and evaluation of events that take place. The appropriation of an event in the form of knowledge depends on the constituents of such knowledge, or better yet, on the tradition of possible meanings and possible changes in meaning. Tradition is never static but a process that transforms knowledge and creates new meanings. The context for experience is not only woven by a desire for knowledge that objectifies an event, but also by a desire for the capability of representing such an event within the historical dimension of a culture that will have an effect on society. The desire for such a capacity of representing an originally pleasurable experience ultimately is a desire to represent desire itself, if not a desire to represent the lack-of-being or lack of happiness.

Historically, representations of desire assigned the task of cultivating political and social harmony to the domain of aesthetics. A happy state of life became a politicized aesthetic goal. This task may be said to derive from an awareness of the historical in relation to the desire for individual happiness. Once this correlation was made conscious in the Enlightenment, the idea of deliberately shaping history became the key to a philosophy of history. The political ideal of an aesthetic state spurned the historico-philosophical model for progress oriented history. But the political goal for such an aesthetic state yet needed to be defined. This provoked a definition of human happiness entailing a teleological representation of desire.

Any practical failure of historical thinking, that is, its failure as a historical critique of signs, stems from the transformation of historical consciousness into an ideology that justifies bad conditions in the present for the sake of a better future. In the case of ideology, people's awareness of unsatisfying conditions was kept in thrall by a propagated image of a utopian state which absorbed the potentially subversive energy of people's desires. The attempt to use controlled aesthetic images to define the subject by representing desire has its roots in a psychological need to dominate the Other as desiring subject. This avoidance (particularly on the part of Kant) of integrating a reflection on what motivates the production of signs distinguishes, for instance, the concept of history in the Enlightenment from that in early German Romanticism. By reexamining and subsequently recycling the mythological past into philosophical and aesthetic discourse, the Romantic philosophers discovered a critical potential in the mythos—the narrative and hence in the aesthetic effects of signifying human experience.[4] In the construction and analysis of stories, the Romantics dealt with history as a linguistic matter in the present, and not as an absolute or inevitable form in itself.

The utopian interpretation of history in temporal form, as the necessary interlude between the lost paradise of the past and its projection into the future, results in a conception of history as regressive utopia. This means that the actual here and now, the historical happening in the present, is forsaken, if not denied in the mind, by the fantasy of a better place. Politically the goal of happiness, of a societal state of happy individuals, underlies historical events and their interpretations that first determine the objects of history in line with the objectives of an officially sanctioned historiography.[5] This political treatment of myths of happiness demonstrates a slide from history into ideology. With the coming of the modern era, induced by the Enlightenment, the distinction between history as political reality and its knowledge or study was blurred. History came to mean both the event and the reflection on it.[6] History and ideology were no longer distinct entities.

By inquiring into the a priori of history and concluding that the prophet creates his own events, Kant[7] set the model for what Reinhart Koselleck has analyzed as *Machbarkeit der Geschichte*,[8] the disposability of history. If history could indeed be planned and calculated, it would require the possibility of a congruence between providence, plan, and its execution. Koselleck states that such congruence, however, is not possible as long as history is carried out by humans, rather than by perfect, godlike beings. Our experience or sense of history rests on the subject's lack of being, the human want for perfection and happiness. Thus, as long as lives are conducted in the here and now, experience is always historical and leads to an awareness of unfulfilled desires and the imperfection of the world. An end of history cannot, therefore, logically be in sight. The future needs to be open-ended, not a postponed fulfilled present. Moreover, any attempt at grasping history requires a misconception since history can only be "had" in its representations. That is, the image of history is always one step behind history's process because time does not merely elapse. Rather, life as physical experience, or eventfulness, goes on. The incommensurability between grasping, and thus getting hold of history, and the ungrasped (after)effects of the events themselves is registered in the structure of the psyche which cannot be programmed to grasp or mirror an objective reality. Displaced in time, the meaning of events has to be mentally constructed within a subjective if not even an unconscious frame of reference. That is, the individual wish for happiness and identity is psychoanalytically rooted in the *unconscious desire* for feeling whole and stems ultimately from an experience of physical dependence on another human being. This state of dependency, though wished for, can never be regained. Yet the subject's perception and sensation of its status quo will nonetheless always register the distance from the other and the missing feeling of happiness.

In his "Theses of History," Walter Benjamin elaborates on what he calls the claim of the past upon the present (*der Anspruch der Vergangenheit an die Gegenwart*) which I take to be a crucial aspect of the structure of experience (*Erfahrung*).[9] *Erfahrung* in German contains the idea of covering a distance, also that of motion, a movement which comes to an end in the present and is thus not something completed in the past. That which is completed in the past Benjamin describes as *Erlebnis*, a lived experience which, once it is over, can be recalled as an episode and as a point in time and space; as an episode that "happens" to a person (which can be later recalled), the experience does not have a significant power that might change a person's habit or thought.[10] *Erfahrung*, instead, implies history as process which has started in the past but goes on into the present. The distance covered is not an empty time space but a temporality in which meaning is produced. Colloquially speaking, we might say that *Erfahrung* involves a process of learning, and history would then mean a learning from the past.

A past experience, *Erlebnis*, has to have an effect on the present for it to be true experience or *Erfahrung*. Since this is an effect of which we are usually not conscious, and also one that emerges only at a later point in time, the original experience that is to have an effect in the meantime undergoes transformation. This implies a layered structure of experience. Yet the effect of transformation will represent itself as significant of the earlier experience only if the subject recognizes the experience and with it the past in a later event. Hence for an experience to be understood it has to be worked through. Significance, now defined as an effect from the past on the present, corresponds to Freud's law of *Nachträglichkeit*, a law that Freud derived from his analysis of subjective perception. It literally means retroaction, and Freud understood and applied this temporal concept to explain states of mind that are triggered by a similarity between an unconscious memory and a conscious perception in the present. The retroactive aspect in perception shifts an arbitrary here and now into re-cognition of objects already seen, known, or experienced. Bluntly put from a psychoanalytic perspective, a person may only see what s/he *already knows*. Making sense out of the here and now requires a previous knowledge, however in a state of anamnesis, which is activated when meaning has to be formed with respect to an event in the present. For the purpose of investigating the relationship between history, experience, and meaning, I prefer to translate Freud's concept of *Nachträglichkeit* as "deferred or belated meaning." The effect that an experience leaves behind, even though the experience might itself be forgotten, is a meaning effect for a later experience or perception of events.

Benjamin's theory of experience and history was clearly shaped by Freud's theory of "belatedness." This includes the concept of "secondary revision," unconscious mental activities through which humans produce meaning. Decisive for both thinkers is the function of time. Without time meaning would not be possible, because meaning always occurs after the event or originary experience. The event, or, rather, the "scene" that is primary for significance, turns out to be a lost object. This object can never be grasped but only inferred through the meaning it may have in and for the present. This meaning is necessarily a secondary occurrence comparable to Freud's secondary revision through which the object is represented in language. Hence, it seems to me that experience and language have a similar structure or mechanism of meaning.

To recognize a past experience in its significance at a later point in time, it must be remembered. However, this remembrance is different from just recalling various episodes or lived experiences stored in memory. Benjamin[11] takes this into account when he expands his concepts of *Erlebnis* and *Erfahrung* by adopting Freud's model of the mind, specifically his distinction between *Gedächtnis* or memory constituted by unconscious memory traces (*Gedächtnisspuren*), and consciousness, which Benjamin associates with *Erinnerung*[12] (recollection). *Erlebnis* names an experience that did not leave a trace in the unconscious and thus does not contribute to the thought structure of the individual psyche—the thought function (in German *Gedanke, denken*) is implied in Freud's term *Ge-dächt-nis* (memory). The reason *Erlebnis* did not leave a trace is its failure to enter the libidinal economy of the psyche which is responsible for the emotional structure of memory; in other words, the experience did not emotionally affect the subject. The affect as energy is actually responsible for leaving the trace that in turn shapes the disposition and responses of the subject toward a future incident. (Hence the experiences that leave a trace contribute to the personal history of the subject.) In this context, Benjamin's citation of Proust's *mémoire involontaire* explicates how his idea of *Erfahrung* relates to the psychical apparatus: "Only that which was not expressly and consciously experienced (*'erlebt'*), which did not happen (*widerfahren*) to the subject as lived experience (*Erlebnis*) can become a constitutive part of the *mémoire involontaire*."[13] In contrast, voluntary memory, as part of intelligence, can recall conscious experiences and use them much like information. Involuntary memory, however, is triggered when the subject remembers the past experience in the interpretation of a later event, most often, however, only in the form of feelings. Feelings in the psychoanalytic sense are already memories, repeated states of mind. They are the residue of an experience that cannot be remembered consciously. These repeated feelings are then transferred on to an object or mental representation, an image, in the present. Indeed, the best example for the repetition of feelings in perception is the feeling of pleasure as part of an aesthetic experience as, for instance, in the reception of a work of art.

Experience became a key issue for Benjamin when, as a cultural critic, he investigated the decline of the work of art in the course of the nineteenth century: the reception and experience of the aura and uniqueness of a specific work of art provided a means of positioning the subject in a certain cultural tradition. Experiencing a work of art, its human createdness, produced a historical awareness of human abilities and ideas thus linking the subject with the cultural past—the specific forms of existence of previous generations. With the reproducibility of art, the nature of aesthetic experience has changed by losing its potential for reflection and critique. In modernity, aesthetic experience no longer led the subject to knowledge and self-understanding within a tradition, but became a vehicle for vicarious pleasure: "The conventional is pleasurably absorbed without any critique."[14]

Given the mechanical copy quality of art, its original work aspect was lost. Without a visible temporality or labored involvement in time, the time of crafting an object, the reproduced work of art elicited a new experience. Smooth reproductions were not contemplated but "consumed." Lamenting the decline of true experience in modernity, Benjamin identifies a relationship between information and conscious experiences which prevents personal experience from interpreting or creating one's reality. Information or ineffective experiences, Benjamin says, distances the individual from his environment and ultimately from himself and thus paralyzes his imagination. Through the power of imagination, the individual is able to appropriate experiences and make them significant for himself.[15] *Erfahrung* bridges or breaks through distances by filling them with significance. This distance, I submit, is the "temporal space" of tradition through which experience passes and emerges as significance. Also of importance to me in this preliminary definition of tradition is the unconscious aspect of experience that achieves meaning only after it has been transformed by the "temporal space" of tradition.[16] That is, time changes from an abstract quantity to a quality of experience, and, ultimately, to the essence of meaning.

Being related to culture, tradition itself is not constituted by historical facts; instead, it entertains ties with a mythological past which is for the most part unconscious. Yet this mythic, cultural past effects the process of the transformation of experience into significance, framing the production of significance. "Experience is, in fact, a matter of tradition, in collective as well as in private life. It takes its shape less from single occurrences fixed in memory (*Erinnerung*) than from piled up and often unconscious data which merge in the mind (*Gedächtnis*)."[17] Tradition, as "temporal space," determines the effect of events retroactively as a belated meaning, as *Erfahrung*. But while it is determined or transformed, the experience as "a matter of tradition" remains unconscious because of the temporal distance covered outside of conscious time. Consequently, the production of significance proceeds unconsciously if not in the unconscious.[18]

Since I intend to link tradition to a concept of the unconscious during the course of this book, I will briefly introduce a useful definition of the unconscious found in Samuel Weber's reading of Freud: "If the unconscious means anything whatsoever, it is that the relation of self and others, inner and outer, cannot be grasped as an *interval between polar opposites* but rather as an irreducible dislocation of the subject in which the other inhabits the self as its condition of possibility."[19] Expanding Weber's understanding of the unconscious as displacement, I would argue that the condition of the self is the existence of tradition, that is, the experiences of others who came before us and who have inscribed their experiences into the language of tradition.

Tradition constitutes a nontangible realm which embraces the relation of selves and others. They need not merely be contemporaneous but may include past and future generations. More importantly, the mediating realm between selves and others, their communication through which the self is shared, is given in language. The German words for communication and communicating oneself are *Mit-teilung* and *sich mit-teilen* and illustrate the psychoanalytic notion of a divided or split self, clearly induced by language. Language as a preserver of historical meanings, which in turn are linguistic sedimentations of social forms of life, exercises a cultural power every time self and other interact and hence share each other in communication.

In imagining the process of division and fragmentation of the self in communication, the question arises, what happens to the various parts of the self? One answer is that they are reshuffled in the subject by each interaction, thus proving a subject capable of change. Another answer is that they are dispersed and sublated in language which renders language as a living, human entity that is nonseparable and "feeds" on the interaction of self and other. The subject, then, can only create meaning from its experiences if it can appropriate these experiences in language, a manifest realm of what I consider an *unconscious* tradition. It is through this tradition that the relation of the self to others is marked and inscribed as sense and as the potential for linguistic meaning in the psyche of the individual. However, what prefigures this relation is a force situated in tradition of which tradition is not a representation. And the force that causes this ongoing process of tradition as the interpretation of experience is desire. It is this desire, that can be faced in the metaphors and rhetorical structure of language, to which I turn in the following chapter.

2

The Representation of History

During the 1970s, Hayden White began arguing that the events and facts of history do not exist independently of their representation in language and therefore cannot be considered as things in themselves. He was right to point out that the act of interpreting a fact or representing a phenomenon as historically significant is dependent on cultural frames of signification. Hence questions like, how do we know about the past? or, how do we intuit a sense of history? necessarily concern the question of the representation (*Darstellung*) of history and its narrative forms. Indeed Hayden White has gone so far as to state that, "the 'overall coherence' of any given 'series' of historical facts is the coherence of the story form."[1] In thinking about such narrative form, White has drawn from Jean Piaget's model of cognitive childhood stages and has argued that in the interpre-tation of experience, the subject moves through an "archetypal plot of discursive formations," hence arriving at an objectified discursive representation.[2] In correlating mind and language this way, White assumes that there is a mimetic consciousness that formalistically encodes data as history, an encoding that could be reversed in order to recapture the event as raw data.

In my estimation, what might really be the case is an *unconscious* inscription of the event as an irreversible sign into a personalized language of interpretation. Here the language and text of history already prefigures reading by forming imaginative alliances with the subject's own memory. These significant alliances transform a text into a scene in which the relationship between subject and event as sign are played out, though not in a predictable course of archetypal figural discourses. In other words, I take distance from White's view which suggests the mechanical imposition of static narrative forms onto the material of history. Furthermore I take issue with White's assumption that language has the function of expressing only consciousness and that no place can be made for the unconscious expression of feeling or affect.

Despite some limitations, White is correct in (1) identifying the role of language use as crucial for the representation of historical facts and in (2) recognizing that cognition and narration are inherently linked. According to White, the effect of narrative forms consists in transforming a fact into part of a story that can no longer be entirely distinguished from fiction. The fact collaborates with the story form in terms of the linguistic construct of the fact's "factuality." Just as any story gains coherence by means of metaphorical aspects of language, the story of history, too, tries to represent something that is not physically present but needs to be imagined.[3] Imagination on the part of the reader is therefore manipulated and activated by the power of language, namely, its rhetorical qualities.

Rhetoric or figuration encompasses everything that cannot be transmitted through the mere literal semantics of a text. Yet if a standard catalogue of rhetorical figures has been in place since antiquity, we should not assume that this rhetorical tropology can determine individual imagination. That is, the relation of imagination to language is constitutive for a history of aesthetics in which "figures of speech and phrases become identified with a pattern of feelings and ideas."[4] History's relation to aesthetic discourse results from the fact that it uses figures of speech that require no proof. James Engell, who traced a history of imagination in aesthetic theories, for example, suggests that if in an account of a strategic attack someone places a bomb "in the lion's den" we do not compare such a statement with its propositional claim. Instead, a figure of speech "gives *carte blanche* to the imagination and encourages us to think of the connections between facts and feelings, the journey of the mind as it considers nature in relation to its own experience."[5] Animating the power of imagination, rhetoric shapes our vicarious experience of the narrated event from which we derive an understanding of history that is contingent on text. At the same time, we are displaced from our presumed detached position as subjects outside of the text and become an effect of that text.

In his work on metahistory, White attributes the understanding of history to the need for plot structure because "the documentary record does not figure forth an unambiguous image of the structure of events attested in them."[6] The task of the historian is to first prefigure his field — "that is to say, constitute it as an object of mental perceptions," which may be said to be a poetic act, particularly as this act also predetermines the modality of the linguistic strategies that will establish the prefigured relationships among the data.[7] Of major importance to White are the modalities of metaphor, metonymy, synecdoche, and irony. Rather than going into the details of White's modal distinctions, I want to discuss the common denominator of these four textual strategies—which White wrongly names "conceptual" strategies—and look instead at the mechanics of linguistic representation as such.[8]

Clearly the most important of White's modes is metonymy, since metonymy is the connecting element between words and concepts that actually drives the narrative development of a text, thus constituting it in a textuality that overrides the lexical meanings of words. Because metonymy is a form of textual grammar, it underlies and combines all the other linguistic or rhetorical devices of language that produce the text's coherence. This is a semiotic view of metonymy that has already been demonstrated at length in psychoanalysis by Jacques Lacan.

In using Roman Jakobson's linguistic model, Lacan theorized the rhetorically overarching role of metonymy as one that, before anything else, combines signifiers so that they can signify. The meaning function of any chain of signifiers is constituted not by any single signifier but through the relationship of individual signifiers to the whole chain. This relationship, as *pars pro toto*, represents the structure of metonymy. Lacan's example of thirty sails for thirty ships illustrates the metonymic structure of language. What happens is the elision of a signifier, namely, that of the ship. The parts come to stand for the whole but also refer to other parts, as ships have more than one sail. The absence of the whole image is represented by other signifiers and their contiguous relationships to one another. But as representation, in which a part stands for the object, and, as part, is absorbed into the text's rhetoric in order to relate to other metonymic signifiers that are parts of a different whole, the signifier soon loses its concrete referential function: the original metonymic reference is lost to consciousness. The elision of a signifier and its substitution by other signifers "installs the lack-of-being in the object relation, using the value of 'reference back' possessed by signification in order to invest it with the desire aimed at the very lack it supports."[9] The concatenation of signifiers is then substituted for the object which in psychoanalysis is considered lost. A lost object can only exist through signification by a subject for whom the text signifies and who senses the discrepancy between representation and desire.

In creating the story's convincing effect of factuality, rhetoric proves to be the link between history and tradition, because desire for the historical fact (object) underlies the advent of metonymies. By way of metonymy, signification not only works formally in terms of the displacement of meaning in signs, but displacements in language act as illusory replacements for the "lost objects" of history. Because we only come to experience history in the form of texts (in White's sense as "stories"), the desire in history as story must then be one of narrative closure or, in Lacan's view, one of *parole pleine* (full speech) which would incorporate the origin, the historical fact.[10] The text would be both the grasping (the comprehension) and the embodiment of the object. Were this desire to be achieved, however, this would mean the end of history. For history only subsists through the force of a desire that is displaced onto language where it misses its object. Finally, desire can never be fulfilled *in* (the time of) history. Instead, the signification of desire in and through texts, as attempts in language to capture history in stories, produces not only a history of texts but also a horizon of cultural signification against which background events are interpreted. Since every interpretation creates a new text, thus enlarging and changing the horizon of signification each time with the expectation of an ultimate meaning, hermeneutic activity propels the process of history, albeit in literary form. Yet the motor of this propulsion is to be located in the lack-of-being of every representation of the event as well as in the irreducible temporal difference between event and its retroactive signification in the present.

Hans Robert Jauss comes close to acknowledging this temporal distance as a space wherein tradition, in the form of continual re-interpretation, exerts the force of desire for meaning. In the repetitive effort of creating meaning by reading texts, the subject renews tradition. In transforming the horizons of signification in this way, history is turned into sense. "As soon as historical consciousness detects the qualitative difference between past and present life in the temporal distance, . . . the identity of the text's truth can only be saved if it is searched for in the process of changing horizons and conceived of as a progressive and always only partial concretisation of sense."[11] The "full word" can never be obtained. Interpreting the past, then, amounts to a dialogical search for meaning—a dialogue between the text that wants to be read and the reader who wants to understand the text. This meaning necessarily varies with each current situation, since it influences the very dialectics of questioning and answering that is ongoing.

Historical understanding—or what Hans-Georg Gadamer calls *geschichtliches Verstehen* (in opposition to a monological historicism)— turns into an event or experience that *is based* on a signifying structure.[12] Horizons of expectation merge with the signifying structure that determines the historical subject vis-à-vis the text. In other words, desire subtends the horizon of signification when the reader-subject translates events or signs into meanings. The mediation of the horizon of the historic text and the horizon of the subject occurs in language.[13] And understanding occurs as a result of this mediation, as a quasi answer to the text's desire. In the process of understanding, the answer consists in signs that "answer" to other signs. This interaction of signs then produces a new text—a text that has translated signs into other signs.[14] The translator's task, and this must also be the historian's task, is then to give form to an archetype of a sign within a (con)text. Working with signs and constituting meaning with his text, the historian becomes a translator and engages, thus, not in a mere hermeneutic that is historically interpretative, but, more importantly, in a semiotic activity. What I mean is that it is not enough to render a new text that tries to capture the historical imagination of the times; rather, the historian must also allow his own imagination, that is, his own cultural horizon and experience, to give meaning to the words of the document he reads. As linguistic signs of the past, certain meanings may simply be no longer available. In that case, the interpreter has to treat them as textually relevant signifiers that derive their meaning from their writerly context and the current associations that it triggers in the mind of the reader.

Before all reflection on historical relevance, the historian's semiotic analysis establishes the readability of signs, whether one is aware of it or not. Positing an awareness of the semiotic process in understanding involves paying attention to the mechanisms of meaning formation in language. Such a position would have to expand, if not transform, the Gadamerian hermeneutic model, which comprehends the interpretation of texts within a dialogue between historian and text. History in this dialogue appears in the form of its determination of the questions asked. A new position toward understanding would have to address the *difference* between the historian's or interpreter's thought or consciousness and language. This is where post-structuralist theories take their departure.

Language, in the process of translation, takes on a metaphorical property, though not in the sense of an alternative to metonymy but through a transferential function: *transfere* = to carry across, that is, to translate. Insofar as this transference in language characterizes the discourse of history, it also involves unconscious expectations and desires that underlie and motivate signification. I dare say, in anticipation of what follows, that these desires determine and underlie the transferential function of language, that is to say, its rhetorical properties. Thus, what establishes our sense of history, or our interpretation of what is called history, does not derive from the events themselves but is dependent on the rhetoric of text(s).

Since Hayden White extends the hermeneutic circle to figurative qualities of discourse,[15] he consequently has to construe the process of understanding as a function of rhetoric. He does this by establishing the basis for the hermeneutic tool of familiarity in the tropes of discourse. "The rendering of the unfamiliar into the familiar is a troping that is generally figurative."[16] History as we come to know it is the product of meaningful configurations. Through rhetoric, the presupposed *fact* becomes noticeable as *effect*. As text that has an effect on the reader, history, in the form of effects, has its own effective history (*Wirkungsgeschichte*).[17] These effects are produced in language, specifically in stories from which we build our understanding of history. Hence the literature on history, itself a product of history, manifests the tradition we engage in and continue, whenever we read a text. Our understanding of history through a text which is not only a story constructed through rhetorical figuration but a text that itself is dated and thus differs from our horizon by its temporal distance from it, embeds us in a tradition that in language has preserved the desire for the lost object of history. Although it might seem provocative to construe history—that is, historical knowledge as the horizon of understanding—as a function of rhetoric, as a relation of signs this historical knowledge is motivated by a modality of understanding that, as White states, is prefigurative and corresponds to a horizon of expectation that is evoked by the emotional moving effect of figurative language.

In adding an excursus into psychoanalytic investigations of representation to White's analysis of historical narrative, the idea of prefiguration may become clearer. Prefiguration is not a conscious effort but a *mise en scène* carried out by the unconscious mind for the purpose of what Freud calls "considerations of representability to consciousness." Figuration contains the unconscious translation of the process of thinking into conscious thought or, better, into images of thought. Freud calls the translation from the unconscious scenario into conscious representation a perception "along the path of the function of speech."[18] Without the memory of verbal representations, perception could never become consciousness. On this premise Lacan developed his structuralist/linguistic theory of the unconscious by suggesting that the "language function" itself is unconscious, given that the consequence of rhetoric is an unconscious mechanism for the production of thought and knowledge.[19]

In contrast to White's attempt at basing the understanding of history on tropological structures (structures of consciousness), another way of determining the tropological nature of meaning formation was described by Freud and formally introduced in his work *The Interpretation of Dreams*. There, Freud first developed what may be considered the tropological structure of the unconscious: displacement, condensation, staging or considerations of representability, and, most of all, secondary revision or *Nachträglichkeit*. Freud recognized this last function as "a psychical function which is indistinguishable from our waking thoughts."[20] In secondary revision, dream thoughts are articulated in language and thus take on the appearance of intelligibility. This linguistic representation of dream thoughts, which Freud himself compared to an underlying text, constitutes part of the dream work that *translates* the signifiers of the dream into a readable text. If the text of history is constituted in a similar manner, then it proceeds in the form of a reordering (*Umordnung*) and transcription (*Umschrift*)[21] that results in a transformation of the events perceived. Rainer Nägele, who has stressed the importance of time in Freud's thought, cites the following features that determine the transformation of events into histories: "(1) the object of the reordering is not the totality of the past, but [selected] fragments which, at the time of the event, could not be integrated into a context of significance; (2) specific experiences and— often critical—situations determine the time and mode of the reordering; 3) all phenomena of 'Nachträglichkeit' are marked by a period of 'latency,' of 'forgetting.'"[22] This period of latency not only marks significance as an "after"-(event), but shifts the descriptive aspect of time to a function immanent in signification.

The law of *Nachträglichkeit,* of the belatedness of meaning essentially determines the relationship between event and history, that is, between event or experience and its meaning. Meaning, or significance, as we have seen by way of White, proves to be a function of textuality and its rhetorical effects on the subject's memory. The operative effect of time, necessary for the actualization of the event, seems to be contingent on the rhetorical structures of language. I attempt to show that this is indeed the case in the next section of this chapter which takes us beyond White's more restricted views.

Constitutive for the belatedness of meaning is a necessary repetition or recollection triggered by a later perception or experience that actualizes the earlier experience (or event). Insofar as the past event needs, on some level, to be recalled in order to gain significance for the present, the qualities of the past must be represented in an image that at the same time also contains features of the present. The political or personal conditions of the present supply the historical form as a perspective for representing the event. Past and present are thus involved in a dialectics between event and conditions of representability, between content and form. But in the subject's perception of this "dialectical image," the demarcations of content and form are blurred. It is this perceptual and experiential phenomenon that Walter Benjamin defined as the "Now" (*Jetztzeit*) of history.

By virtue of the image, history can be recognized. History does not simply refer to a past event but to a knowable relationship that is made visible by certain phenomena. With his notion of the Now, Benjamin tried to initiate a new way of thinking about history and historical cognition. He juxtaposed the temporal aspect of the past and the present to an essence of what has been, *das Gewesene,* and what we experience as the Now, *das Jetzt.*

The latter two terms merge in the recognition of an experience, in its meaning, which the subject can only grasp in an image:

> It is not that the past throws its light upon the present, or the present throws its light upon the past, but the image is that in which what-has-been collides with the Now, as in a flash, in a constellation. In other words: the image is [a] dialectic that stands still. For, whereas the relationship of the present with the past is purely temporal and continuous, the relationship of what has been to [what is] Now is dialectical: it is not [a] process, but [an] image, abrupt.[23]

In this chance-like constellation of past and present typical of the dialectical image Benjamin sees a historical redemptive structure. That the phenomenon of belatedness transforms events into significance helps us understand what for Benjamin must be the ultimate essence of time: its redemptive quality. In Benjamin's theory of history redemption means nothing other than the potential conditions for recognizing and understanding the object of history. "History is the object of a construction whose place is not homogeneous empty time but a time that is fulfilled by the Now."[24] The idea of a fulfilled time might become more familiar if we think of it preliminarily as a time filled with meaning, or at least with potential or "latent" meanings. The moment in which the image is formed is itself a historically significant moment because it disrupts the progressive flow of empty time when it signals to the subject the "Now of a specific recognizability" of historical formation.[25] Benjamin's expression indicates the moment when the past becomes relevant for reading a configuration of signs or phenomena occurring in the present.[26]

In Benjamin's concept of the "dialectical image," the individual, imaginatively, partakes of her past as it defines her present. What can be recognized by the individual in the present defines her as a historical subject. In its perception, the historical subject translates a potentially significant element of the past into the present as objects or signs at hand. Through perception the existence of the subject is unthinkable without history, for only through history are phenomena and objects transformed into signs. Hence it is through the referential nature of signs that the subject is referred to its past in every perception of the present. Benjamin's "claim of the past on the present" strongly infers the structure of *Nachträglichkeit* inherent in the event and its transformation into a sign by means of which history is constituted for the subject. The signifying structure that results from *Nachträglichkeit* is a language whose mimetic features, as Benjamin says, are dependent on the semiotic effects of words derived from their relational inscription *in a text*:

Everything that is mimetic in a language can only emerge, like a flame, with the support of some kind of carrier. This carrier is the semiotic. Thus the textual structuring of the meanings of words or sentences is the carrier in which the similarity [to the signified] appears in a flash. Man's production and perception of these words and sentences, in many and especially in the most important cases, depends upon their flashlike emergence. They wisk by.[27]

Benjamin's use of the term "semiotic" refers to a mental creation of meaning which exceeds, and differs from, a perception of semantic contents of words. It refers precisely to the (creative) operation of reading which pays attention—even unconsciously—to their formal or textual correspondences. An exemplary reading of this nature has been performed by Werner Hamacher on Benjamin's text *Berlin Childhood*.[28] Hamacher weaves his text from formal similarities of words such as "Wolke," "Worte," "violett," "Ge*walt*," and "*Walter*" which he presents in a meaningful assemblage that stands for what I would, however, call an unconscious meaning of Benjamin's text. Hamacher makes visible a signifying relationship among these words by paying attention to both their orthographic-phonetic gestures and their location in a specific configuration with other words.[29] In supporting textuality, this kind of associative meaning structure is based on metonymical relations between signs. If these signifying relations are not immediately obvious to the reader, they nevertheless serve as a vehicle that transports meaning (or the building blocks thereof) between text and mind.

Returning to the quote from Benjamin, the "semiotic," which from a critical stance we ought not confuse with the semantic, is the vehicle that transports signifiers and brings about meaning. For the semiotic displaces the semantic content of words into a relationship with the subject's history, as the unconsciously perceived textual correspondences between words trigger past experiences in the subject's memory. Through reading, a hitherto unrecognized experience from the subject's past is actualized and, with the help of the textual signs at hand, appears as an image or intuition. Since the image is brought about in a "constellation of what-has-been with the Now,"[30] facilitated by the semiotic vehicle, it can be called a dialectical image. In terms of both "constellation" and "dialectical image," Benjamin claims, "Only dialectical images are authentic (i.e., not archaic images); and the location where you encounter them is *language*." (Emphasis added.)[31]

In addressing the mimetic quality of language, Benjamin rejects the mirroring of an objective reality in favor of a historical, signifying relationship—the dialectics that goes on between the subject's own history and the history of language. In the essay, "On The Mimetic Faculty," Benjamin says that language is our "canon of non-sensuous similarities."[32] In the essay, Benjamin opposes theories of language that insist on the conventional, arbitrary nature of signs. The non-arbitrariness of the signifying quality of language consists in its inscription of those dialectical images that human beings have grasped and written down over time. It is from these historical records that turns of phrases survive and become part of conventional language use. History lives on not as memory of a fact but as the fact's figural and temporal meaning for human existence.

When Benjamin distinguishes homogeneous time from fulfilled time, he introduces a new avenue for uncovering what is at stake in thinking about history as an object in itself. It is our conception of time that foregrounds such a concept of monolithic history. Benjamin's goal is to free history from the abstract coordinates of time and space that turn history into an object of science that dissociates history from the field of human experience.[33] The upshot of Benjamin's critique of time is the importing of human perception into the understanding of history.

Perception or what humans "take to be true"(*Wahr-nehmung*) has its basis not in a chronological sequence of prior events but rather in the affective quality of experiences that are translated into signs of consciousness. The progression of time, which catalogues events as past, present or future, is but secondary in perception. The subjective "truth" in perception, then, rests on an unconscious interaction of past with present scenarios of situations as well as with projected desires for happiness and concrete change. In fact, only psychoanalysis offers the hermeneutic tools for dealing with the representations of the subject's memory as they are formed in conjunction with the perception of an other being. These time-marked representations induce the subject to consciously mistake a past experience for a perception *in* and seemingly *of* an objective-temporal present. In the case of reading, for instance, the reader inscribes his or her past experience into the text at hand. The language of the text signifies as much the reader's past as it signifies itself. Hence the reader's historicity always mediates the historically conditioned meanings of words.

Our perception of time rests on the interruption of its flow by an event. But the awareness of the historicity of such an event does not arise until something about the event is remembered at a later point in time. Hence the mark of time is not consciously registered until the event is reconstructed in the subject's mind. It is perceived through the lens of the present situation. The need for familiarity in any perception of something new is satisfied by a psychological shift that transports a similar event from the subject's past into the present situation. A new experience, in the present, remains conscious. It is remembered and "taken for truth" (*wahr-*

genommen) as a significant point in time. However this "truth" in perception rests on the subject's capacity for comparing two phenomena over the course of time. Psychoanalytically, this capacity always relates a primary, never consciously available, event with a "secondary" event, and what appears to the Ego—the conscious self—as a first and decisive historical event is the second event only. Yet its significance stems from a prior, primary event.

In the psychoanalytic model, the mark of a primary event or experience imprints itself in the individual's psyche, a process that, as stated, will never become conscious in itself. This impression leaves a memory trace (*Gedächtnisspur*) behind. As it interacts with other such traces of impressions, it forms the matrix for (belated) significant experiences which shape the individual's history. Resembling an unconscious text, these marks effect future perceptions of events or experiences in the sense that by being recalled they prefigure their interpretation and significance. Since the event that caused the impression will never become conscious, it can only be inferred or posited in the analysis of a later element of significance. Even though the spatial-temporal constituents of the second event are different from the first, the event in the subject's perception is a repetition of the first. Repetition does not suggest a duplication of the experience, for the temporal forward displacement of a primary event has changed the latter's character and significance over time, adapting it to the life-history and circumstances of the subject. The difference here results from the event's displacement which shifts the assumed originary event into different contexts and onto different levels of signification. This difference in repetition marks the difference between an unconscious structure of significance, based on the unconscious capacity of memory, and conscious understanding in the form of perceivable and interpretable signs.

Time is of the essence in the constitution of this difference. The transference and consequent translation of one event into another later one is contingent on time. The time that elapses between the first and second event is, however, filled with unconscious meanings. In this sense, time is no longer a progressive and automatic entity, but assumes the nature of a temporality instantiated by repetition. Repetition merely organizes conscious perception and experience in a temporal structure, and history comes into being in this temporal structure as a string of overdetermined signifiers. Consciousness emerges only from this temporal structure (i.e., history) in which it is linked with the past through unconscious memory.

3

Repetition and Experience

GOING BACK: FREUD AND THE DRIVES

IN THE DISCUSSION OF THE DRIVES IN SIGMUND FREUD'S LATER WORK, a distinction is made between death drives and life or sexual drives. Freud calls the former death drives because he defines drives as tendencies to return to an earlier state of equilibrium. In doing so, he assumes that organic life developed through an impetus of force out of inorganic matter whose lifeless state existed prior to the organic. Thus the goal of life must lie in a return to an original state of death. In his evolutionary model, Freud shows that all drives except the sexual drives are of an inherently conservative nature. Drives aim to bring about not a new and different state of life but a primeval state of life: "It would be in contradiction to the conservative nature of the drives if the goal of life were a state of things which had never before been attained. On the contrary, the goal must be an *old* state of things, an initial state from which the living entity has at one time or other departed and to which it is striving to return by the circuitous paths along which development leads."[1] For Freud, development consists in an adaptation to changing exterior conditions. This process of adaptation often entails a regression in development (*Rückbildung*) in another area of the organism, possibly to balance its economy.

Evolutionary development and regression, Freud speculates, may be the result of a developmental response to something exterior that drives the organism. Dominating the psychological economy, the interior drives facilitate the necessary assimilation of these developmental changes by converting them into a source of pleasure. The experience of pleasure would be a reaction or secondary development to changes in the organism, changes that, even though they can be considered as moving forward on the evolutionary scale, also involve a movement backward to an earlier state of life. To support this possible explanation for the generally conservative, and thus regressive, nature of drives, Freud cites Sandor Ferenczi who had already conceived of the same possibility: "If this train of thought is pursued to its logical conclusion, one must make oneself familiar with the idea of a tendency to persevere or regress dominating organic life as well, while the tendency towards progressive development, adaptation, etc. would become active only in response to external stimuli."[2]

Freud's attempt to posit the pleasurable experience of change implies an ontological recognition of the force of repetition in the course of organic life. Repetition acts out the conservative, regressive nature of drives. As a movement or tendency of *moving* backwards to an earlier state in life that consisted of a pleasurable experience of satisfied needs, this regressive nature of the drive is experienced psychologically as *motivation*, since motivation is, at least in part, experienced as a form of pleasure associated with a certain activity. The force of repetition is thus derived from an early experience of pleasure remembered only in the unconscious, though it is nonetheless manifest in its transformative aspect of motivation which rules the subject's behavior.

Through this motivating force, the subject's activity can be seen as always controlled by a past that the subject can never consciously recollect as a concrete incident but, at best, only become aware of by recognizing emotional responses to specific situations that relate to the past. In recognizing parts of the self in the other, parts that the Ego projected, self-reflection comes about, and, of course, in such self-reflection the subject's attention is drawn to its own representations. Since self-reflection releases the subject from adapting to its environment with equivocating representations, the subject can actually explore its power of representation by following its own imagination as it is put in *motion* by *emotions*.

These emotions, whose derivative force I will call motivation, are brought to awareness in the state of reflection by realizing their relation to images. (After all, the ideal state for such reflection is an aesthetic experience.) Since in the self-reflective state no interaction with the environment occurs, motivation which normally might cause actions makes itself felt as desire for a state of feeling whole. This desire or yearning (cf. *Sehnsucht*) is accompanied by fantastic representations whose unspecific matter of content cannot be judged with categories of reason or understanding, and therefore do not correspond to what Freud calls the reality principle. These representations might thus be called "fantastic" precisely because they do not correspond to the expectations set up by reason; instead, they are experienced as affected mental images. The difference between fantasy and (reality bound) imagination may well be stated as this affective component: a residue of and allusion to a past which the mind struggles to recreate in fantasies of a pleasurable state. In literature, these representations have taken the form of utopia, a fictional or figural topos motivated by an unconscious past attempting to capture the imagined state in adequate representation.

Desire, according to Freud, stems from the past. Experience of *Sehnsucht* (affect) articulates desire by directing the perceptual faculties toward the past. Since desire and its object is for the most part unconscious, the feeling of longing must also be connected to the unconscious which incorporates into the self what is past and cannot consciously be remembered. A concept of the unconscious might thus prove inseparable from history. This is why I venture the thesis that without history there is no unconscious. For as unconscious memory, the past impinges upon our experiences and gives us a sense of historical being. Though an originary scene or event, the primal past does not reemerge. Rather, it determines the specific feeling that is triggered in an experience. This feeling is not newly created at the moment of the experience, but is merely repeated and only then recognized in its quality. This quality will influence how an experience is interpreted and incorporated into the psychical economy of the subject. In the mind, the feeling will figure as representation or fantasy, which means the remembered feeling has an impact on an imagination that tries to find representations adequate to the subject's state of feeling. In this way, imagination is a faculty for mental representations that is ultimately "affected" by a past that makes itself felt in the repetition of feeling and the images that accompany it. Still, these images are not just representations of a past event, since they are also triggered by a present experience or object that requires comprehension. Nonetheless, the manner in which the subject comprehends and interprets this object is influenced by the past or *history* that directs the subject's imagination.

However, we must recall that Freud posits the longed-for situation in which the subject's needs were satisfied as an original state of equilibrium of drives that can be compared to death. Failure to acknowledge one's desire for such a state involves a denial of feelings that result from a repression of the regressive drive toward an ultimate satisfaction. The fantasy of an ideal state therefore conflicts with the fear of death. The repression of the death drive, or desire for an inorganic state of (e-)motional extinction, therefore concerns a conscious ignorance of any regressive tendencies in the psychological reaction to an outside stimulus, to an object. Therefore the subject misrecognizes his or her reaction and interpretation as emanating from the object or the other rather than as being determined by the subject's own past. Positioned vis-à-vis an object, the illusion of the subject as being-present-to-himself prevents him from recognizing his being affected by a memory.

The failure of such a recognition also discourages a sense of history within acts of interpretation. Instead, the sublimation of the desire for an experience of total satisfaction, manifest in a drive oriented toward the past, produces the idea of a perfect human being. In the history of culture, this idea has been stylized, that is, made into an ideal toward which people strive. As historical force, the "drive" toward a more ideal person, toward what in the eighteenth century was established aesthetically as the "beautiful soul" (*schöne Seele*), propels intellectual and artistic achievements that were indeed used as a measure for cultural progress.

The drive toward perfection underlies a one-sided notion of history and culture that registers only progress. Oblivion to and suppression of the past consciously leads to a value judgment of earlier stages in culture and human organization as either inferior or outdated. Time thus becomes a sole criterion for meaning. The concept of perfection assumes a constant temporal movement that prohibits the arrest of time in a moment of self-reflection; for example, the looking back upon one's path that the Ego has "driven" (*gefahren*) in experience (*Er-fahrung*), or, appreciating those experiences that have formed the self.

In contrast to this idea of time as progress and history as perfectibility of mankind, the moment of arrested time represents, in its quality, a moment of remembrance, of *Eingedenken* in the Benjaminian sense of a confluence of self-awareness and the awareness of history in memory. In merging the ideas of Benjamin and Freud with those of Jacques Lacan, who has mapped out some structures of desire, this moment proves to be one of recognition and tolerance: recognition of a certain past in the present and the assumption of an unfulfillable desire rooted in the fantasy of a pleasurable past. Lacan argued for the acceptance of one's desire as the goal of the psychoanalytic process, because it is desire that causes a misperception in which past and present are confused and misconstrued. The goal of analysis in general must be the recognition of one's history, even if it means the construction of fictional events that "explain" the repetition of feelings and mental states in the present.

Freud himself did not believe in a "drive towards perfection," a false drive that, as he says, would have to produce "superman" [*Übermensch*].[3] Instead, he attributes this drive of restlessly moving forward and toward different situations, for the ever-new, to a fear of coming into contact with what is only too familiar and therefore old. It is familiar, of course, only in the unconscious mind, which keeps track of every experience. As Freud says, the unconscious never forgets.[4] To the conscious mind, however, such contents seem unfamiliar and uncanny. Moreover, the mind interprets the uncanny as a threat of death that would cut the life of the organism short by returning it to its origin. Evading "death" or, by extrapolation, a former state of being, channels the organism's energy into a "flight forward."

As forward movement, this progress is actually caused by the forgetfulness of the past. The Ego's resistance to the past is the same resistance of total satisfaction which, just like death, takes on the function of a taboo in the individual mind and in culture.[5] Ambivalence toward the taboo, the unconsciously desired experience of original satisfaction, shows up in the symptom of the wish to be perfect. Perfectionism may merely be a displacement of death as the end of history, since once the perfect state of man has been achieved no further development is necessary. The unconscious past is thus transferred into the future in a conscious striving for a different state of being. Striving toward perfection proves to be an acting out of an unconscious desire for a state of "perfect," complete satisfaction. Here, history as a series of actions toward a better state of being converges with unconscious tradition as a past that affects the present in the need to bring about a future state of perfection. *In this historical context tradition is translated, or displaced, into conscious progress.*

Freud criticizes the "drive toward perfection" indirectly by identifying this kind of behavior and attitude as a sublimation of desire for the past experience. I have interpreted the progress of "making history" in terms of a translation of an unacknowledged past, that is, of the unconscious desire for a search for a fulfilled life. This uncompleted process is the experience of tradition, since there, too, the goal of perfection is unconsciously motivated by a desire for the happy past. In spatial terms, the projected future of perfection represents the same "place" as the past that Benjamin has described as a place of "free fulfillment," liberated from the taboos that were made necessary by the fall into culture. This place, which is also a time, opens up the notion of a messianic time when the world's past will be fully redeemed in the present, an untimely present that is precisely not a succession to the past. This kind of present will incorporate the entire history of culture. Such a messianic nature of time as pure presence, that is, as a standstill, is intimated in the fleeting moment of bliss—as *Erfahrung* which structures our sense of time as a signifying history.[6]

RETROACTION AND TRADITION: BENJAMIN'S MOMENT OF "NOW"

Benjamin's philosophy of history resembles Freud's theory of the unconscious past in that Benjamin also considers a death drive that is not entirely separated from the drive of pleasure.[7] Initially, Benjamin declares that striving for happiness is the purpose of history whether it be sacred or profane. In fact, for Benjamin history and tradition merge in a notion of messianic time that serves as the orientation of one's life time:

> The order of the profane has to establish itself by an orientation to the idea of happiness. The relationship of this order to the messianic is one of the essential teachings of philosophy. Conditioned by this relationship is a mystical apprehension of history whose problematic can be represented in an image. If one arrow signifies the direction of the goal, which is effected by the dynamics of the profane, and another arrow signifies messianic intensity, then of course a liberated mankind in its search for happiness will strive away from the messianic direction. Yet, just as one force through its course may propel another in its course, so the order of the profane can advance the coming of the messianic kingdom. It is true, the profane is not a category of the kingdom, but it is a category of the truest nature of its most unnoticeable coming. For in [the moment of] happiness, all earthly being strives for its dissolution, and only in happiness will it [all earthly being] find its destination of perishing.[8]

The divine kingdom associated with the time and place of "free fulfillment" is not the telos of history but its end and it occurs as a disruption of history. "The messiah breaks off history (*bricht ab*); the messiah does not appear at the end of a development."[9] The perishing of the organism, of nature, and the end of "earthly" history are the conditions of happiness. In this sense, the life of the organism, nature, names the same category as history. The history of the organism is also its nature. Although the course of conscious history organizes itself along the lines of a teleological striving for a state of well-being—that is, for perfection or *tradition*, the concept that I derive from Benjamin's notion of the messianic—it unconsciously motivates the actions of historical agency. The messianic time of a Now arrests the course of happenings (*Geschehen*) and forces the subject to acknowledge the present not as a transitory moment but as an experience (*Erfahrung*) of the past, not as relived memory but as a meaningful constellation within the present.

Unlike Christianity, which orients itself by the teleology of the second coming of Christ as well as by the future of a better life after redemption, in Jewish tradition life on earth is not a transitory, and therefore devalued stage, but a possible stage for the coming of the messiah at any time. Therefore the tripartite historical model, past (golden age of paradise), present (worldly history split off from God), and future (utopia of a recovered paradise and union with God) is determined by Christian belief. This is radically different from the concept of history in Jewish thought. For example, Benjamin's notion of *Jetztzeit* is derived from a Jewish concept of history that is not defined by a temporal linearity of past, present, and future, but rather by a tradition that links these temporal aspects meaningfully within a unified and deeply experienced present.

A view of the future does not consist in representing and striving for a utopian moment or place. Rather, as Benjamin points out, through remembrance (*Eingedenken*), Jews are instructed to integrate the past into the present as a meaningful construct like a story. Potentially, the present is at any moment the redemption of the past, and, in the Now of recognizing the meaning of the past for the present, "splinters of messianic time" manifest themselves. As for the future, it is but a possibility of the Now as the coming of a messiah, and it folds into the present.[10] As such, the future is the possibility of a meaningful Now, created in the act of remembering the past.

The effect of this hermeneutical act conflates past, present, and future into the present of the Now. This constellated Now not only explicates a process of experience but also describes the material or linguistic task of the historian who, in this instance, takes on messianic qualities when he interprets the documents of the past. With respect to tradition, the historian transmits by translating the past into recognizable linguistic images that are dependent on a treatment of language that no longer repeats but interprets or works through a *sense* of meaning. The historian is therefore like the poet, for through his linguistic work tradition is passed on as a sense, feeling, and experience that links personal history with a *sense* of history in language.

Of course, tradition is not something merely ready to hand, but has to be constituted by interpreting the past. Interpretation retroactively constructs history as knowledge from the perspective of the now, a knowledge that serves as the intellectual basis for deciding on future actions. As a way of commemorating the past, interpretation hence functions as the origin of any kind of historical sense, decisive action, and speculation about the future. As a human need, it is anchored in the individual's psychological organization of past and present. The need for interpretation, as a coming to terms with the past, must be attributed to memory, but not to memory as an entity but as a process that emanates from the past.

Benjamin's distinction between two kinds of memory, *Eingedenken* and *Erinnerung*, provides a cognitive equivalent to my psychoanalytic differentiation of history and tradition. In his work on Baudelaire, Benjamin works out the historical as well as psychological difference between *Eingedenken* and *Erinnerung* and illustrates the reifying character of *Erinnerung* in the idea of the souvenir. Souvenirs represent memory as entities that can be identified in time and space and voluntarily recalled. Benjamin even sharpens this association of *Erinnerung* with souvenirs when he criticizes Baudelaire for being obsessed with fetish-like souvenirs. Benjamin analyzes Baudelaire's relationship to the past, to history and temporality, as one of repression and avoidance.

For this purpose, Benjamin introduces the notion of a spleen that designates the neurotic avoidance of dealing with one's past in experience. Spleen precludes any new experience through which the person might incorporate, acknowledge, and work through the past in the present. In other words, new experience always involves interpreting the past which then enables the subject to designate the past as history and separate it from the present. As a result of this process, the subject can experience itself as living in the present and project itself through action into the future. The "need" for such an interpretation of life is, in Baudelaire's case, displaced and distorted into an obsession with specific things or events that merely represent and symbolize a past experience. While the past is caught up in these souvenir representations, Baudelaire's desire and, with it, the temporal development of his experience is brought to a halt. His libido has unconsciously cathected the objects by means of a conscious obsession with things. In the condition called spleen, this kind of unconscious-conscious interaction receives a fixed mark, since with every new move and every new perception the same images are associated. Memory always precedes any reflection on the past that might be triggered by chance. And chance is nothing but the temporal existence of experience which is prevented by spleen. The road to the distant past that cannot be traveled in experience, *Er-fahr-ung*, is cut by blocking the feeling of *long-ing*. This feeling of desire, made conscious, invokes a search for the past, a motivation that resounds in the German word for longing: *Sehn-sucht*. History, for Baudelaire, consists—and is tangible—in the form of souvenirs, *Andenken*, specific things that he can think of (*denken an*) in the event of a (potential) experience.

What is at stake in the atrophy of experience is the loss of tradition. Benjamin uses Baudelaire as an example in demonstrating this sense of (objectified) experience in modernity, given that for Benjamin modernity means the neglect and repression of the past. Only experience, *Erfahrung*, keeps tradition alive, because only an interpretation of the present event unfolds the event into an experience that reaches into the past and brings it into the present. What we experience is then not tradition itself, as content matter, but an unknowable scenario of the past which resonates in the present situation. What up to this point in time was an unconscious experience, in the sense of *Erlebnis* or perception, is now activated by an event, and the interpretation of this event-cum-memory produces a historical experience or *Erfahrung*. I have already described this transformation as deferred action or *Nachträglichkeit*, an effect of meaning imparted by the past. Through the effect of belated meaning, tradition manifests in how we make sense of experience by recognizing the feeling that our past plays in our evaluation of the present.

If we accept history as a retroactive semantic construct, and think of tradition as the unconscious cultural memory that carries over the past into the present (recognizable in one's affective response to the present event), then the concepts of history and tradition join in the psychoanalytic phenomenon of a belated meaning effect. This is even made manifest in psychoanalysis where the therapeutic process consists in the construction of a history of events that "fit" the symptoms. The reconstructive process of history in psychoanalysis is, in fact, guided by a series of unconnected memory images or screen memories associated with a feeling state evoked by the present. It is the analyst's task to connect these memories in a meaningful way by reconstructing scenarios of the patient's past that seem plausible in regard to the symptoms and associations. In this task elements of fiction help establish the individual's history so that the effects of the past become readable as a coherent, re-membered story which the patient can understand and identify as *his* or *her* past.

Likewise, tradition as unconscious cultural memory carries the past until it is redeemed in the meaning of the present. This meaning formation is essentially that of the retroactive construction of history in an act of interpretation. Its aim is to bring the present (the symptom) into relation with the past (experience). Hence the notions of tradition and historiography (i.e., story) overlap in a concept of history that Gadamer called *Wirkungsgeschichte* (=operative history) in order to underline the fact that history operates through its effects rather than as a thing-in-itself. The "object" of history is thus a *relationship* between the past and the present, a *relationship* that characterizes historical consciousness as the reality and efficacy of past events and experiences.

> Real (*wirklich*) historical thinking must think its own historicity at the same time. Only then will it not chase after the phantom of a historical object which is the object of ongoing research, instead it will learn to recognize in the object the other of its self and hence it will recognize both the one and the other. The real historical object is not an object but the unity of this one and the other, a relationship in which the reality of history and the reality of historical understanding is established.[11]

The reality of history (the German word is *Wirklichkeit*, a noun derived from the verb *wirken*, which means to effect) encompasses what is effected and produced by a certain mental *work*. It consists of a relationship between a present position of thinking that reflects on its own historicity, its being determined by historical factors, and what this thinking takes to be an object of the past. What has the appearance of an object, however, can only be a sign for the past, since it must first be interpreted and thought about in an act of evaluation. The significance of the object is interpreted within the horizon of the present situation that is already effectuated by a not fully known history. An awareness of present symptoms or sensitivities will shape the interpretation of the signs of the past into a plausible meaning that relates to these present symptoms. The result is an insight into their determinedness by a past that is expressed in distorted images only.

Instead of symptoms and sensitivities, Gadamer uses the notion of prejudice for naming the unconscious meaning effects of the past in the present. Gadamer's model of understanding aims at the suspension of prejudices. "For as long as a prejudgment determines us we do not know it and do not reflect upon it *as* a judgment."[12] On the basis of psychoanalytic findings, we can safely say that underlying unreflected judgment is either a (traumatic) past experience or the need to rationalize the denial of an interior conflict that would otherwise threaten the stability of the Ego and its ideology. Both experience and the threat are forces of the past that secretly exert themselves in the judgment of the present. We can also say that prejudice is a prefiguration of the present by the subject's disposition. In prejudice, the past and the unconscious are one and the same. They are, however, stirred when the mind encounters signs, objects that indicate a past yet unkown. In this context Gadamer uses the word *reizen,* which means several things: to provide a stimulus; to irritate; to provoke; to entice; to attract and arouse. The sensuous allusions in this word would suggest an affect, if not the body itself, as a mediation between understanding and history. To become aware of a prejudice, it must first be irritated. "To [mentally] represent a prejudice cannot succeed as long as this prejudice is a persistent and unnoticed part in the game [of understanding], it can only be represented when it is, so to speak, irritated. That which has the power of irritating it, is precisely the encounter with the (literary) works of the past. For that which entices to be understood must already have manifested itself in its otherness. The first thing that understanding begins with is . . . that something attracts us (*uns anspricht*)."[13]

Concluding from Gadamer, what is at stake in the hermeneutic situation, the encounter of understanding, and the signs from the past is finding a "reason" for what attracts our attention and activates our prejudice or sensitivity. Why do we want to understand the other? Why are we provoked into prejudice? Maybe because before any reflection something related to this otherness communicates with our unconscious mind and hence with our past. Embedded in the phenomenon of attraction or provocation lies a dialectical relationship of past and present, self and other, that will guide any interpretation of the sign of the past. This dialectic occurs without our awareness and establishes a transference that, when unacknowledged, makes familiar the otherness of the historical object. The other is thus taken to be the object and cause of one's symptoms, sensitivity, and perception. The other is thereby pulled into one's horizon of sensitiviy, or as Gadamer would say, into the horizon of prejudice or pre-understanding (*Vorverständnis*) through which our attention becomes fixated on specific things in the encounter with the other. Here the past becomes more and more difficult to distinguish from the present. In fact, the past is paradoxical because the past is never over, never "history" in the colloquial sense of the word, since it is also residual in the present. A hermeneutical understanding thus rests on the awareness of a flexible past. "A hermeneutic situation," Gadamer explains,

> is determined by the prejudices which we bring along to it. They form the horizon of a present to the extent that they represent that beyond which one cannot see. Here it is necessary to ward off the error that it is a fixed stock of opinions and values which delimit the horizon of the present, and that the otherness of the past would detach itself contrastively from the present like from a firm ground. In reality, the horizon of the present is constantly in the process of formation insofar as we constantly have to put to test all our prejudices. Part of such a test is, not least of all, the encounter with the past and the understanding of tradition from whence we come. Hence the horizon of the present does not establish itself without the past.[14]

The otherness of the past is not really distinct from the present if one avoids a narrow concept of the present conceived of presence in the here and now. This present merely refers to the horizon of the present which is misleading, for this horizon is shaped by the past and is merely activated and transferred in a present encounter with an other. This interpretative horizon of prejudice marks us as historical beings. And consequently, any interpretative understanding performed within this horizon can only be valid and make sense *at the time* of interpretation. The constructed meaning is necessarily relative to the historical horizon of understanding. As such, it is a variable product of a historically changing horizon. If meaning and interpretation are mediated by the historicity of the horizon of understanding, they themselves mediate the historicity of the horizon by preserving it in the act of affecting the present in terms of probing the unconscious past in the prejudices. Unconscious to the subject, this second quality of the historicity of meaning and interpretation is the *work* and effect (*Wirkung*) of tradition.[15] The definition of tradition is now deepened in that it means the unconscious transfer of the past into the present by way of a hermeneutical construction of meaning.

In contrast to a conventional conception of history in which it is thought that history can be empirically known, an effective history or *Wirkungsgeschichte* functions in terms of "meaning effects" from an unconscious past that is never fully known and can only become conscious to the extent that we are conscious within a hermeneutical situation. However, the problem with this *wirkungsgeschichtliches Bewußtsein*, as Gadamer points out, is that it does not stand outside of the hermeneutic situation, but rather takes place within it. Thus the hermeneutic situation itself can never become an *object* of itself. Instead, reflection on the hermeneutic situation is an infinite circular process, a *Reflectionskontinuum* as identified by Gadamer if not by the German Romantics before him, who realized that this represents the essence of historicity per se.

Knowing oneself (one's self as other) is contingent on reflecting on the particular hermeneutic situation in which the self and the other are constitutive parts. The historicity of the self, which is to say, the ongoing historical process of being engaged in acts of interpretation, defers an absolute knowledge of the self that would arrest the historical process of interpretation in one fixed meaning. This meaning could claim to be universal, for it would have to be understood immediately, and without mediation, at all times. Such an absolute self-identity would be congruent with the end of time and history. "Historical being [being historically] means to never suspend oneself into the knowledge of one's self."[16]

Gadamer further describes the possibility of self-knowledge as emerging from a historical antecedent which, in analogy to Hegel, he calls substance.[17] The substance of subjectivity, the self, is thus history, a person's past where subjective opinion and current behavior have their origin and which prescribes the possibilities of interpretation and understanding in the present. To make the self the object of understanding, as is the case in the psychoanalytic situation, one is forced to take the detour through the subject's history before arriving at the self. In the psychoanalytic situation, the prescriptive origin for present behavior and the horizon of understanding (the prejudices) is reconstructed in the form of the fiction of a meaningful event that "explains" the current response to things, the individual's symptoms and affects. In a psychoanalytic context, this fictional story serves to overcome the trauma of the loss of the (m)other in the constitution of the self. The recognition of the self's castration, its state of being separated from this needed other, facilitates the active revision of one's history in terms of an originary loss.

Like Gadamer's hermeneutic situation, psychoanalysis aims to start a reflection on the effects of the past on the present by working from the present backwards to the past. For one's prejudices to become the object of reflection, they have to be understood as disfigured representations of something else. In other words, they are not merely ideological representations of their image content. For example, to say that nonwhites are inferior does more than represent racism, since it may well be a displacement of one's own experiences of powerlessness. The attempt to isolate a prejudice as a theme in analysis requires triggering and irritating it (*reizen*) which the analyst or the intersubjective situation has to simulate through repetition of an unconscious response to the other.

The emerging relationship between the analysand and the analyst, between a self and an other, consists, on the surface, of a dialogue; but on the level of the unconscious, the dialogue develops a relationship between the individual's past and the present. In this case, the past is simply one constituent of a split present, and the so-called past becomes a paradoxical notion, since it is also always present. In the analytic relationship of self and other, the diachronic quality of the present takes shape in discursive representations. These discursive representations are treated as figurative scenarios for the analysand's psychological context. Both analysis and the hermeneutic situation are built primarily upon a transferential relation. In the transference,[18] the analysand draws the other, the person of the analyst, into his historical horizon and unconsciously treats this other as a familiar object of his past to which he reacts sensitively and with an "old" pattern of behavior and thought. This transferential relationship is necessary for the unconscious past of the patient to surface and play itself out in this dialogical, intersubjective space.

Since the analyst is actually not an object in the patient's distant past, the patient repeats a reaction formed in response to an experience in the past by displacing it into the present and mis-taking the analyst for the object and cause of the instigation. This situation represents a model for the psychical processes involved in the interpretation of what is called history, or experience, namely, a formally unacknowledged dialectic between past and present due to a transferential displacement of a specific past evoked by the present. If the unconscious past effects meaning in the present and cannot in itself be made fully conscious, it has to be inferred by way of constructing a plausible history through the transference.

The *transfer* of a past "hidden" in affects, sensitivities, symptoms, and/or prejudices may be said to be a condition for tradition, in the sense of *traditio* (= to hand down). The "plausible history" accommodates in its creation the non-representational creative, or as Freud says "dynamic," unconscious which fosters tradition as a process of changing representations, as a repetition with change. Tradition, in the usual sense, exists because the origin of history, the true event, is lost. From the biblical history of the Jews, Benjamin derived the notion of "being exiled into history,"—historical being as a detour toward a reunification with God, the place of self-same meaning, a place where the linguistic remembrance of history reveals the latter's essence in meaning.

Freud also illustrates his theory of the drives with a model of life as a detour to the desired inorganic state, the state of an energetic equilibrium beyond the search for temporary pleasure. Though Freud relies on a biological model to legitimate regressive tendencies, the compulsion to repeat with the aim of reconstituting an earlier familiar state nonetheless applies to the dynamics of experience. If one links Freud's concept of the repetition compulsion with his advances concerning language and the unconscious, (the hyper-cathexes of word representations), then a connection between repetition aimed at binding new stimuli and linguistic signification can be detected. Once the stimulus as incoming bout of energy is bound to a word representation (lingering in the "preconscious," where it receives the cathexis from the invoked thing representations), the activated psychical apparatus is put to rest again. The new experience, the encounter with the seemingly strange other, has been mastered by the Ego.

Tradition contains the capacity of the past to project itself into the future, and with the dynamics of repetition in language the signified, or rather the future experience to be signified, is translated into a signifier for a motivated word in the past. In this capacity, tradition is inextricably linked with an individual psychical economy and with language as a transmitter of historical experiences. The individual unconscious is contingent on language for its representation in memories. What is "handed over" in language from the past into the present is the capacity to make sense, that is, the experience of meaning in language, or the capability of meaning via the same old words only with a different sensibility.

For an understanding of the projection of the past onto the future through an unconscious repetition, it is crucial to keep in mind that what is repeated is not a past actuality, not something that already *was*, which had a present. One should think rather of this past as a possible meaning or concept that did not get a chance in the temporality of the past to inscribe itself in language. Therefore, what is stored in unconscious memory, which is thus dependent on the passage of time for its actualization, supplies a set of possibilities for future significations. These possibilities are "handed down" (*überliefert*) in the movement and giving of tradition belatedly. This tradition does not give an account of past events. It only creates history in the narration of a rather subjective experience in which the past was belatedly recognized in an imaginative configuration of images. What the historian records is this configuration of images which represent to him a belated image of the past. Only to this record, to this story of his experience, does Benjamin give the name of history, a notion that is exactly parallel to what I have been calling tradition.

> The historical materialist cannot do without a concept of the present which is not a transition but a present in which time stands in place and has come to a standstill. For it is this concept that defines precisely *that* present [a place] in which he writes history for himself. Historicism captures the "eternal" image of the past, [but] the historical materialist captures an experience of it which is unique.[19]

History as Tradition

As we have just seen, Walter Benjamin's understanding of the historical and of history conforms to what I am calling tradition. So far, I have examined the concept tradition in terms of the past. However, Benjamin is of particular interest in that he also views tradition as history in terms of a messianic moment that is instantiated in the arrival of a now or presentness that always seems to be immanent. This presentness which is always about to come is that Now (*Jetztzeit*) in which time becomes readable. It is the now of recognizability that is, in fact, the birth of an authentic historical time, a time of truth. That this time about to come is allied to the coming about of an interpretation that is itself a time and place of truth suggests that reading and interpreting are themselves to be considered a part of the messianic moment in which history reveals itself as truth. Indeed, this truth reflects a critical moment of which the crisis of representing truth in signs is constitutive. Because this crisis is itself historical and requires an understanding of the past, one could say that the now which is about to be disclosed in the messianic time is mediated by an interpretation of the past as tradition.

The interpretation of the past as an experience passed on for interpretation is even somewhat visionary and dreamlike in a way quite compatible with Freudian thinking. We should recall that for Benjamin imagination plays a key role in historical understanding because without imagination the significance of the past for the present cannot be grasped. Indeed, Freud's theory of dream interpretation served him as a model for the historian's work. "The utilization of dream elements upon awakening is a textbook example of dialectical thinking, which is thus the agency of historical awakening."[20] The remembrance of the dream, according to Freud, is already a selective and hence interpretative process which distorts the actual dream as it occurred. Like the dream, history is a complex of images that have to be brought into a sensible alliance. It is only by creating relationships between the various enigmatic parts of the dream that manifestations of an unacknowledged past or experience can come to light. Psychoanalysis takes the dream to be a response from the unconscious to a current situation in which the relevance of a past experience appears disguised in the content of the dream. The dream elements function like signifiers that can be read within a constellation of exhibited symptoms that are merely signifiers of a past experience. In the psychoanalytic view, there is no present per se, but only the unconscious repetition of the past on the one hand and the site of interpretation and "historical awakening" on the other.

If the unconscious memory in the dream repeats a past scenario by recalling it as a response to the present, and if the dream is also defined as a product of unconscious fantasy, then whatever gives the images to the dream must have the same source or agency as whatever gives the involuntary memory mental images. In a similar fashion to Freud, Benjamin tries to explain how the historian's mind works. Benjamin says that the historian's presence of mind grasps the dialectical image from the assembly of images that appear to him as a constellation in which the past engages the present. In other words, his presence of mind recognizes the power of memory that effects and affects any experience of the present. The work of the unconscious and the work of tradition on the mind are in effect the same, because both "hand down" the past in images that the historian's mind takes hold of in the meaningful experience of the present, that is the moment of awakening. Benjamin transposes the concept of the dialectical image from the individual psyche into the realm of the social. What the historian reads in the moment of readability is a figure of social hieroglyphics. These enigmatic images are revealed to him in terms of concealing the struggle and physical suffering of individuals in societies of long ago. For Benjamin, these enigmas are hallucinatory images and actually represent the residue of a society's dreamworld.[21] The historian-interpreter, then, reads the dialectical image as a chronotope that uncovers a relation between society's collective memory and its historically concrete experience.[22] For Benjamin, this relation constitutes the primal phenomenon of history.

Since historical cognition is an experience that comes about through a specific constellation of images whose appearance the subject does not willingly control, cognition cannot but be informed by imagination.

Reading these involuntary images as signifiers in their *combination*, as Freud has suggested for the interpretation of dreams, will lead to a construction of the significance of the past in the signification of desire. Experience cannot take place without the acknowledgment of this desire in the instant of the dialectical image. Even though desire cannot be known in itself, it can be experienced in the dialectics of past and present which is at stake in the specific arrangement of images. The desire, unacknowledged and made strange because it is feared (for which Freud has adopted the word *unheimlich*), is what usually remains repressed in conscious thought. Historical cognition, in the Benjaminian sense, is therefore analogous to psychoanalytical insight in that it always tries to account for desire. Because it is a generic human desire that reaches from the past into the historian's present, the historian has to acknowledge it in his own life time. In effect, the past lives on as desire because it originates in the unified fantasy of its fulfillment, the lost historical moment of bliss which motivates all experience.

An intricate relationship between desire (fantasy) and the past (experience) underlies the conscious feeling of longing and the fantastic images of our imaginary. But only through these feelings of longing and their concomitant images can experiences in the past be inferred and worked through. Inversely, repression of the past leads to a repressed history, or, rather, a repressed tradition, because the past will never be redeemed in a present, since the present is then not the place of historical recognition and, consequently, of an acceptance of the threatening otherness of one's desire as represented in fantasies and fiction. The dialectical image of the instant of the now is thus a historical phenomenon in our own minds. It constitutes, we might say, the relationship between individual psyche and cultural-literary history in the imagination. The subsequent work of interpretation then creates history as we know it, as knowledge represented in language. It is our imagination (informed by tradition) that produces the connections between what has already been and what is perceived as Now. As Benjamin infers the necessity of the imagination of historical cognition, "while the relationship of the present to the past is a mere temporal one, the relationship of that which has been (*des Gewesenen*) to the Now (*Jetzt*) is a dialectical one: its nature is not temporal but that of an image (*bildlich*) [i.e. imaginative]. Only dialectical images are really historical, and hence not archaic images."[23]

The instant of the dialectical image in which "the has-been [*das Gewesene*], flashlike, convenes with the Now in a constellation"[24] has the same psychological quality of what we usually refer to as intuition, a form of understanding or an insight not achieved through explicit rational logic. The concrete site of these dialectical images, Benjamin adds, is clearly linguistic. If tradition rests on a process of translation, then language indeed represents the vehicle for the interaction of imagination and experience, for the past and for meaning in the present. A sensibility to the historical materiality of language would then prove indispensable for any venture into the constitution of meaning in the present. Benjamin points out that these images are not phenomenological essences, for a historical index inheres in them:

> These images have to be delimited against the categories of the mind, the so-called habitus, style, etc. The historical index of images not only indicates that they belong to a certain time, it also indicates, above all, that their readability does not occur before a certain time. This achievement of readability constitutes a certain critical point in the movement of their interior. Every present is determined by those images which are synchronous with it: Every Now is the Now of a certain recognizability.[25]

What brings about the "recognizability" of the Now that is also synchronous with the readability of the images? Something in the present must lift the repression imposed by ideological consciousness and give way to nonobjective fantasy that is propelled by an unconscious desire for (undefined) bliss. Such an experience of one's imagination most vividly finds its "object" in the beautiful. Since I devote a whole chapter to Kant and aesthetic theory, it is sufficient to suggest here that aesthetic experience represents the prototype of all experience in the Benjaminian sense of reliving an unconscious, previous scenario.

Without the recognition of the past and the continuity of desire in images, and without remembrance, the experience of the beautiful elaborated by Kant as the experience of the self could not take place. Having taken the place of cult rituals, the realm of the aesthetic maintains the former's importance for an interruption of the mundane, arresting the conscious flow of time with the purpose of creating conditions for reminiscence whereby the past has a chance to penetrate the present. The beautiful, then, is but the present in which the repression of the Ego is lifted and a historical awakening can take place. Moreover, the experience of the beautiful may just be *the* experience of tradition or an experience in which tradition can be grasped. Benjamin indeed sees correspondences in the beautiful with a primal, preontological past (*das Urvergangene*) conveyed in aesthetic experience not as an object but rather as our capability and desire for interpretation which keeps us in touch with an unconscious bliss. Both the fantasy of happiness and the power of interpretation in language assume messianic qualities that can stop the cycle of blindly repeating the same event. The coming of the messiah would put an end to the "mindless" happening of history by sorting out and re-membering, connecting in a meaningful way, what has happened. In the beautiful, the fantasy of bliss and the feeling of longing for a perfect state of being link the generations to one another in the history of mankind. For Benjamin, it is in art history that the history of mankind is represented.

If, for Freud, the death drive and the compulsion to repeat represented a phylogenetic phenomenon, then, for Benjamin, imagination is, by virtue of its tie with desire and a primal past, the power of tradition that repeats the fantasy of bliss in every generation.[26] The experience of one's imagination as a power that represents at will refers the person to the phenomenon of a given. In aesthetic experience, the faculty of representation is freed from comprehending anything specific; the images that nonetheless emerge are *triggered* by the beautiful object; for example, the craft of language, but they are *created* by the remembering mind. Since feelings are but repeated memories, the feeling of pleasure in the beautiful refers the subject to a similar object in the past. The pleasurable response to an awakened desire for that same, once pleasurable past is, however, insufficient, since a true and thus durably cathected representation of the primary experience can never be achieved. Instead, the unsatisfied desire for this primal state of bliss shines through in the ensuing feeling of longing.

> What makes the pleasure/desire of the beautiful insatiable is the image of a prior world (*Vorwelt*), one which Baudelaire calls veiled by the tears of longing for home. "Ah, you were in bygone times my sister or my mother"—this confession is the tribute which the beautiful can demand as such. To the extent that art aims at the beautiful by reflecting it, no matter how modestly, art dredges it up (as Faust did Helene) from the depth of time.[27]

What the object of art reflects, however, is, as Kant has shown, an activated imagination. In aesthetic experience, imagination interacts with memory—the *memoire involontaire*—to produce images that the Ego can project onto the object so as to perceive them outside of itself. Benjamin tries to further describe the role of fantasy in this experience as

> perhaps a faculty that can make wishes of a special kind; these are wishes whose fulfillment can be thought of as "something beautiful." (. . .) A painting . . . would reflect in an instant that of which one's eyes cannot get enough. That which in the painting fulfills the wish that is capable of being projected into its origin is something which incessantly also feeds this wish.[28]

This is the experience of feeling whole and the dream of an alterior state of being that can be recognized in the familiarity of its images. This familiarity stems from the unconscious memory of a past state, Baudelaire's image of a *Vorwelt*, that is inscribed in the psyche as fantasy. "L'homme y passe à travers des forêts de symboles / Qui l'observent avec des regards familiers."[29] What "looks back" at the dreaming subject is a reflection of himself, a self that he, as the author of the dream, has unconsciously projected onto other figures or symbols in the dream. This displaced part of the self signifies an aspect of the subject's past of which he is unaware in the waking state. In psychoanalytic practice, the dream serves a key function in establishing the subject's history from these fragments of the displaced self. The unconscious familiarity with what seems alien to waking consciousness reveals the subject's ambivalence with respect to objects of desire. The subject does not know what the unconscious self desires; hence s/he often feels alienated from the representations of his or her own fantasies. Yet these fantasies are but disguised if not disfigured (in the Freudian sense of *entstellt*) memories of the self's history. In the case of the beautiful where the cognitive defences are, so to speak, lowered, the subject's mind is open to those images that respond to its desire by recognizing this desire as a feeling that evokes the subject's past.

Removing the disguise from the fantasies and reincorporating the representations as historical images into the structure of the self, that is, that part of the self which has been displaced into the dream, is the task of a messianic consciousness with which the Benjaminian historian should be endowed. It is, after all, the idea of the messiah who puts the image of history right. The historian recognizes in the disfigured representations a future oriented desire that aims at the state of bliss. Historical consciousness requires the interpretation of profane historical experience in terms of an idea of happiness. Benjamin makes a radical distinction between his concept of the messianic and the idea of a transcendental God or realm of God. The messianic refers to a state of human bliss which serves as a necessary guide for living in the order of the profane. What he also implies is a psychological and emotional experience of happiness, "the immediate messianic intensity of the heart,"[30] which endows humans with the capacity of the desire for such a state of well-being.

In the case of the artist, the aesthetic combination of the disguised images of desire can bring about a figural construction, a *Gebilde* or *figura*, that conforms to Benjamin's idea of the dialectical image in which features of the past are mingled with those of the present. What belongs to the past is usually recognized by the dreamer, but what motivates its relationship with the present in the dream image requires an interpreter or art critic.

> In the dialectical image, the has-been of a certain epoch is, at the same time,
> that which "has for ever been" (*Von-jeher-Gewesene*). As such, it appears
> before the eyes of a very specific epoch only: namely that epoch in which
> mankind, rubbing their eyes, is just recognizing in this dream image the
> past as such. It is in this [visionary] moment that the historian assumes, vis-
> à-vis the image, the task of dream interpretation.[31]

Benjamin states further that the use of these dream elements, that is, the
cultural signifiers, in the moment of a (social) awakening, or cultural crisis,
is mandatory for the historian, because "the processing of dream elements
at the time of awakening is the canon of dialectical thinking."[32]

As in the example of aesthetic experience, the awakened desire for a
return of the pleasure, associated with experience of the beautiful, emerges
when the subject's or a society's imaginary is finally contrasted with the
conditions of its very existence. The conscious experience of the discrepancy between desire, on the one hand, and historical existence, on the
other, engenders the sense of nonfulfillment and longing. In this subsequent or secondary experience, the subject is placed in the epistemological
split between imagination and the knowledge of life conditions. This is a
special cognitive moment in aesthetic experience in which the subject is
identical with neither. Experiencing this psychological schism, the self is
thrown off balance, because it is at a loss for a meaningful subject position.
Benjamin even speaks of "shock" when he describes the effect of rupture in
the psychological tendency toward identification. However, Benjamin's
interpreter-historian must articulate just this experience of a lack of meaning and its consequent ambivalence in historical manifestations if s/he
wants to avoid a one-sided story. Yet, articulating mankind's ambivalence
amounts to nothing less than the representation of desire. For it is desire
that figures in the crucial experience of a nonfulfillment that causes the
longing for plenitude and the subject's wish for total identification with an
idealized other.

For the interpreter to assume a desire that motivates present representations (*Vorstellungen*) means to signify desire as a causal relation between
mind, imagination, and reality. What the interpreter does in his task of
writing history is to reflect upon his role as writer when representing his
experience with the past. Making this reflection upon writing part of the
representation—so as to avoid a narcissistic transference—implies a dis-
tancing device in the text that will also prevent the reader from identifying
with the text as the representation of a self-identical past. Rather, the reader
will have to recognize the possibility for further interpretation, making
sense of how he is affected by the text or the past or his desire that is activated by the effects of the textual images. To the degree to which the writer

reflects on the representational process in language and includes it in the linguistic representation, he does engage in a style of writing comparable to romantic irony. Rooted in the self-reflexive style of such Romantic writers as Novalis and Schlegel, romantic irony displaces the writer and reader in relation to the text, pointing to the force of aesthetic production that exerts a signifying logic of its own. For Benjamin this aesthetic production reveals the theological nature of language, that is, the awareness of longing in the experience of reading and writing puts the reader and writer in touch with the proleptic aspect of signification.

When in a "tradition" of literary criticism, oriented by aesthetic values, critics in their commentaries emphasized the genius of a certain poet or writer, they alluded to the way in which the poet represented his imagination in language. "The cult of the *Genie* reduces language to the dead letter by investing the I with the power of speech."[33] In this way, Rainer Nägele has identified a certain treatment of the concept of genius, which substantially differs from a view of genius that is not ego-bound. Nägele distinguishes between *Genie* and *Genius* whereby the latter refers not to a person or the I of speech but to a signifying force that emerges in an intersubjective realm where it is language that constitutes the significant relations in culture. "One can *have Genius*, but one can *be* a *Genie*. (. . .) *Genius* comes from the outside to the subject, or so it is viewed from the perspective of a world where the I is subject. (. . .) There are many *Genien*, but no *Genius* of the I. He might appear as *genius loci*, as *Genius* of a language, of music, of a people, etc. He steps forth and emerges from an interior created by two or more subjects."[34] Accordingly, we could say, the "genius of representation" (*Darstellung*) rather than individual imagination controls the meaning formation in interpretation. The way or path of meaning cuts through language whose tradition interacts with the mind in the displacement and transformation of what is thought and remembered.

Part II

Faculties of the Unconscious in Kant

4

Desire and the Body in Kant

NO ONE HAS BETTER EXPLAINED THAN KANT WHAT IS AT STAKE IN THE genius of representation, since it was he who formulated a philosophy of the aesthetic as a way to rationalize the psychological gap opened up between *Vorstellung* (mental representation) and *Darstellung* (linguistic or artistic representation in a medium) in the Enlightenment's investigation of aesthetic experiences. Given its status as a human faculty, Kant admonishes that genius be kept in check by taste so as not to risk madness. According to Kant, genius represents a danger to the mind. Powered by desire for self-expression, the individual's imagination may run wild with ideas and cross over into hallucination. The ensuing artistic representations (*Darstellungen*) would therefore no longer hold any sense for the recipient who judges them by means of a taste that can be attributed to just anyone. Hence an implicit tension exists between a potentially ego-centric genius and a social if not universal judgment of general taste.

Genius has indeed been a problematic notion throughout the eighteenth century. But this troublesome faculty, which always wavers on the border of insanity, suggests a use of imagination that no longer represents phenomena of perceptions or sensation but, on account of its creativity, transforms reality according to an individualistic law that cannot be easily discerned. This is the law of desire that governs the imaginary space in which genius creates representations. Through artistic representations, the beholder has the opportunity to gain hold of his own desire for self-completion (the pleasurable memory of being one or whole), something that by way of an investigation of the body in the context of Kant concerns the figure of the (m)other. As I will show, aesthetic experience is mapped on the unconscious memory of the mother. Moreover, the aesthetic space in the mind which takes place between *Vorstellung* and *Darstellung* is the space of a desire that can be recognized in feelings of longing as well as in the remembrance of early, blissful experiences.

Even though Kant's treatment of desire is intended to negate history in the formal analyses of aesthetic judgments, desire—in my psychoanalytic reading of Kant—undermines the Enlightenment's official break with history and its futurist orientation. It is therefore my aim here to recover the retrospective quality of an aesthetic experience that is situated in the body's memory and based upon pleasure.

In aesthetic experience, a mechanistic historical division of the past and present is overcome, laying the ground for what later was fully developed as a hermeneutical understanding by the Romantics that was expanded in the twentieth century by Hans-Georg Gadamer. Since Kant insists on a noncognitive concept of aesthetic judgment, there must be an understanding or interpretation of art that links us synchronically as well as diachronically with others who are equally affected by aesthetic representations. However, what we share with others is not only our corporeal nature of being but also an unconscious part of the mind in which existential experiences exercise their significance on how we think and feel. In the aesthetic realm we can reflect on this intricate dynamic of thinking and feeling. This much Kant has realized in the *reflective judgment* which is ultimately determined by a fantasy that, as we know from psychoanalysis, is sustained by a lost object: the body of the mother.

◊ ◊ ◊

In his attempt to explain the universality of aesthetic experience and, especially, the judgment of the beautiful, Kant, though a philosopher of rational morality, grapples with the phenomenon of desire (*Begehren*) in a surprisingly psychoanalytic way: he links desire with the idea of unfulfillment as the cause for representations of imagination. He views desire as a cause for representations, particularly those he calls "fantastic desires." These are often accompanied by affect, particularly the affect of *Sehnsucht* (longing). Even if Kant changes his position somewhat in the introduction to the *Critique of Judgment* when he tries to delineate the relation of desire and representation (*Vorstellung*), he still acknowledges a relationship between one's abilities, actions, and *desire*. In other words, there still is no such thing as an experience that changes the self's reality without desire.

Kant begins with a definition of the capacity of desire (*Begehrungsvermögen*) "as the capacity to be the cause of, through its representations [*Vorstellungen*], the reality of the objects of these representations."[1] He opposes the criticism that wishes alone could not produce their objects by stating that even though "there are also desires through which human beings stand in contradiction with themselves," these desires nonetheless

motivate behavior and actions geared toward trying to bring about the
desired state of being. Trying to bring about the desired state, he suggests,
involves the *trying out* of human powers that produces a knowledge of
one's capacities and limitations as agents, in short, a knowledge of self:

> It seems that, if we were not determined to the application of our powers
> before we were assured of the adequacy of our faculties to produce an
> object, these powers would remain in great part unused. For we commonly
> learn to know our powers only by first making trial of them.[2]

Since representations (in)form expectations according to which human
beings act and even think, these expectations are psychological, emotionally based reactions to a reality wherein the desired objects are lacking. The
gap or conflict between one's expectations that orient a subject toward an
envisioned future state of the world and the state now experienced conditions the experience of temporality out of which a sense of oneself as a historical being arises. Contingent on one's imaginary representations, this
experience of the difference (the gap) creates a horizon of expectations in
terms of which the subject operates. Though Kant reckoned with desire as
an influence on imagination and experience, he could not go so far as
defining experience in imaginary and historical terms, for this would have
meant giving up an Enlightenment project based only on rational insight.
Only rational insight, it was believed, could change human behavior to
achieve the enlightenment goal of a happy social state.

Given the gap opened up between the representations of one's desires
and reality, the temporal space in which actions are motivated and performed manifests itself as that temporal space or moment in which history
is actually made, given that it is the realm of the possible. But what is possible is not predetermined. Instead, the possible is a function first of testing
the impossible, to which Kant alludes in his discussion of the capacity of
desire and representation. When Kant slightly changes his definition of
desire in the same passage from "a *capacity to be* the cause of the reality of
the objects it represents" to a desire that *is* not the cause of reality but
merely *represents* this causality, he acknowledges, however obliquely, the
role of feeling in mental representations.[3] Even more so, he is saying that
through desire we are capable of representing the otherwise obscured
causal relation between mind and reality. This kind of representation
occurs by way of desire in the realm of the beautiful:

> Although in such fantastic desires we are aware of the insufficiency of our
> representations (or their inadequacy) to be the cause of their objects, never-
> theless the fact remains that the *relation of these representations, as cause, and*

hence the representation of their causality, is contained in each wish, and this is eminently visible when this wish is an affect, namely longing [*Sehnsucht*].[4]

If the relation between desire, representation, and reality is seen by Kant in terms of a causality that is itself represented to the subject, the subject can reflect on this relationship, as Kant in fact does here. In aesthetic experience, the subject becomes like a psychoanalytic patient who gains access to the unconscious by slowly recognizing the difference between his biographically conditioned fantasies and his perceptions of the present circumstance. The subject reflects on the difference in what Kant consequently calls the *reflective* judgment of the beautiful. In reflecting on the relation of causality, the subject is, in his/her mind, moving in the space opened up between representation and reality. This kind of imaginary space is created by the capacity of desire and its representations which, in the *Critique of Judgment,* are a product of imagination. Indeed, cultural critics since Kant, such as Jürgen Habermas, have addressed this mental space as a sociological space of aesthetic experiences, an aesthetic realm that supplements the political and economic realm of a social existence that would otherwise restrict the individual's sense of freedom.

Although Kant's definition of experience was restricted to sense experiences, we could nonetheless apply his category of experience to his treatment of feeling since feeling is always the remnant of a forgotten sensuous experience. If Kant goes so far as to recognize a relation between the feeling and a mental state, he does so with the aim of eventually cognizing these mental states as well. Such cognition becomes the task of judgment. For Kant, it is this task of judgment that prompts a theory of the mind and representation. The resistance of Kant's model of the mind to any elaboration of cognitive processes lies not only upon the emphasis on judgment but in a systemic approach that is modeled on natural processes. Cognition repeats nature. Hence, he does not conceive of experience as a function of subjectivity. However, typical of Kant's ambivalence about a complete subject-object split is that he nevertheless acknowledges that human cognition cannot fully grasp nature since nature lacks systematicity. Kant therefore shifts the focus of cognition back upon the subject who engages in perceptions. If nature is heterogeneous, the form of perception that takes something for truth, *Wahr-nehmung,* is only identical with itself. As concerns the subject, the heterogeneity of nature is sublated into the homogeneity of perception, and this form of subjective perception is warranted only by the categories of time and space:

> For the unity of nature in time and space and the unity of our possible
> experiences is one and the same, because the unity of nature is the essence

of mere phenomena (modes of representation) [*Vorstellungsarten*], an essence that can find its objective reality only in experience that, as a system, has to be possible even according to empirical laws, provided one conceives of the unity of nature (as one must) like a system.[5]

Because the frame of time and space defines perception as a perception in and of the present, experience of nature can only be determined as an experience of presence. The notion of the past or of an unconscious motivation for perception and feeling in experience does not enter Kant's model.[6] Thus, the unity of nature is merely posited in analogy to the unity of the cognitive mind on the basis of a priori categories. In Kant's theory, the past would have to be the past of a former present, unchanged by any later experience that might rework this past toward a new meaning in the present. As to the aesthetic experience in which the individual might become aware of such a reworking process, he experiences an interaction of feelings, images, and associations of past experiences and thereby gains insight into his relationship to the world as he is able to acknowledge wishes and longings for a happier state of being. In as much as a person also reflects on this confluence of images and feelings in aesthetic experience, by way of remembrance, he may recognize a force of motivation that affects his mood and creates a particular experience of the present in the aesthetic realm. Recognizing the connection of this motivating force with a remembrance of things past, the subject is manipulated into a state or process of self-reflection; and self-reflection can only mean reflection on the subject's past. However, this emerging past does not encompass concrete events but reveals the ways in which the subject has been shaped up to that point. These ways, or manners, are a matter of feeling and respond to the present with a particular mental state or attitude that has developed as a reaction to an unconscious event. A child, for instance, creates a fantasy about an experience that it cannot process; in the child's psyche, the fantasy mediates the event and the feeling. In the aesthetic experience, the subject comes to sense himself as a historically constituted being without, however, knowing the "facts." The subject becomes aware of the fantasies (*intuitions* in Kant's model) that trigger his feelings.

Walter Benjamin extended this psychological relation between fantasy and feeling and attributed this "historical" sense to the feeling of belonging to a tradition: the commemorative and interpretative claim the past has on us as historical agents in the present. Kant was forced to exclude such a nonprogressive notion of history from aesthetic experience, since a nonprogressive history implies that the meaning of the past is deferred onto a future experience. In the context of the Enlightenment, Kant's interest in history was first of all a cognitive interest in thinking of the future as being different from the political status quo. In a secondary move, the aesthetic had to be brought in line with such a philosophy of history. It was to take on the function of preserving cognitive ideals for shaping individuals in the appropriate course of political history. Formulating such a purpose for aesthetic practice attests to an attempt at dominating subjective experience and fantasy. He hoped to achieve such domination in theorizing about the *form* of aesthetic experience.

Kant's illusion about the formative power of the aesthetic implies that the force of desire can be controlled as long as one can find "appropriate" artistic representations for experiences. Yet desire cannot be formed into any permanent representation, and because it resists the cognitive appropriation of experiences, it is able to act as the repetitive force in, and even as, tradition: the repetition of an affective experience inscribed in the human body.

Desire emerges in the gap between the experienced affect and a harmonizing fantasy that integrates self and other into a manageable experience. In other words, a child surrounds the overwhelming impact of an affect with a soothing fantasy through which it could register and record the experience as memory. The fantasy, however, remains unconscious. Desire thus never pertains to any identity in experience, because what really happened was never experienced as such. *Fantasy changed the event.* Hence, desire pertains to the difference between the imaginary (transformed) scene of the event and the suffered affect which is always greater than the fantasy that tried to contain it at the time. The difference or *differend* as Lyotard would say is felt as longing. As a psychological force in tradition, the fantasy and its retrospective awareness to the unattainability of the fantasized object is kept alive. Memory is active in tradition as longing; its psychological motor is an unsatisfied desire. Desire in its capacity to represent the causality of the fantasized object juxtaposes tradition to history, that is, subjective, adaptive, and imaginative experience to abstract, rationalized, and canonized knowledge. In its feeling of longing, desire testifies to the loss of nature often symbolized in the maternal figure of nature.

It is important to recall that Enlightenment philosophy dissociated nature, of which affects are its sensuous part, from the world of myth and magic, revelation, and the church. The relevance of these historical institutions in the cultural development of individuals was finally rejected by the idea of refining nature by controlling aesthetic practice. From this vantage point, the Enlightenment project has to be viewed as a break with "history," since, due to the Enlightenment's preoccupation with defining the future, the question about the historical determination of individuals or a retrospective personal history is never asked. However, aesthetic experience could lend itself to such an inquiry if one keeps in mind Kant's definition of desire "as the capacity to be the cause of, through its representations, the reality of objects of these representations."[7] In aesthetic experience, representations are the products of imagination, and hence, imagination acts transferentially as a power of external reality that causes *subjective* representations. Kant's eventual avoidance of acknowledging such a power of reality may be reflected in his decision to separate aesthetic experience and aesthetic judgment from other cognitive capacities. Cognition for Kant, and in principal for the Enlightenment, has always been object-oriented. "To cognize the other as the other of the self," might serve as a useful description of the unconscious strategies that underlie the concept of cognition in the eighteenth century. Such a view of cognition also illustrates a lacking awareness of what "traditionally" differentiates people in their transformation of the desire into their relation with an other. History was interpreted as the history of the object and its properties and was sublated into the cognitive categories of reason and understanding. Assessed as emancipatory faculties, reason and understanding represented the basis for equality among human beings. At the same time, this categorical equality enabled the repression of cultural-historically determined psychodynamic structures that create different experiences and meanings.

To the extent that desire is a manifestation of the past in fantasy, this desire expresses itself differently for various peoples and cultures. A denial of such difference has consequences for both the project of a prospective history and aesthetic repression. In the latter case, difference is acknowledged as a sensuality to be kept in check. And to the degree that sensuality comes into play in the presence of an other, of being affected if not touched by an other, the question of self and other is at the heart of a "politicized" Enlightenment aesthetics. As part of a political program, art will always approach a view of experience that satisfies the narcissistic drive that wants to appropriate the other. Working against this drive, taste also—in its capacity for a sensuous cognition of nature—had to be redirected into a universal instead of a particular expression of pleasure. That is, in aesthetic judgment, taste must not be separated from imagination—a mediation of one's sensuality (that experiences the affected body as an other) in imagination.

As Samuel Weber points out in his reading of Kant,[8] if desire contains a reflexive element because it causes the subject to represent himself as the agency of reality, then the relation of the subject to reality is mediated in imagination, in representations of which the subject becomes aware in aesthetic experience. Desire motivates representations through which the subject experiences himself as the creator of a reality that can be construed as tradition, a transfer of a fantasy (formed in the past) into the present. According to Weber, the problem for Kant consists in his inability to successfully include "the other side of reflective judgment" in the power of judgment. Imagination needed to somehow absorb this comparative side of desire, that is, the subject's capacity for distinguishing between reality and possibility in his awareness (memory) of the desired state. Desire as the power of the past impinging on the present, in the event of experience, can thus be considered the temporal component in (aesthetic) experience whereby the subject is brought in touch with his past. Reflection on or awareness of his relation to the past makes aesthetic experience the progenitor of all experience in that it effects the subject's sense of himself as being historically constituted.

In aesthetic judgment, the subject becomes conscious of the effort of finding or forming representations for the perception/sensation of the particular. It is an effort that may also be addressed as a struggle between exterior perception (*Wahrnehmung*) and interior representation (*Vorstellung*). This struggle within aesthetic judgment, in which the cognitive and representative powers are freed from the application of rules and concepts, leads to the realization that perception and representation are not easily separated and that they are brought about by engaging the individual's psychical economy. The psychical economy, and hence the person's history as it is also physically felt, is always at work when representations occur.

Of course, the power of imagination cannot function without memory, including the body's memory of pleasure and pain, when it conjures up representations in the form of sensuous intuitions (*Anschauungen*) as opposed to sensuous (affective) experiences. For the mind, therefore, memory performs the task of repeating events in the imagination. The initial difference between a perceived other and a lack of representations for this other is overcome by the desire to incorporate the other into the context or history of the self. Desire, as the motor of representation, mediates the gap between self and other, transferring to the imagination an impulse to repeat a memory-image. Contingent on memory, experience cannot be universalizable, since what is unconsciously reinstated is a subjective past. Thus the idea of a universality in experience is limited to a formal relationship with thought. Such an idea supports the psychoanalytic approach to meaning which treats experiences not so much as objective events than as the person's emotional reaction to an object. Instead of knowing the object, experience indicates to the subject how the object has affected the self.

Abbé du Bos, apparently an early example of a psychoanalytic psychologist, was also interested in the effect that art elicits from human nature.

Similarly Rolf Grimminger, who cites du Bos in his aesthetics of sensuality, asks "what are the processes involved in the constitution of the phenomenon of art, processes that can be invested with affects but which seem to harmonize, in the end, in producing a comprehensive artistic event."[9] With this question Grimminger hints at an essential relation of human nature and art, possibly one which would put art in charge of organizing all of human affect. In this task, art indeed joins in with modern day psychoanalysis.

Indeed, the work of psychoanalysis is concerned with the nature of these affects. Aesthetic criticism, at least in the eighteenth century, has analyzed these affects in the form of "aesthetical ideas" which artists bring to bear on language. These are "ideas" which have no representation but merely an effect on the reader's state of mind; they are a trigger of feeling that connects the reader's body with the intellectual act of reading. Psychoanalysis treats these affects as belonging to old experiences that (in)form the present state of mind. Since these experiences can no longer be recalled, they must be inferred from the affect experienced in a similar, but later situation. With the focus on affective experience being similar yet temporally different, psychoanalytic theory grounds itself in the signifying quality of temporality through which the past and present are related in a particular state of mind. Affect needs the duration and change of time to play itself out in the genesis of experience—*Er-fahr-ung*, moving across the distance between the present (later) event and an unconscious, primary experience. In "traveling" this distance between an unconscious past and a conscious present in experience, affect shows itself embedded in a process of remembrance linking the past with the present.

Experience involves remembrance. In remembrance the affect is unhinged from an unconscious representation of a primary physical experience and attached to the current representation of an event. This kind of psychodynamic is often described by psychoanalysts as an acting out of an unconscious memory in the current situation. Remembrance has unleashed the affect and turned it into a mobile force that is now able to engender new perceptions. Yet without the temporality of repetition, affect would lose its historical force and interpretative character. First, affect is a function of the past in the subject's psychical organization and in his life. Second, remembrance generates the mobility of affect and thus its power to modify future representations. Since affect is always connected with an unconscious fantasy of a satisfaction of desire, its representative status of history in the mental activity is inseparable from a fantasy of happiness. History as remembrance is never a pure memory but one distorted by unconscious fantasies about past experience.

Especially in the case of the beautiful, aesthetic experience is determined by the feeling of pleasure. Since the subject does not cognize the beautiful object, he is free to reflect on his being affected by the object, that is, on his feeling of pleasure, his affect. In this reflection he may realize that he is momentarily influenced by a past experience that he can no longer recall as such but that he can infer through a series of fragmentary images, Kant's "intuitions," that flicker in the subject's contemplation of the work of art. The feeling of pleasure transports the subject back to yet an earlier state in which the feeling first arose. The unconscious memory of this state transfers this past into the present in the occurrence of a (triggered) feeling.

In this way, I suggest, experience can be linked with a notion of an unconscious tradition. Tradition—conceived of as an unconscious process of memory, enacted by desire and carried out by the power of imagination that pictures (*vorstellt*) the triggered feeling—transmits a knowledge of the past in the instance of aesthetic experience. In this instance of experience, time comes to a standstill in order for the constellation of the past and the present to occur. Such a moment is "reminiscent" in the sense that it allows the significance of the past to shine through in the present. Since the force of desire that instigated this remembrance cannot be immediately contemplated, much less grasped in any cognitive form, there are only the imaginative representations that contain a "knowledge of the past," but this knowledge takes shape only in the present, in the form of an experience. Tradition can then be said to prepare the mental scene for an affective experience to take place in the space and time of a particular cultural event, that is, interpreted by the cultural signs at hand. In short, tradition transmits the impulse for experience to repeat itself in and as culture once the subject is in a position of reflecting on what is happening to him, how he is affected or touched by the Other. In this process of self-reflection, the judgment of taste tends toward a tactile (physical) rather than a transcendental experience of the aesthetic impact.

5

The Maternal Ground of Aesthetic Experience

IF KANT PROPOSES AFFECT AS THE BASIS FOR AESTHETIC JUDGMENT—THE relation of the subject's feeling of pleasure or displeasure (*Lust oder Unlust*) to a representation—this also implies some notion of the body that Kant intuits but never quite develops. I will attempt to bring out this bodily dimension that informs the judgment of taste and, by extension, aesthetic experience. In aesthetic judgment a certain knowledge of one's body, its re-action to certain situations and representations, is made possible in the form of an experience. Since the body is the place where the mind and "physical" reality meet, it serves as the substrate for a knowledge engendered by the interpretation of sense impressions. The body stores, so to speak, an unconscious knowledge that determines the body's reaction to physical stimuli. Such reactions are already embedded in an unreflected though established, hence unconscious, relationship of the subject to the world. Conscious access to this relationship is bound up in the body's reactions and is possible only through the faculty of imagination which finds images for physical states caused by external stimuli. Hence, we actually do not know the body directly, as it is being affected, nor the affects in themselves; we only know them through the accompanying, forever newly created images with which the mind, involuntarily, tries to represent sensuous experience.

Kant complicates matters because he neglects to mention the body, leaving the reader to wonder about the medium of reflection.[1] If the exterior (beautiful) object is abandoned for the subject as the object of reflection, then the "object" must be the subject's body as it "suffers" the affects. Reflecting on the affective experience, as the body's "sufferings," may not trace a genealogy of affect so much as it masters a *pathology* of past experiences that have not been worked through or consciously put to rest in the subject's memory. (An affect is put to rest when an image or imaginative scene can be constructed to absorb the affect as remembrance.) The

79

pathological or "pathetic" (from Greek: *pathein*) quality of experience and its memory in repetitive affect, rather than indicating a clinical label for disturbance, hints at the temporal structure of experience in the sense of *Erfahrung* which requires a belated completion. Before such a completion of experience in the present, the subject remains fixated on the past. Because of their suffering bodies, subjects might well be in a perpetually latent melancholic state.

"Melancholia" names the emotional attachment to the unmastered other in hitherto unconscious experience. Unmasterable affect resembles the psychological shock experience of trauma. Referring again to Benjamin's model of experience, I contend that every experience affects the subject's mind not entirely unlike the belated effects of trauma. The contingency of trauma and experience is the unconscious and unknowable physical event in a person's life. In the aesthetic experience of the present, the experience is no longer one of the body but of the mind. It is here that all the attachments to the past event are played out. As such an attachment, the melancholic state of mind serves as a cognitive catalyst for remembrance—the fusion of a new image with an old affect that results in a conscious feeling of satisfaction.

In *reflective* judgment, the subject reflects upon an interplay between affect (pleasure) and image that produces a subjective satisfaction—subjective, because it is disinterested in the existence of the object. We may conclude that the external object merely served to start an internal process of forming and dissolving representations in alternation with the feeling of pleasure or pain. This latter process could be called autoaffection insofar as the subject enjoys his subjectivity in imagination, a process that results in feeling.

Kant himself speaks of "autoaffection" in the *Opus Postumum* where he tries to think the mediating power of representation in the relation between subject and object: "Perception is the empirical representation whereby the subject affects himself a priori in the intuition [*Anschauung*], making himself the a priori object of transcendental cognition, according to a principle of the synthetic representation [*Vorstellung*] that follows the system of categories, and then passing over into physics."[2] (Intuition here refers to indefinite representations of the past.) The original affect, or rather the state of being affected by the stimulus, is, through the intervention of imagination, turned into inner feeling which we assessed earlier as a sign of the subject's past that is repeated in "disinterested satisfaction." Disinterested indeed, because the satisfaction or pleasure produced does not consist of an enjoyment of the object in the present, but rather describes a state of mind that is brought about with the help of imagination.

Hence Kant's notion of disinterestedness implies an uncathected object, something that suggests a self-cathexis in aesthetic experience. As a power that is both productive and reproductive, imagination has the capacity to repeat a past state of mind, one associated with feeling pleasure in response to the beautiful. Reflecting on the movement of imagination in the beautiful, the subject may gain a knowledge of his sensuality that would otherwise remain unconscious and be expressed in the form of automatic physical reactions to various situations.

But how is such knowledge of the sensual (i.e. pleasure) represented to the mind? For Kant, the process of cognition is identical to the process of forming mental representations. How then can he discern representations that are not cognitive, or what are the criteria by which he denies cognitive value to representations? Finally, if Kant actually relates the power of judgment to understanding—for imagination and understanding are both involved in judgment—what is it that aesthetic judgment cannot cognize with respect to the subject if not the body?[3]

If it is the task of imagination to represent feeling and sensuality so that the subject might comprehend her feelings and experiences, then first and foremost the questions to ask are, what kind of relationship exists between sensuality and mental representation, and what role does imagination play in it? In the mind's attempt to represent affect, the affect's connection to imagination is referred, as we have seen above, to the subject's unconscious desire for pleasure which stems from a past experience with/or of the other. Put differently, the subject's memory of the past intervenes in, and thus constitutes the relationship between imagination and the body.

However, in Kant's concept of sensuality/sensibility (*Sinnlichkeit*), the body is difficult to discern as the materiality of experience, since in this concept (spelled out in the *Critique of Pure Reason*) he already relates sensations to representation: "The faculty (receptivity) to receive representations in the manner in which we are affected by objects is called sensuality [*Sinnlichkeit*]."[4] Sensuality thus implies a mediation of sense impressions that are perceived in the form of representations corresponding to affects. The body gets lost in this mediation, and Kant's notion of sensibility/ sensuality is implicitly supposed to substitute for this loss by covering over an apparently a priori relationship between body and imagination. He even goes so far as to say that sensuality produces intuitions: "Objects are given to us by means of sensuality [*Sinnlichkeit*] which alone supplies us with intuitions."[5] In the *Critique of Judgment*, in which Kant is more concerned with the status of imagination, intuitions are attributed to the power of imagination and, conversely, he calls imagination, at least in its freedom, a faculty of sensuality (*Sinnlichkeit*).[6]

Kant's overemphasis on cognition clearly emerges from this perceptual array of sensation, intuition, and imagination which he sublates into the posited faculty of sensibility. Sensuality thus seems to be, again, a theoretical construct whose bodily basis—sensations and affects—is passed over. As a consequence, he offers no conception as to how such affects are made intelligible or are differentiated from one another. He just posits their transformation into intuitions that are perceived. In this sense, the transformative mind is always already involved in and interferes with the body, for the goal of these transformative processes is to achieve a mental representation, that is, to impose (cognitive, conceptualizable) form on the amorphous mass of sense impressions and affects (*Sinnenreiz*). Form names an a priori category of consciousness.

Here it is most interesting to note how Kant circumvents the body, the affect of pleasure and pain, supposedly the sole ground for the judgment of the beautiful, when he posits the a prioriness of form. He does this by first assuming an ideality of objects given to the senses on the basis of which objects can be cognized as representations. With respect to the beautiful where cognitive faculties are not concerned with the determination of the object but with the subject's feeling of pleasure, Kant nonetheless follows through with the mental ideality of the object's form. Instead of making the affect of pleasure the "object" of reflection—and hence the body the focus—he stays with the beautiful object per se and treats it as a potential object for cognition by referring it to an "idealism of purposiveness:"[7] the object's purpose is the representation of form. The feeling or affect never becomes the "object of sensuous intuition" upon which the power of judgment might reflect in a secondary elaboration. Instead, Kant starts with the entity of intuition (*Anschauung*) when he analyzes the production of representation. The quality of disinterested satisfaction (of pleasure), in contrast to sensuous pleasure, hinges on the difference between sensation and intuition as the object of reflection:"The satisfaction in the beautiful must depend on the reflection upon an object, leading to any concept (however indefinite), and it is thus distinguished from the pleasant, which rests entirely upon sensation."[8] The object is given to the senses as an intuition, and reflection upon the intuition then must lead to a concept. Intuition thus represents a necessary intermediary step in developing concepts of objects. From this we may conclude that Kant omits the entity of feeling, avoiding the need to conceptualize both the feeling and its conditions. What makes feeling and affect intelligible is a question that cannot be answered by Kant's theory of mental representation (*Vorstellung*). By defining imagination as the faculty of a priori intuitions,[9] Kant, for his purposes of linking aesthetic judgment with the presumed

intellectual freedom of imagination, can stop with the a priori status of intuition. For our purpose of investigating the relation of feeling to imagination and representation, we will have to question this a priori status of
intuition.

Certainly a place to begin is the idea of a tactile and sensuous intuition
that already implies the body of the mother; after all, it is *Mutterwitz* that
underlies Kant's concept of judgment of taste in its modality of disinterested satisfaction. Kant's recourse to the natural talent of *Mutterwitz* serves
him well if he wants to reflect the psychological structure of a mimesis in
which the imaginary body of the mother—that is, the lost object of experience—not only produces a concrete sense of relation but also the intuition
of the mere possibility of a relationship between different and seemingly
unrelated objects. This facilitating capacity in mimesis (mimetic imagination) seems to resist further abstraction and must legitimate itself indeed
as a natural talent. Otherwise, as Luiz Costa Lima has argued in his book
The Control of the Imaginary, imagination needs to rely on fictional language as necessary examples for grasping human nature. Costa Lima asserts, "it is impossible for us to think without fictions,"[10] an insight that
merely elaborates a much earlier insight of the eighteenth century by
Jeremy Bentham who wrote on the importance of language for training the
mind. This ability to abstract an intuition of metaphysical concepts from
language is, however, the condition for philosophizing as such. Without the
body in language, philosophy would not have any basis.

Kant, however, needs to hold on to a pure metaphysics and therefore
leaves vague the transposition from language (*Darstellung*) to the mind
(*Vorstellung*). Instead of acknowledging a historical imagination, he tries to
ground the metaphysical, and, for him, ahistorical nature of humans in
pure form. He does this by pursuing the possibility of a framed image
without content; in other words, he tries to think the formality or
schematics of representation. He calls this mental product "purposiveness
of representation" so as to distinguish it from any definite image or meaning. His whole treatise on the aesthetic judgment thus reformulates the
question of the beautiful as a question of formality: How can the beautiful
form be reflected or constituted in the mind so that its subjective judgment can find universal consensus? Kant's analysis of aesthetic judgment
gradually funnels into an analysis of the power of imagination. How can
imagination produce form if it does not work with concepts? It should not
come as a surprise that Kant needs to abandon an empirical, body-bound
concept of imagination for a transcendental power of imagination that can
stay free from a sensuality that involves the body in representation (*Vorstellung*). The putative power of this imagination produces pure intuitions,

representations of mere possibilities of experience. The question, however, remains whether the idea of transcendence can indeed dislodge human cognitive faculties from physical contingencies.

Kant's insurmountable task in the *Third Critique* is to rationally combine a definition of taste with a concept of form that is not cognitive. Such a noncognitive form cannot be issued by the faculty of reason because it would have to be an idea, a completed representation. Hence, the noncognitive form must be a form that is an intuition of pure formality, or transcendence as a mental state. Since the judgment of taste pertains to the feeling of pleasure, the problem naturally lies with the objectification of this feeling in representation. Transcendence and feeling are the two states that need to be represented to the mind. Concrete, sensible and, to be sure, sensuous examples—what Kant calls "the wheels of the faculty of judging" that determine "mother wit"[11]—might well be the only vehicle available for Kant to succeed in his move from the sensuous to the conceptual realm. Such body-bound examples may, however, turn, as Derrida has shown in his reading of Kant, into a "parergonal" movement[12] that diverts the imaginative attention toward the frame and the mechanics of representation rather than allowing imagination to conjure up the forgotten pleasure of the mother's body, the *jouissance* repeated in the experience of the work of art.

Kant's formal/material impasse in representing the beautiful reveals philosophy's ambivalence toward imagination as a sensuous *and* intellectual faculty. And yet, why could feeling not be the mediating instance between form and matter? If so, we would then have to presume that imagination has an affective character. In any case, this impasse in the sensuous and intellectual faculty of imagination proves that thinking the "imaginative" state—Kant's purposiveness of representation—is impossible, because such a pure or rather empty state serves no purpose in the psychical economy of emotional cathexis.

Consequently, trivialized to carnivalesque folklore, "mother wit" in its manifestation of an affective cognition had to be excluded from the philosophical paradigms of the Enlightenment. But this means that Kant never came to terms with the phenomenon as well as the *feeling* of creativity, despite Kant's fascination with it in his cosmological theory. (Let me note here that, in his pre-critical writings, e.g., the *Theory of the Heavens*, Kant's discourse is saturated with metaphors of the maternal to describe the generative and creative powers of the universe.[13]) Philosophy indeed could not come to terms with it because, as we see in the example of Kant, the implicitly acknowledged source of creativity, the nurturent body of the mother, had to be explicitly suppressed for the sake of developing an autonomy of the individual. And, lest we forget, what warrants the undividable status of the individual is the power of reason. After all, Kant relegated the status of "mother wit" to a footnote in his *Critique of Practical Reason*. This represents a missed chance in Kant to think through the potential of an affective cognition or that which (aesthetically) unconsciously mediates the body and the mind.

And what happens to desire, philosophically and psychologically? The inevitability of the desire for an other manifests itself only negatively, namely, in the subject's attempt to split off his affective nature from his cognitive self so as to deny his (imaginative) dependence on something or someone prior to rational consciousness. Since the individual nonetheless has social needs, the possibility for relating to an other on existential or emotional grounds diminishes once the foundational (m)other is killed off in the self. Psychoanalysis has defined such people as narcissistic, as incapable of transference and of a libidinal investment in the other.

While an Enlightenment philosophy of *Bildung* stressed individuation in a conscious effort to struggle free from the comfortable embracement by the maternal body, the Romantic goal of *Bildung* emphasized the remembrance of the relationship with the mother and an awareness of one's own body. The self's relation to his own and the body of an other was seen as basic to developing a sensitivity toward another human being as well as for developing one's imagination through sensuous experience. The arts and the aesthetic realm eventually found their legitimation in the cultivation of the individual's sensibilities. Eventually, aesthetics occupied its own cultural space. Only in the form of beauty can matter and the self's affective grounding in nature be acknowledged. The aesthetic pleasure does not exist without the feeling of an original separation from a nurturent, maternal body. Hence, the pleasure of beauty attests to an ambivalence toward the mother whose remembrance is also experienced as pain—the pains of reason to overcome the desire for the mother:

> The principle "noli tangere matrem" locates its economy of reason and desire in the *categorical imperative*. Fear and awe of an all powerful nature forbid man to touch his/the mother and reward his courage in resisting her attractions by granting him the right to judge himself independent, while at the same time encouraging him to prepare himself to continue resisting dangers in the future by developing (his) [intellectual] culture.[14]

Reason must replace the imaginary in an attempt to create a social culture merely through the circulation of *ideas*. Of course, if society legitimates itself through an intersubjectivity borne by the realm of ideas, the individuals in this society are only all the more susceptible to vicarious experiences of sociality supplied by mass media images; and, in the twentieth century, these electronic images have replaced both (intellectual) ideas and the sensitivity/receptivity of the body as mutual ground of a relational existence.

If Kant wants to define imagination as a formal power, capable of detaching itself from the body, his critical move must aim at abandoning affect altogether. With such a move, however, he erodes all material basis of experience. Imagination then operates without the resources of experience and memory and desire. Such isolation of imagination from the body and from sensuous experience necessarily assimilates the power of imagination to the faculties of understanding and reason. Yet, the bodily experience, namely sensation and affect, is what supports imagination and makes it an effective power for self-experience. Experience supplies the material for an imaginative translation into meaning. And it is this translation that represents the central issue in aesthetic judgment. What else could a "reflective judgment" imply, if not the subject's reflection on how his imagination tries to grasp his own feelings in the aesthetic moment? Is not this reflection and awareness of the interplay between imagination and feeling what Kant means by *Lebensgefühl*, a feeling of being alive that he himself attributes to such a reflection, as its result of an aesthetic experience?

Through feelings, the body has an impact on self-consciousness. Kant also determines aesthetic experience as one of self-consciousness, even if it is the body that mediates between self and environment, between self and other. One might be prompted to wonder what might have determined the self up until the moment of self-awareness triggered, according to Kant, by a feeling. An answer to this question might be that the subject actually decides the meaning of past experiences once they coalesce in a nameable quality of that feeling. For, without previous experiences, preserved in unconscious fantasies, the present experience could not motivate the subject's imagination to produce an intuition. Past experience is actually needed for the creative power of imagination to draw on. For a theoretical reflection on experience this means that, without recourse to history and a concept of the past, the very concept of experience loses its cognitive validity. Experience only has significance because of its genealogical structure. If the judgment of taste does not rest on experience and history, as it surely cannot when it is regarded as the result of an abstraction from feeling and body, then it represents little more than a conceptual construct of an intellectual feeling and is but a heuristic device for mediating imagination and understanding.

As I have argued, Kant's understanding of aesthetic experience is derived from a separation of mind and body. Because his reasoning is caught up in constantly opposing the categories of materiality to those of formality, he is therefore unable to link these categories plausibly without the insight of a third "category," the category of an unconscious translation, or what Benjamin calls the "correspondence" between memory and experience. In the aesthetic judgment an involuntary memory surfaces and calls attention to its power over how we experience the present moment. In the aesthetic judgment, the faculties are not preoccupied with cognizing the (beautiful) object. As Benjamin might put it, what is nonetheless cognized is the impact of the past upon the present, or even, how history conditions our consciousness.

If reflection on feeling were to bring about a cognitive judgment or understanding, then it would have to evoke a lived past for an assessment of the present experience. A hermeneutic process of the mind would thus indeed bring about an understanding of the self as a historically constituted being. Kant, seemingly handicapped in this case by an epistemology of universal reason, cannot allow such subjective, and necessarily historical, understanding of the status of cognition. His aesthetic philosophy, however, manifests an attempt at combining the subjective category of experience with the universal truth of beauty. He follows through in this attempt by analyzing the function of various cognitive faculties generally involved in experience. This maneuver, necessary for postulating the universality of the judgment of taste, exposes Kant's ongoing struggle with the concept of knowledge; he is unable to theoretically separate knowledge from cognition. His bias toward an objective, universalizable knowledge, a knowledge that results from a priori logical categories of consciousness, prevents him from recognizing a hermeneutic process of cognition. When he associates materiality with sensation, which is variably subjective, he means by "reflection" only the formal, mental movement that is at stake when a phenomenon is apprehended into a representation, like an image. The mental process in reflective judgment leads to an accord of the faculties, which Kant stresses as the same psychological result in everyone. It is here that Kant's moral underpinning of the aesthetic judgment shows through. Since the mind's interest does not lie with the object but with the subject's feelings, Kant can come up with the idea of a disinterested pleasure of the beautiful. Since for Kant reflection only implies an apprehension according to form, the question remains: what is the form of a feeling?

Because feeling does not have a form, it has to be treated like an inner sensation which can only be understood in terms of the images it triggers. These images do not, however, represent the feeling as such, for they are independently existing representations or fantasies that are merely associated at the moment of pleasure or pain. In the case of the beautiful, it is not the mental representation of a rose that is pleasurable but the images remembered *along with* the subject's affection by the rose.

What should have become evident by now is Kant's movement from nature to culture, in the disguise of an aesthetic theory. He starts out with the sense impression of the beautiful object, and hence with nature; but, rather than analyzing how affect becomes mental image, he dwells on the mental processes which bring about the formality of aesthetic judgment. Both sensation and nature, precisely because they resist subsumption under concepts and hence constitute an unknowable other in the aesthetic judgment, need to be regulated by laws of representation. The establishment of such laws forces Kant into a concern with the formality of representation.

This focus on formality rather than the physical support or context of reflection prevents him from taking into consideration what his contemporary Novalis has defined in his *Reizlehre* (theory of stimulation) as "the subject's inner sensibility," its sensitivity, which affects the subject's power of intuition. *Sensibilität*, or sensitivity, is a requirement for perception and aesthetic experience. Hence, perception names a capacity that is patterned after the subject's past. This view subverts a concept of taste which reduces taste to its formal properties in judgment. Such a reduction of taste to its form demonstrates Kant's avoidance of historical considerations for conceptualizing the subject's experience of the present. In the following, Kant's epistemological innovation of criticism (*Kritik*) shall, however, reveal its grounding in history, in a critique of taste rather than in a "transcendental aesthetics."

The *method of critique* (*Kritik*) takes as its object the particularity of taste, one that is contingent on the capability of discrimination. One cannot have taste without the ability of comparing the present sensation to a previous one; without experience or history, the tradition of taste, for instance represented as literary criticism, would literally not make "sense."

6

The Unconscious Hermeneutics of "Wit"

Since my aim is to excavate the inherent psychoanalytic supplement to Kant's critique of judgment, constructed in part by the Romantics, it is appropriate to advance a possible distinction between the function of judgment in Kant and in the Romantic thinkers. After all, what Kant works into the form of a *critique* (*Kritik*) the Romantics transformed into a *hermeneutics* based on the idea of an unconscious memory from which imagination derives its power for representation. The value of an experience, like the value of a potentially beautiful object, is determined by the reflective and transformative process that compares the present with the past. An interesting aspect of this determination of (aesthetic) experience concerns the original definition of aesthetics in the eighteenth century as a science (*Wissenschaft*). One has to keep in mind that in the eighteenth century *Wissenschaft* was a notion that did not necessarily imply pure analysis of the material; rather, it also preserved the practical aspect of the object of study. We should not forget that many theoreticians and philosophers were what we would today call creative writers, which is why aesthetics not only functioned as a theory of the beautiful but was itself supposed to *lead to* the beautiful. Hence, aesthetics *facilitated* experience and creation. Kant and the Romantics are important for the development of a theory of experience that found its completion in Walter Benjamin, since experience in the sense of *Erfahrung* is patterned on the temporal and anaclytic structure of memory and the subsequent remembrance of the lost object in the prototype of experience, the aesthetic moment. You cannot have an affective/aesthetic experience without the conditioning fantasy of a recovered lost object.

If aesthetic experience can be treated as prototypical for all experience in the temporal delay of self-completion ("the perfection of man"), then the history of aesthetics may indeed yield another valuable insight into the psychological development of the individual. That is, it is much more than

Kant's apparent mechanical investigation into the faculties at play in the judgment of the beautiful. Rather, the *critique* of aesthetics tends toward a hermeneutical understanding of experience and how that experience relates to the individual's overall formation (*Bildung*).[1] Hermeneutics as it concerns the interaction of a subject with a work of art, or the reader and the text, engages the subject in a transferential relationship not only with the text but also with parts of his hitherto unacknowledged self. It is not only a question of making sense of the text, but also of making sense of one's "split-off" or repressed selves. Hermeneutics adumbrates a psychoanalytic strategy to create a whole, that is, a mutually integrative figure between self and other.

As a philosophical concept introduced by the German Romantics, hermeneutics focuses on the process involved in sense-making. Since Romanticism, hermeneutics has come to represent an alternative epistemological grounding of a mode of knowledge other than rational cognition. Hans-Georg Gadamer finally elaborated consciousness as a hermeneutical instrument tuned by tradition and language rather than instrumental reason. It is also no coincidence that hermeneutics emerged at the same time as did philosophies of history. Historical experience simply cannot be reduced to categories of deduction, or cause and effect. The Romantics understood that history cannot be planned, because the temporal structure of individual experience is nonlinear. Moreover, experience constitutes individual differences that, in order for them to be socially synthesized, need to be mediated by a certain kind of language. The Romantics saw the possibility of such a mediation in the creation of an allegorical culture in art. By implementing experience as a new grounding for knowledge—in the sense of insight rather than cognition—a conceptual integration of individual difference into a theory of knowledge (*Wissenschaft* as *Kritik*) could be achieved. What eventually became clear, in the eighteenth century's struggle over subsuming the particular under the universal, was that the concept of taste relates to individual difference that can only be addressed in terms of feeling and imagination. And, as both imagination and feeling derive from the subject's previous experiences, taste is less a formal category than it is a historical one. Kant himself, though foremost concerned with the formality and universality of judgments of taste, cannot entirely exclude the historical contingency of the faculty of judgment, since judgment always compares the object at hand with one already perceived. Judgment needs experience to know the difference.

Kant's reflection on critique is, after all, aimed at a mode of knowledge different from that established by causality and the application of laws. Critique and judgment use "sentiments" as their modes of knowledge; but a sentiment comes from the heart, not the head. Therefore, in contrast to doctrine, the principles of critique cannot be taught.[2] They must previously exist as part of the subject's faculties and merely need to be developed and stimulated by experience. Experience and the empirical realm do, in fact, have their place in Kant's conception of the judgment of taste. Taste designates the capacity that enables one to compare oneself with others when making a judgment. Consequently, in taste, the Ego can actually assume the stance of another to judge itself. By comparing oneself with others, the subject demonstrates a social contingency of thinking and feeling. This comparison in one's judgments implies that taste is also a capacity for self-criticism, and, derived from that, self-knowledge. Taste determines a value judgment, though it is also an expression of the capability to judge, particularly from the perspective of wholeness. From the standpoint of knowledge, this is precisely the hermeneutical perspective of judgment, even if Kant, of course, did not state the relationship between taste and the power of judgment in these terms. Instead, he conceived of a social utopia when he defined judgment as that power of the subject which focuses on "the proper" of the object. This required a comparison of the concrete appearance of the object to an *idea* of the object proper. But whence does one get the idea of the proper in the object? How does one know what it should be? What is the ideal object—or subject—in self-criticism? How do we acquire an ideal notion of the other? Finally, what does the proper—in German: *das Schickliche*—refer to in Kant?

Since *das Schickliche* is concerned with the comparing of two things (self and other, self with the whole, other with a notion of the whole), it must refer to a harmony or congruence of contiguous intuitions in the mind. After all, the proper attitude eventually brings about the experience of pleasure in the subject, which means that it is linked with a mental state in which different items are easily connected with one another. If they are not connected, they are not *schicklich*, and the result is the feeling of displeasure and frustration. We could then say that the power of judgment supplies the connection between two things to create a *schicklicher*, pleasurable state of mind. The mind does this whenever it can find a *tertium comparationis*, a reference point which activates the psychical maneuver of connecting two things comfortably. This psychical maneuver then creates a context or structure in which objects are brought into contact with each other by means of the proper reference point which mediates the contiguity of intuitions prompted by the objects. A network of such mental relationships turns objects into signs and grants them meaning.

The concept of purposiveness (*Zweckmässigkeit*) is such a reference point, or *tertium comparationis*. If the object must be referred or related to a purpose, the *tertium* in the subject's mental apparatus is a movement or motion, the movement of relating. This aspect of mental movement relates the activity of comparing to a *sense* or awareness of movement in the proper itself. The adjective *schicklich* in German derives from the verb "to send," *schicken*. Sending, however, is a directed movement. As Derrida has pointed out in his work *The Postcard*, sending implies an addressee, or telos which the posted letter may or may not reach due to the postal system's detours, hold-ups, interceptions, and so on. This underlying movement in determining whether something is proper—or rather properly or purpose-fully "sent"—or not, ultimately enacts an interpretative process that effects what in language is called "metaphor," which in Greek (*meta-phora*) means to move from one place to another. In theories of signification, metaphor designates the movement of translation or the transfer of meaning from one realm of signification to another. In judgment, of course, all this moving about takes place in the subject's mind where it is part and parcel of the psychical economy of the person.

In the eighteenth century, the comparative and transferential agency of the mind was conceptualized as the faculty of wit or—at least in the first half of the century—as spirit (*Geist*), both of which were regarded as very distinct from reason. Reason represented scholarly or bounded thought (*das gebundene Denken*), whereas *Geist* generated free roaming and creative thought (*frei schweifendens und gestaltendes Denken*).[3] *Geist* is really no dif-ferent from the concept of fantasy fashioned by the Romantics in relation to thinking. Before the Romantics placed a new emphasis on fantasy as a power of thinking, eighteenth-century philosophers of aesthetics had ac-knowledged a mental capacity or talent in wit (which never occurs sepa-rately from *Geist*) that was responsible for the psychical translation process and its rhetorical representation in language. The presence of wit in a person accounts for his translation of *Vorstellung* into *Darstellung*. This conception of wit foreshadowed an aesthetics of genius to which Kant fully subscribed. Philosophers before Kant had already reflected on the connec-tion between psyche and language, and interpreted wit as a faculty whose power was dependent on language, the medium of witty metaphor.

One can only be affected by language if the faculty of wit has previously assembled the parts of language in such a way that the receptive mind can easily compare different things that would otherwise never be associated with one another. With reference to Benjamin, this comparison may only be possible by means of a tradition in which language and the individual psyche are related by a historical continuum. Tradition presents itself as what Benjamin has called the "canon of non-mimetic representation" in language.[4] The capacity of wit turns written signifiers into figurative signs.

Wit was therefore acknowledged as a significant power of artistic representation in the burgeoning critique of aesthetics: "Wit shows itself mainly in the happy invention of a 'flowery manner of speaking' [*verblümter Redensarten*], i.e. metaphors, through which we are brought to [recognize] similarities among things, as metaphor is only a 'short allegory.'"[5]

A re-reading of the notion of poiesis (*Dichtkunst*) in the eighteenth century reveals the analytic and philosophical struggle involved in expressing the semiotic interaction between the mental apparatus and language. In a careful study of Johann Christoph Gottsched's *Critische Dichtkunst*, for instance, Alfred Bäumler uncovers the prerequisites of what I will call a psychological theory of language. The all-encompassing concepts that continually emerge at the conceptual impasse between psyche and language are "soul" and "genius": "Comparing is an activity of the soul."[6] A passage through this impasse is granted by the mediation of wit: "In wit is thus found the psychological ground of the most important capacity of the poet; it is metaphor and allegory that poetry actually depends upon."[7]

In the eighteenth century, the concept of wit was enmeshed in a view of metaphor that had yet to be articulated in terms of a linguistic theory. The notion of metaphor had been borrowed from the realm of painting, which means that the movement of *meta-phora* as effecting a translation, and hence a semantic difference, was not yet recognized. The relationship between *Urbild* (original) and *Abbild* (copy) was merely understood as one of imitation. Yet, when Christian Wolff, the proponent of *Vermögenspsychologie* (psychology of faculties), realized the transcendent aspect of imagination which combines things freely, he not only expanded the concept of imagination but, at the same time, shifted the focus of the relationship between *Urbild* and *Abbild* from a concern with identity to an appreciation of the transformative quality of imagination. This shift allowed him to acknowledge difference. Wit represented an ingenious faculty to perceive similarities in different things. Again, in his essay on the mimetic capacity, Benjamin's notion of *unsinnliche Ähnlichkeiten* (non-mimetic similarities) lends itself to an interpretation of wit as that mimetic capacity (*mimetisches Vermögen*) that mediates between language and mental image, transforming both in the process. Such a rendition of wit inevitably ruptured the static mimetic model of representation that had been established on the premise that appearance merely resembled identity.

This rupture of mimesis also opened the door for a psychoanalytic model of representation in which desire and history skew the linear equation of *Abbild* and *Urbild*. Wit, the faculty which listens to desire, interferes in the mirror relationship of *Urbild* and *Abbild*, distorting and distracting imagination in its attempt to represent the object. Wit causes imagination to be creative by assembling the various parts of the object in different and unexpected ways so that different things can be compared and subsequently associated with one another in the perceiver's mind. It is this surprising quality of an unexpected but nonetheless understood meaning which is still preserved in German in today's meaning of wit as joke (*Witz*). Freud elaborated on this quality in his analysis of the unconscious in the joke.[8]

It was also Freud who rehabilitated the commemorative power of wit in the organization of the mind. In fact, Freud alludes to an "ingenious" faculty of the unconscious mind that causes the understanding and hence the punchline of a joke. The "genius" of wit lies in an unconscious knowledge about a secret relationship between things. Because of cultural taboos, this knowledge can only emerge in an oblique or non-mimetic linguistic representation. The fact that an awareness of the tabooed meaning is accompanied by explosive laughter shows the repressive tension involved in the socio-cultural regimentation of thought and meaning. By analyzing people's mental constructions, Freud has demonstrated that conscious thought requires the repression of certain similarities between incongruous experiences and thoughts. The joke's effect does not stem from an innovative connection between things but merely reveals an already cognized but repressed familiarity with tabooed ideas attached to these things. Freud's notion of the uncanny (*unheimlich*) elaborates this phenomenon of an unconscious familiarity (the aspect of *heimisch* in *un-heimlich*) that expresses itself in an irrational, that is to say neurotic, fear.

That we are able to associate very different objects or ideas with one another when reading a linguistic representation results from a linguistic creativity that produces an appearance of similarities between things that are normally unrelated. This appearance or semblance is only artificially created as the "artefact" of an artistic representation. Such representation depends on rhetoric and hence on the fictional quality of language which initially produces an appearance of similarities between things or signs. From this vantage point, language exerts a psychological power by prompting additional meanings that would otherwise be forgotten in the referential or mirror function of linguistic signs. This referential notion of language prevails in the science of linguistics in a way that is not dissimilar from the positivist assumptions of historicism. The antidote to such a constrained view of language is the aesthetic which positivists decry for its poetic license.

Walter Benjamin, however, introduces the aesthetic status of literary texts within a historical framework often dominated by positivism. He insists that aesthetic and allegorical strategies are necessary for the purpose of constructing historical consciousness. Such strategies of representation (*Darstellung*) parallel the concept of psychoanalytic transference and the essential temporality in the formation of thought (*Vorstellung*). The similarities produced by the rhetorical and figural power of language can be viewed as examples of a belated, intuitive connection supplied by wit. And wit, we must recognize, proves indispensable for imagination as a cognitive power in aesthetic representation.

The talent of a perception that "finds" nonobvious similarities in things was not, however, recognized in the eighteenth century as a cognitive faculty. Rather, wit was interpreted as the faculty of inventing and representing something new that surprises the senses, and if it was not to be cognitive, then it must be something new in the sense of the sensational. But what sets this search activity of the psyche in motion? Why would the individual, encountering textuality, "see" something differently than before? And why then would the subject, when perceiving separate things, indulge in a vision of their similarities? Such questions aim at identifying the motivation of wit and fantasy. They try to address the emotional relationship between the subject and the object. The process starts, again, with affect.

Depending on its force, affect triggers an emotional interest in those objects that motivate the subject to perceive their similarities. The knowledge supporting the perception of similarities can only emerge once affect has set the mental translation process in motion, the movement of *meta-phora*, that turns affect into images and conscious feelings. Once the affect is "reflected" in a mental image, it becomes a feeling. The power of affect depends upon the impact of an experience in the subject's past. This past experience is then unconsciously repeated through the sense impressions from the current object. The subject's disposition vis-à-vis the object is thus influenced by the past as it triggers the subject's desire for a memory of bliss. This animated desire ultimately forms the subject's vision of the object. It is this desire-driven vision that constitutes the basis for a value judgment, such as "this rose is beautiful."

Given the view that an unconscious past is represented or reproduced only in feelings, what the mind compares is not so much the particularities of external objects. Rather, it checks the current affect against the unconscious desire for bliss. The degree of satisfaction of this desire determines whether affect is reflected as a feeling of pleasure or pain. If there is pleasure, the affect has satisfied the desire for self-completion and tapped into the unconscious memory/fantasy of being whole. In the *Critique of Judgment*, Kant obviously recruits this kind of pleasure as a basis for the judgment of taste. In Kant's theory of aesthetic judgment, the feeling of pleasure imports a subjective purposiveness (*Zweckmässigkeit*) into mental representation.[9] Purposiveness precedes the cognition of an object and sets in motion the psychical activity of comparing the affect with the unconscious desire of the subject. The activity of comparing will "find," that is, create, invent (*erfinden*), similarities between the pleasurable experience in the past and the one in the present, all projected, at first, outward on the objects. The creative power that finds such similarities in artistic representation is the imagination which articulates itself in language as wit. Although Kant had merely renamed this creative power "Genie mit Geist," he had at the same time also named the mimetic capacity that can link *Vorstellung* with *Darstellung*, or a purposive (historical) imagination with language.

Because affect is a-structural and initially free-floating, it cannot be represented in itself; it must attach itself to an object. The mediating services of imagination for a representation of an arbitrary object are necessary for such "objectification." The power of imagination reproduces an intuition which in turn causes a feeling.

In the history of aesthetics it was Christian Wolff who first formulated a theory of pleasure in connection with the beautiful. He associated pleasure with the intuition of perfection.[10] Perfection also intends the subject's desire for feeling whole, a desire that predisposes him in his intuitions. In the unconsciously remembered experience of wholeness lies the potential for the repetition of feeling and hence the recognition of perfect being as a pleasurable state.[11] The sense that an aesthetic representation is perfect is supported by an underlying desire for self-completion in the other. As a sense, the beautiful, in its form of perfection, relies on a sensation of the body: the pleasure in having all one's physical needs satisfied, which originally induced the fantasy of a body-Ego that is perfect.

It is therefore problematic to talk about the "idea" of the beautiful when it can only be appreciated as a sense, a feeling derived from an affect and hence from the body. Kant tried to circumvent this conceptual problem by addressing the beautiful as a non-conceptual idea. But more generally, even, this problem lays open the double meaning of *sense, Sinn,* and *Sinnlichkeit.* Meaning is manifest in the presence of signs. The establishment of signs, however, presupposes the inscribing of matter, the body matrix, and the leaving of a trace.[12] The beautiful object also functions as a sign, which means there needs to first have occurred a sensation in the body. Without this sensory or affective trace of experiencing pleasure, the beautiful would not have gained the status of sign; hence the notion of the beautiful or, in general, aesthetic experience would not exist.

If affect is a crucial aspect of how signs make sense, a genealogy of the sign reveals the sign's contingency on a history as prehistory, a history that is preserved in an unconscious memory where affect is active. Grounded in "sense" the aesthetic judgment builds upon a fundamental connection between body and mind from which knowledge first of all derives. Kant was not unaware of this, and it is reflected in his ambivalence toward assigning absolutely either cognitive or noncognitive status to aesthetic judgment. By situating the faculty of sensation between cognition and desire, he inadvertently acknowledges feeling as an interface between the subject's past (his desire) and intellectual cognition, even though cognition, in Kant's mind, seems only to be concerned with the present.[13]

If Kant insists on the feeling of pleasure in the aesthetic judgment—that is, to "know" whether something is beautiful or not—then this pleasure must be known to the subject, and it must repeat a very early and basic affect in the person's life. Indeed, without affects that are constantly repeated throughout life, the idea of "sense" would lose its original grounding in being affected by the senses. Psychoanalysis has shown that affects are connected to experiences that in the unconscious are often interpreted by fantasy. Affects are then associated with unconscious fantasies.

In the pleasure of an aesthetic experience, the "sense" of being whole is transferred or "sent" (*geschickt*) from the past into the present where the power of judgment reflects the *Schickliche*—the sending as well as the *proper* form or intuition of the past in the present, hence its ap*propriation* in the judgment of taste. If wit stands for the capacity to compare an unconscious fantasy with a similar construction in language, it must itself be partly unconscious and partly conscious. Because of this ambivalent status, wit was conflated in eighteenth century philosophy with equally ambivalent cognitive as well as creative powers such as *Geist* and *Einbildungskraft*. The unconscious component in these faculties, which I have developed as the historical contingency of representation and feeling, surfaces in Kant's critique of imagination, namely, in his discussion of genius as related to *Geist*. If in the *reflective* judgment the subject reflects on his affective state, then he necessarily compares an old memory, the memory of bliss, with the present feeling of pleasure. Kant's invoking of *Mutterwitz* as a natural talent of judgment can only mean that there is a mechanism that translates between the real and the unreal and uses both to make sense. In other words, Kant's reference to the folkloric mother wit demonstrates his need for another faculty that could connect the power of imagination with a historical affect. Mother wit is both a conscious and unconscious faculty. The intuition of the beautiful relies on the mediating capacity of such a natural talent.

If mother wit is a more down-to-earth version of wit that transforms an intuition (fantasy) into a representation (imagination), then the exact status of imagination in representation remains unclear. Is it indeed a formal power (i.e., transcendental) or an image archive (i.e., empirical and based in experience)? In the next chapter I will make it my task to clarify the function of imagination in representation by questioning Kant's a priori status of intuition. What I hope to arrive at is a firmer link of imagination with unconscious or past experience, that is to say, with memory.

7

Intuition versus Representation

LACKING INSIGHT INTO AN UNCONSCIOUS PAST THAT INFLUENCES THE mental image of the present, Kant was not really able to establish what I take to be a constitutive connection between imagination, representation, and feeling which shapes our perceptions and subjective interpretations of phenomena. In fact, psychoanalysis has taught us that there is no such thing as an unmotivated perception; perception is already to some degree, even if only unconsciously, interpreted. Given this premise, I would like to push Kant's concept of intuition to the extreme in order to reveal another aporia in Kant that, like the case of mother wit above, points to a need in Kant for another mental agency or prior ground to which he could only allude in the faculty of desire.

In aesthetic judgment, desire determines a mode of representation by motivating the production of pleasurable images which do not replicate the present reality. What is perceived in the mode of desire, which is to say, what is produced by imagination, Freud has designated with the term "perceptual identity" (*Wahrnehmungsidentität*)—an intuition, in Kant's vocabulary, that is linked to the memory of a total satisfaction of needs. In Freudian terms, this special kind of representation—the result of a mediation between intuition and memory—is but a sign of the drives that are satisfied in the experience of the beautiful. The recognition or *Wahrnehmung* of this perceptual similarity between a happy past and the present causes the affective transition from pain to pleasure. Freud called this representational process based on desire *Vorstellungs-Repräsentanz*. By that he meant that the affective drive for pleasure has found a representative in the mind. We may comprehend Freud's term in the context of Kant as the representation of an intuition, a mental process that applies itself to the framing and completing of a mental image, what Kant has tried to articulate in the *reflective* judgment. He couches the pleasure of this kind of (process of) representation in remarkably similar terms to psychoanalytic theory:

> To apprehend a regular, purposive building by means of one's cognitive
> faculty . . . is something quite different from being conscious of this repre-
> sentation as connected with the sensation of satisfaction. Here the represen-
> tation is altogether referred to the subject and to its feeling of life, under the
> name of feeling pleasure or pain. This establishes a quite separate faculty of
> distinction and of judgment, adding nothing to cognition [of the object],
> but only comparing the given representation in the subject with the whole
> faculty of representations, of which the mind is conscious in the feeling of its
> state.[1]

By a "quite separate faculty" of judgment, Kant alludes to the special
case of *reflective* judgment of taste. When judgment is only reflective and
not *determinative*, imagination is free to pursue the subject's (unconscious)
desires. Desire motivates the course of imagination and thus determines
the mode, if not also the mood, of representation. In this (aesthetic) state
of mind, the subject experiences his thoughts as pleasurable because they
take place, as Kant suggests, in indeterminate, nonformal representations.
Motivated by desire, imagination is driven to synthesize the past and present without, however, producing any intuition of finality, say, the closure
of an image. This means that, unlike the case of cognition in which imagination operates in a formal mode prescribed by a finalizing concept of history as teleology, representation, when aligned with desire, is freed from
such a teleological closure and purpose; it may postpone closing the frame
of the mental image indefinitely.

This distinction between intuition (*Anschauung*) and representation
(*Vorstellung*) might be better understood in terms of the difference between *Vorstellung* and *Darstellung* (figural presentation). *Darstellung* involves the formation of signs. In the mind, the equivalent of written signs
are framed images, what Kant calls representation proper; whereas, in the
process of *Vorstellung*, that is in the interim between imagination and understanding, intuition is still waiting to be comprehended, *zusammengefaßt*
under a (framing) concept or purpose. Kant, it seems to me, has tried to
grasp this interim or, rather, this interface in the aesthetic judgment. In distinguishing a mental representation from an intuition, Kant introduces the
idea of "purposiveness"—the awareness or sense of a *possibility* of form
and thus of a potential signification. Intuitions have the potential power to
become a mental sign—or, as Freud would say, imaginary derivatives of
drives:

> Now the purposiveness of a thing, so far as it is represented in perception,
> is no characteristic of the object itself (for such cannot be perceived)
> although it may be inferred from a cognition of things. The purposiveness,

therefore, which precedes the cognition of an object and which, even without our wishing to use the representation of it for cognition, is at the same
time immediately bound up with it, is that subjective [element] which cannot be an ingredient in cognition. Hence the [beautiful] object is only called
purposive when its representation is immediately combined with the feeling of pleasure, and this very representation is an aesthetical representation
of purposiveness.[2]

When concerned with the sheer purposiveness of an object, the imagination is not limited in its function of apprehension. The procedure of apprehension is portrayed by Kant as a kind of syntagmatic, horizontal
movement of representation.[3] In contrast, when the imagination, under
the rule of understanding, has to gather partial representations or intuitions into a complete image, it reaches a limit. This limit sets up the necessary frame and delimits, as it were, the content of the image. Beyond this
limit, the intuitions either disappear or simply cannot be registered any-
more as part of an image content:

> For when apprehension has gone so far that the partial representations of
> sensuous intuition at first apprehended begin to vanish in the imagination,
> while this ever proceeds to the apprehension of others, then it loses as much
> on the one side as it gains on the other; and in comprehension there is a
> maximum beyond which it cannot go.[4]

What gets lost in perception or has to be ignored in order to comprehend the
object according to its form is recovered in the act of reflective judgment.
Since this is an act of intuitive imagination, the power of judgment hovers
between the feeling of pleasure and the attempted representation of the
beautiful but stops short of any delimiting comprehension (*Zusammenfas-
sung*) so as to apprehend or gather up (*auffassen*) ever more intuitions. Kant
has even called imagination the faculty of a priori intuitions,[5] which is as far
as Kant will go in his materialist determination of imagination.

But what does constitute an intuition, and from where does that which
appears in imagination come? Also, why does Kant define intuition as an a
priori, treating it like an object when it is really only part of a mental
process? It seems as if by introducing the a priori status of intuition, he
acknowledges the impossibility of dealing with imagination as only pertaining to consciousness.

Perhaps the "a priori" in Kant's pre-psychoanalytic epistemology might
be taken to point toward something that is unconscious and thus must be
excluded from a model of the mind based on conscious structures alone.
Yet, his discourse on imagination reflects an ambivalence as to its status.

On the one hand, he tries to delimit imagination formally by calling it a power (*Einbildungs-kraft*); on the other hand, he withdraws this status of a formal *power* (lacking in image content) when he defines it as the *faculty* of a priori intuitions. The latter would imply that imagination is in part an unconscious faculty, filled with preconscious ideas and unconscious fantasies, as in the case of a psychoanalytic view. Kant's distinction between "comprehensible" mental representations and "apprehensible" intuitions suggests that the latter appear prior to the cognitive process of the mind; that is, intuitions develop before the desire to com-prehend, gather, and press the visibilities (*Anschauungen*) into representational objects. Such a distinction between (mental) representations and intuitions suggests a representational structure of consciousness, that is to say, intuitions are transformed into recognizable signs. But since only the conscious mind is formative with the aim of cognition, intuitions as a priori phenomena must, in their emergence, belong to an unconscious structure. This unconscious structure is, consequently, not representational but merely generative; it only supplies consciousness with the "material" of intuition. The "a priori" modality of intuitions may well identify precognitive "categories" that inherently structure Kant's model of the mind. Kant would thus be forced to refer the process of forming representations to preformal "forms" of thinking. If consciousness can be defined as the formation of representations (*Vorstellungen*), then this *preformal* nature of thinking must be an unconscious thinking which manifests itself in the power of imagination as it apprehends the beautiful in the form of a priori intuitions.

Kant seems to be well on the way toward the idea of an unconscious mind when he fashions the concept of an aesthetical idea. In his discussion of genius, Kant conceptualizes intuitions as "aesthetical ideas" that arise in response to a work of art. As aesthetical "ideas," or intuitions, they defy the category of a particular conscious thought. They merely indicate to consciousness that there is presently a kind of thinking going on, but that this mental process is regulated by the feeling of pleasure. The pleasure is only prolonged if this intuitive process is allowed to go on. Only if pleasure has a certain *durance* can it be reflected upon and turn from mere affect into a conscious feeling. And feeling is always already linked to imagination, that is, the production of an aesthetical idea. By an aesthetical idea, Kant understands "that representation of the imagination which occasions much thought, without however any definite thought, that is, any *concept*, being capable of being adequate to it; it consequently cannot be completely encompassed and made intelligible by language."[6] This is so because Kant's notion of cognition is tied to a discursive model of the mind. Intuition, however, is nondiscursive and is therefore a product of the imagination,

not of reason. The linguistic transformation of an intuition requires a secondary process which already acts as a censor for the content of images. In
the status of "primary process," intuitions appear "a priori" and escape, as
Kant insinuates, the control of any other power. Thus, in Kant's model, the
status of an a priori may reflect an impact of the unconscious past on the
mind whenever an aesthetic experience occurs.

When Kant first defined imagination as empirical and free roaming (in
the introduction to the first edition of the *Critique of Pure Reason*) only to
later establish imagination as a transcendental and formative power that
never acts quite on its own but solely in accord with understanding or
reason, he developed a conception of an inner censor. As in Freud, this
censor works toward the repression of the past and the formation of an unconscious in the subject's psyche. Kant's distinction between intuition and
representation in the *Third Critique* ultimately preserves both functions of
imagination, either free (inventive) or controlled (formative). In the formative function of representation, imagination already acts as an interpretive agent comparing and selecting the (freely found) intuitions with a
view to the memory of a pleasurable experience. Intuitions are sorted according to their relationship with the Ego's desire. In the psychical economy of representation, the Ego plays the role of desire's agent.

In my psychoanalytic reading of Kant, it is the desire to repeat the experience of wholeness what finally determines the faculty of imagination in
the aesthetic judgment. Judgment turns out to be the result of interpreting
what is given to the mind from the interior. The process of representation
is not directly governed by the Ego's desire but is directed by the imagination which selects intuitions according to that desire. The comprehending
power of imagination—which leans to the faculty of understanding in
Kant's definition—performs the transformation of the unconsciously produced intuitions into a mental image. With this psychical movement,
imagination, in its task of judging, engages in a process of semiosis. By assembling an image from fragments of memory in the mind, imagination
creates a sign. Following Kant, it seems as though intuition provides the
raw material—taken from memory—from which imagination, in its interpretative moves, produces understandable signs.

If we, however, follow a different model of the mind and sign production, as in the case of C. S. Peirce who criticizes Kant for his limited view of
the sign, we have to address intuition itself as already being a sign. Whereas
in Kant's passive act, the external object acts as a stimulus on the mind and
activates mental processes for forming a representation of the object, in
Peirce's theory of semiosis, perception already implies an interpretive act in

which the object is taken for a sign. This activity of perception comprises a triadic model consisting of consciousness, the sign, and the object. Though the object might never be completely known, Kant theorizes it as the *Ding an sich* of which the mind contains only a representation. A mediation of consciousness and the object via the sign, however, does not exist in Kant's view of perception. The quality of a sign not only opens up the possibility for various interpretations but also establishes meaning as a historical variable. Whereas for Peirce, consciousness is not a mechanical apparatus but is itself a sign precisely because it has been conditioned by previous experiences that have left a trace.

The activity of an unacknowledged, unconscious, "a priori" production of intuitions also performs an interpretive task in the apprehension of such traces as signs. As sign, the memory of an experience is interpreted by the transcendental power of imagination in the cultural-historical horizon of signification. The mental sign becomes a culturally determined representation or conscious image. If we expand Peirce's concept of semiosis with Freud's theory of primary and secondary process, we are brought back to the mimetic faculty of wit, and hence to *Mutterwitz*. For, wit acts in a semiotic and metaphoric capacity when it finds similarities between the past and the present in an aesthetic representation. If the child fantasizes about pleasure in perceptual identities (*Wahrnehmungsidentitäten*), these identities become metaphors or signs for a satisfied drive in the translation from perceptual identity into an image or representation (*Vorstellungs-Repräsentanz*). In the perceptual identity of what in Kant is an intuition, the Ego may well regress to an archaic fantasy of the mother for an experience of pleasure as bliss. If such a psychodynamic regression can indeed be assumed, then the category of intuition already incorporates a shift from affect to imagination. Imagination tries to recapture the experience with the mother in another, nonsimilar image. Involved here is actually a tension between unconscious fantasy, the fantasy of the mother, and an imagination that gropes for the appropriate image to both represent this archaic fantasy and reflect the present perception at the same time. Since this primal experience of bliss cannot be consciously recalled in a mental representation, imagination is always compelled to generate approximate representations that at least trigger the familiar feeling. In the beautiful, imagination is free to engage in the process of infinite intuitions, a process which does not have to be arrested for the purpose of producing one specific or true representation. Imagination's only duty is to keep up the pleasurable feeling that associates those intuitions. In the mere attempt at forming a representation of the beautiful, imagination is ruled only by the faculty of feeling, the primary affect of pleasure or pain.

Since aesthetic judgment is merely reflective and not determinative, the representation involved does not conform to a concept of a thing. It is a kind of representation that does not reproduce or copy anything; rather, images are sought and used as signifiers for an unconscious memory of pleasure. Hence intuitive associations produce a figural network in the mind—Peirce calls the mind a sign(!)—that dis-figures the memory of experience. As Freud pointed out in the dream work, the past is always re-inscribed in this figure of a memory.[7] Freud's theory of dream interpretation posits an alternative mode of representation and cognition, namely, that of desire which is not based upon the pictorial or representational content of a mental image but on the associative relation of images to one another, a relation of meaning which he designates as the primary process.[8] In primary process, the mobility of libidinal cathexis is preserved and re-sembles a drive that can only be satisfied in the perceptual-consciousness system of representation.

When Kant tries to resolve the struggle with the nonconceptuality of representation in aesthetic judgment by disregarding the content of representation in order to focus on its form in relation to pleasure, he may have thematized the Freudian mode of representation in which nothing is cognized, but only pleasurably (dis-)figured. For this kind of representative process in the beautiful, Kant speaks of "purposiveness without purpose." As opposed to purpose, involving the presence of a concept, purposiveness suggests that figural representations are potentially meaningful, given that they are made of the same material as images. However, the specific meaning, or purpose, of such representational figuration is either withheld from consciousness or postponed. Instead of arresting and thus inhibiting the flow of libidinal cathexis in a determinate object or representation, which is what the secondary process does in the formation of representation, imagination as the dominant power in reflective judgment keeps the primary process of intuition going.

Kant, of course, could not think behind the notion of intuition and re-fused a historical constitution of imagination and of the individual's faculties. In contrast, the early German Romantic philosophers were able to link history with mental faculties. They saw the value of a fluctuating movement of imagination for the formation of the individual, precisely because it puts one in touch with the past as potential significance for and in the present. Romantic theories of the individual proliferated, touching on the idea of Bildung (formation) as an interpretive process. Like the formation of a mental representation of the beautiful, the individual finds himself in a continuous process of formation. If there were a static representation of the beautiful, the closure of form in the mind would render the power of imagination nil as there would no longer exist a need to translate intuition into metaphors of pleasure, since the past has already been recaptured in a disposable image. No mediation between the present and the past would be necessary. Instead, the past would be conceptualizable in always the same image, and this one image would also be universally true. It would mean, finally, the atrophy of experience, as experience (*Erfahrung*) consists precisely in the changing significance of the past in and for the present. There would be no experience of difference to support the evolution of meanings. The notion of tradition as an ongoing, unconscious process of interpretation, of an exchange between the past and the present as experience, of a desire to be transmitted in the activity of imagination, is of no use if there exists a static representation of the origin.

Tradition and the idea of an unconscious are founded on the loss of a definite origin, of a definite past that merely calls attention to itself as a feeling of longing. In Kant's definition of taste as "common sense," the nostalgic feeling linked to this loss can be communicated as a feeling of pleasure. Even so, it involves an *algia*, an ever so slightly painful awareness of loss that mixes with the feeling of pleasure in the surrender to one's fantasy about a happier past. In this shared pleasurable pain of longing, tradition is universally confirmed as a loss of plenitude and meaning, a meaning that is reconstructed in subjective, though universally occurring, fantasies. Based on the common experience of the loss of the past, tradition testifies to a primal repression necessary to motivate the translation of an unconscious past into the presence of the sign. The status of the sign entails its interpretation. Every interpretation is itself a translation into the living horizon of signification. As translation, interpretation is an activity that produces other signs. Thus the recognition of loss engenders tradition as an ongoing semiotic process—a process of cultural transmission in the production of signs. And this transmission we can comprehend as the historical process of meaning.

8

The "Genius" of Tradition

IN THE 18TH CENTURY, THE PROPER FORMATION OF THE INDIVIDUAL WAS attributed to an aesthetic education or *Bildung*. The meaningful unfolding of the individual's history requires that one participate in tradition, because the traverse through tradition enables the individual to interpret experiences in the form of cultural, historical, and hence readable signs. But, insofar as an aesthetic education is concerned, the training of imagination and interpretation through art, and, ultimately, the question of an ideal of education, as well as an ideal of art, enters the picture. Such an ideal is unnameable, since, in the aesthetic judgment, the beautiful as the form of perfection cannot be conceptualized. For the faculty of judgment does not operate with concepts but with intuitions based on feelings of pleasure.

If in the aesthetic judgment imagination forever produces and dissolves images to capture the feeling in an intuition, then an analogy exists between imagination, perfection, and education as formation (*Bildung*). As in the process of aesthetic judgment, in which representation (*Vorstellung*) reveals itself as an indeterminate and interminal process, the *Bildungsprozess* implies a formation of the individual whose ideal is not representable in an image. At least, such an image cannot and should not reach closure; otherwise, it would detach from the material world of experience and historical change and live in the realm of ideology and disposable images or idols.

Kant's rendition of aesthetic education first and foremost involves the stimulation and practice of genius, a faculty that everybody has, at least potentially. But genius and its counterpart, taste, Kant says, cannot be learned; it can only be practiced. This practice is none other than the practice of *Darstellung*, which is the translation of *Vorstellung* into signs for which the medium of art is the prime example. Yet, art is also a life form, a mode of being, because in it the formation of representation merges with the formation of the individual as creative and created being (*gebildetes Sein*). Indeed, for such a being there is no firm image (*Bild*) or model that might serve as a standard and, once it were achieved, arrest the process of creation, or formation. Art and *Bildung* go on indefinitely; they are the life forms of tradition as a historical process. Because genius has no final representation, any law or standard would annul its properties:

> There is, therefore, for beautiful art only a manner (modus), not a method of teaching (methodus) . . . Nevertheless, regard must be had here to a certain ideal, which art must have before its eyes, although it cannot be completely attained in practice. It is only through waking up the imagination of the pupil to accordance with a given concept, by making him note the inadequacy of the expression for the idea, to which the concept itself does not attain because it is an aesthetical idea, and by severe critique, that he can be prevented from taking the examples set before him as models (*Urbilder*) for imitation, to be subjected to no higher standard or independent judgment. It is thus that genius, and with it the freedom of the imagination, is stifled by its very conformity to law; and without these no beautiful art, and not even an accurately judging individual taste, is possible.[1]

Asserting the importance of art and the expression of genius, Kant recognizes the medium and mediality of language. The import of the mediality of language is tantamount to the validity of genius in representation. It is what Kant tries to capture in his notion of the "aesthetical idea," a nonconceptual sign that uses language to express the unnameable, the indeterminate idea of the beautiful, in a word, *Geist*.

For Kant, it is *Geist* that expresses the genius in language. If linguistic or artistic representation can be said to have *Geist*, it can be said to represent an aesthetical idea. Here Kant is actually quite ambiguous about whether *Geist* pertains to language or to the mind. Whatever the case, it does name the essential link between the mind and the emotional or rhetorical capacity of language: "[It inheres in a representation] which adds to a concept much ineffable thought, the feeling of which animates the cognitive [cf. representational] faculties, and which combines with language, as mere letter, spirit."[2] If feeling endows the letter with *Geist* or spirit, *Geist* is then dependent on feeling as an effect of reading. In other words, *Geist* is contingent on signification. If we can differentiate *Geist* from an "aesthetical idea," it would appear that *Geist* tends toward being a linguistic faculty, while the production of "aesthetical ideas" remains a mental faculty.

At this point I would like to introduce a more familiar distinction in order to clarify Kant's grappling with another intermediary faculty that links language and mind. If the aesthetical idea expresses the unnameable state of mind in the experience of the beautiful and yet is not a conceptual sign, not a determinate image, and if it is the capacity of genius to represent aesthetical ideas, and if *Geist* has to be added to genius to express these ideas in language, then Kant inadvertently questions the unity of the sign. In other words, with his notion of an "aesthetical idea"—essentially a product of imagination, an intuition[3]—Kant is approaching the Saussurean distinction between signifer and signified.

Indeed, it is in the gap between signifier and signified that the aesthetical idea seems to be articulated as *Geist* in language. *Geist* then designates a nonconceptual signifying power that may well be the differential between signifier and signified—hence, the intermediary faculty that Kant seems to have been looking for all along. If genius is a power of the mind, rooted in imagination, then *Geist* refers to the articulation of imagination in language.

Kant is clearly aware of a difference in representation when it comes to art, given that art translates *intuitions* into representations, not objects in nature. This shift in representation foregrounds the problem of communication in art. How do you communicate in your medium that what you are representing is an intuition and not an object in nature? The answer is that a feeling has to be effected in the receiver, and as we noticed above, this feeling can only come about if the work has a *Geist* or spirit that will transfer itself to the mind of the reader, who is in touch with his own imagination or genius.

Kant also calls *Geist* the animating power that emanates from the work and motivates imagination to "think more, yet in an undeveloped manner, than could be comprehended in a concept and therefore in a determinate expression of language."[4] To think in an undeveloped manner is to imagine, to free associate, to tap old memories, to have intuitions which, in the previous chapter, I have shown to be mental signs of the past. But here I am concerned with what it is in the language of a work of art that causes such intuitions to come about in the reader. Since Kant acknowledges an indeterminacy of signification in art, what he must refer to and does by introducing the concept of "hypotyposis" is the act of poiesis that names the relationship between genius and language. Poiesis is the creativity attributed to signification that rests on the metaphoricity of language.

In metaphor, genius becomes a manifestation of the spirit of language in that it combines signs in such a way that they communicate with the reader on an emotional level. However, as figuration, language expresses the power of tradition in a mimetic commonality which endows the subject with sense. If an indeterminate, figural, or even non-mimetic level of expression abounds in language, it is the emotive capacity of language which not only enacts genius but also is enacted by genius in the creation of an imaginative nature of being. This imaginative nature of representation that one can sense without cognizing is a realm of thought that is independent of any current object at hand, even though it nevertheless acts as a trigger for the stimulation of thought. This is the modality in which involuntary memories hold sway and inform our imagination. We usually refer to such a modality or state when we say that we have just had an association or intuition. Within the medium of language, genius as the creative faculty of imagination also has the capacity to link an otherwise unconscious past with the present. Since it is metaphor within language that carries out the signifying movement in which a memory is linked with the present, one may hypothesize that it must be genius that is behind this movement—or *meta-phora*—a metaphoric process of the transfer or transference between intuitions and affective language.

In his discussion of what amounts to the metaphorizing mental process based on a transfer of intuition, Kants refers to the mimetic mechanism of "hypotyposis" as a way of dealing with the difference between mental representation (*Vorstellung*) and material representation (*Darstellung*). To read signs as hypotyposes is to use them merely as props for the associative power of imagination, and it is these associations that are signified within the "aesthetical idea." Kant calls this aesthetic effect of the work an "idea" because an idea has no direct, sensuous representation. In the transformative or interpretive process, the power of judgment proceeds only analogically to understanding. It "exercises a double function, first applying the concept to the object of a sensible intuition, and then applying the mere rule of the reflection made upon that intuition to a quite different object of which the first is only a symbol."[5] The beautiful object is only a symbol or a sign for the object of memory or imagination that it evokes. What is reflected in the aesthetic judgment, then, is the subject's former experiences that are now translated into meaning as they finally make sense in the context of the present. This capacity of transferring or translating experience into meaning is the core of a literary education. Through such an education we are both affected by and can make sense out of the metaphors in language.

Central to the formation of the individual is the development of the capacity to create meaning, the development of a judgment of taste. Genius, as the innate disposition by means of which "the nature (of the subject) . . . gives the rule to art (the production of the beautiful)," becomes, in the individual's formative process, the mode in which nature is transposed, displaced into representations that we know as culture.[6] The power of representation produces an imaginary nature of signs, a mode or medium through which, in education, we come to interpret "nature proper" while appropriating and understanding our own nature. This "appropriated" nature is our sensuality (*Sinnlichkeit*) which has little to do with the empiricist-psychological concept of sensation given that it includes all the psychosomatic aspects that Kant accumulated in his vocabulary of affect, feeling, emotion, sensitivity (*Empfindung*), mood, passion, and mind (*Gemüt*). All of these body-mind relations are, in the end, aspects of the power of a judgment that distinguishes between pleasure and pain.

Through desire and imagination, merged in the power of judgment, the subject is always kept in touch with experience and the past. Without this psychological recourse to the past, the faculty of wit could not rely on the talent of mother wit for creating a metaphoric mental structure between the subject's body and a culture of signs. Why do we have taste at all, or even care about taste if not as an ability to participate in cultural forms of life which are pleasurable for us as an expression of sensuality? The Enlightenment idea of a culture's goal was the evolution of happiness or *Glückseligkeit.*

Happiness is first of all a sense determined by feelings of pleasure. Culture merely forms our nature into a sensuality whose expression causes pleasure for both self and others. As the individual who is in formation learns to negotiate experiences with cultural signs, taste becomes the memory of such a negotiation in terms of what is pleasurable. Experiences become aesthetic whenever the link between *Vorstellung,* the relation of self and other as affection, and *Darstellung,* the visibility or imaginative representation of this relation or affect, makes "sense." Whether it makes sense and also feels good—and therefore makes sense to us—is a judgment based on the memory of a successful congruence of feeling and image that implies a cultural history of artistic representations. What is then transmitted of the individual's past is the body's experiences as sublimated in imagination where the past exerts its power as sensuality in cognition—Kant's schematism underlying concepts as physically related *Begriffe.* Taken as a whole this process is what grounds and informs genius.

Here we are very close to the theorizations of Walter Benjamin who learned much from Kant in precisely this context. For in Benjamin's theory of historical consciousness the sense for history is also created in terms of aesthetic experiences which constitute a *Jetztzeit,* or time of recognition, that concerns genius. As part of the subject's nature, genius forms the image of the present by way of recollecting the past in such a way that the present is turned into an imaginary sign structure. Here we have to note that for Benjamin there is no temporal distinction of past and present, only a psychical, emotional distinction that relates an image to an experience, and, as in the beautiful, relates the feeling of pleasure to the desire for an ideal form of being. This form is inseparable from the unconscious materiality of experience.[7]

In the formation of a dialectical image, which corresponds to the aesthetic experience and the notion of *Jetztzeit*, imagination could be said to carry out Freud's secondary process that constitutes meaning with the forms of cultural signs. This secondary process relates the individual's psyche, or past, and the cultural environment in an act of imagination. If it is the capacity of genius to create cultural and aesthetic signs, then a link exists between the artistic genius and the more common genius of the reading subject who translates those signs into a remembrance of his or her past experience.

This commemorative link consists in an intuitive labor of imagination accorded by language or the materiality of the sign. Especially the aesthetic sign exerts a commemorative power on the subject's mind. It is in literary tradition that language develops this power of engaging the past in the subject's imagination.[8] When judging the beautiful, the subject reflects upon the past and the purposiveness (*Zweckmässigkeit*) of experience. Such reflection informs the subject's sense of the meaningfulness of those experiences for her way of interpreting the world. The reflective judgment performs a mental act of redeeming one's experiences, an act that affirms one's life history for the production of meaning.

Finally, Kant well anticipates Benjamin in acknowledging that, in the judgment of taste, the role of desire is to recognize the past in the subject's present. Genius translates desire into signification, hence the peculiar status of genius pertaining to both psyche and language. In his treatise on genius, Kant even uses imagination synonymously with genius by specifically designating the former in the production of aesthetical ideas as a "productive cognitive power"[9] that turns nature into signs. According to Kant, without this signifying power, we would not have the concepts of nature and of sensibility to conceive of the individual as a "being in formation." If the subject is formed into an individual, just like nature is formed into interpretable signs, both meet their possibility in the idea of the purposiveness of form and meaning which is transmitted and activated in the event of every signification. If purposiveness indeed implies a signifiability that is enacted by the signifying power of genius, then the notion of genius can no longer be confined to the mental capabilities of a historical subject but expresses the purpose of a literary tradition.

Both tradition and genius are the creative and innovative force in the practice of art. Artistic expression of signification demonstrates, as Kant says, an originality and is thus

> not an example of imitation (*Nachahmung*) (for then that which determines genius and the spirit of the work would be lost) but an example

(*Nachfolge*) for another genius which, by it, is awakened to the feeling of its own originality to practice art in freedom from the constraint of rules, that thereby a new rule is created for art; in that, the talent shows itself to be exemplary.[10]

The effect and origin(ality) of genius is succession, *Nachfolge*, which is constituted *in* and *as* temporal delay in order for it to produce aesthetical ideas that signify through an indeterminacy of language.

As for the concept of *Bildung*, it was Novalis who pointed out that genius is infinite; thus, the process of *Bildung* is not terminable, since language is not a determinate entity. There may be infinite aesthetic representations and subjective expressions of nature because "in the products of genius it is the nature (of the subject), and not a premeditated purpose, that gives the rule to art (of the production of the beautiful). . . . [and serves] as the subjective standard of that aesthetical but unconditioned purposiveness in beautiful art that can rightly claim to please everyone."[11] Here Kant's "nature" almost forecasts Freud's model of the psyche which integrates both the conscious and the unconscious in a synthesis that also effects the production of art. Kant has ascribed the expression of such a mental or psychical synthesis to genius. With this highly ambivalent concept of nature, Kant transgresses the epistemological boundaries within which human faculties are defined. Besides nature, genius is given the status of a faculty, because it is capable of producing beautiful art. But when Kant links nature to the notion of a "supersensible substrate of all the faculties" he admits to a larger unity, if not purpose, of the mind that he can no longer grasp except in theological terms.[12]

As it turns out, the notion of genius not only causes Kant to transgress conceptual boundaries, because of its power to transgress any given form, it also permits the conceptual fusion of nature and culture in its transition "from a [Kantian] discourse of human experience to a discourse of reason."[13] In his work on Kant and the sublime, Jean-François Lyotard considers a transition in genius from the sublime to that of enthusiasm, which is a feeling located on the outer extreme or edge of the sublime. This is relevant to us, too, because it concerns Kant's idea that making a judgment about the sublime requires a sense of culture and tradition even if its foundation is to be located in human nature.[14]

For Kant, the significance of culture and, by implication, tradition, lies in its recruitment of ideas, namely freedom, for the (nonconceptual) sense of a historical event like the French revolution. In contrast, what Lyotard wants to demonstrate is that such a cultural conditioning of a feeling is also cognitive with respect to the human condition, and that the Enlightenment tried to theorize this as a cultural progress toward happiness (*Glückseligkeit*). It has to be noted, of course, that in the critique of teleological judgment that comprises the latter parts of the *Third Critique*, Kant actually retreats from the import of happiness as the purposiveness of human nature and, in compromising this telos, seems content with the production of culture alone. He can admit this, given that here his philosophical *raison d'être* is the existence and creation of ideas: One first has to have an idea of happiness as a state of being before one can create the empirical conditions for it.[15] This is decidedly an argument for a historical agency that legitimates itself through an existing culture.

In thinking "idea" and "history" together, Kant arrives at the notion of a subjective "sense of history" which I have evoked in terms of Benjamin as a resistance to an objectified history, isolated from the human sensorium. There is some precedent in *Idea for a Universal History from a Cosmopolitan Point of View*,[16] in which Kant compares the ideal state to a body (*Staatskörper*), and derives the idea of a perfect world from a "feeling in all members" which preserves the whole while the existing state may indeed disintegrate.[17] This feeling for the whole engenders the hope that, after several necessary revolutions, the universal cosmopolitan state will emerge.

It is actually on the basis of feeling (in this case a feeling-for-history), that Kant evokes the human potential for political development stimulated by a cultural context. According to Kant, culture makes humans sensitive to ideas, for in culture "nature strives purposefully towards a formation which makes us sensitive to purposes higher than nature itself could supply."[18] Lyotard interprets this relation of culture and sensitivity as follows: "[Culture] is the condition which broaches the thinking of the unconditional."[19] This unconditional state has no historical representation and can only be presented through what Lyotard elsewhere calls a libidinal economy, a shared recognition of intra- and intersubjective tensions which align themselves in an enthusiasm for the incomprehensible, a phenomemon of the sublime.

Contrary to what one might ordinarily imagine of Kant's views on politics, he is arguing, in fact, that a political economy must first of all work through a libidinal economy and reckon with a radical, repressed subjectivity that periodically exerts its force (desire) in terms of, say, political revolutions. That is, for Kant such revolutions synchronize, for the historical moment, subjective desire with cultural formation.

According to Kant, the development of a sense of history demands skill; Kant calls it a formal cultural skill, though we might call it genius. Whereas I see no difference between culture as such and the development of skills,

Lyotard determines this skill within the feeling or rather the state of enthusiasm that Kant would actually caution against precisely because it cannot be contained in any form of reason. Yet, it is this formlessness that the enthusiastic spectator of a historical event detects as its potential for change. This formlessness of the feeling corresponds to what the subject senses as a beyond of cultural experience, an experience of freedom *in potentia*. But in order to identify and be aware of this beyond as a freedom, individuals must have already been acculturated to a vision of Kant's cosmopolitan peace. Such peace rests on a neutralization of competing forces. Psychologically speaking, it is the same as the harmony among the faculties that Kant invokes in the aesthetic judgment.

Enthusiasm raises the human condition of desire to consciousness. As a force that overwhelms the faculty of understanding, the sublime nonetheless aligns itself with the purpose of reason: to proceed toward a better state of humanity, a state whose idea, lest we not forget, is intrasubjectively predetermined by an experience of pleasure as well as fantasies of wholeness. In enthusiasm, this idea (of wholeness or a better state of being) is shared intersubjectively as a communicable feeling. In this intra- and intersubjective sense, based on feeling, the idea of freedom is an aesthetical idea. And the presentation of aesthetical ideas, Lyotard reminds us, is, to get back to our theme, the task of genius, since genius manages the transition from a historical-philosophical postulate of the idea to its (impossible) intuition. It treats the idea *as if* it were something concrete which is then something else; hence, genius produces the "sense" of an idea through an indirect representation. Insofar as this idea is a historically necessary representation, genius would be responsible for writing the history of mankind.[20]

From a Benjaminian point of view, we have been considering the historian as a genius-artist rather than as a mere scholar. Central to Benjamin's point of view, of course, is Kant's notion of the aesthetical idea rather than a notion approaching Lyotard's understanding of enthusiasm. Within the aesthetical idea, it turns out that more historical material is presented than the faculty of understanding can apprehend. Thus genius gathers the excess of the material in a fictional mode of representation. The sense of history is, in fact, a transference of a subjective sensuality (sensibility) that becomes the reference point for a political-historical idea as well as for an incomprehensible political spectacle. From the Benjaminian perspective, the purpose of this fictional mode of representing history is to change the mood of the recipient spectator, to create a "better" state of mind for experiencing a "sense" of freedom. As reflective judgment, this "sense" may liberate imagination to synthesize feelings and images into new and different representations of desire, that is, a successive or diachronic imagining of culture (*Nachfolge*) instead of a mere imitative copying of a represented telos (*Nachahmung*).

Diachronically, the subject is addressed as a historical power to effect change through representation based on a historical sense that carries out the tradition of a desired state of being. This sense is a gift of nature, since genius gives the rule to art as part of nature. Passing a judgment of taste, then, expresses the historical sense of a subject with the cultural skill of comparing aesthetic as well as historical events with the "idea" of enjoying complete or fulfilled being. However, this idea is not a universally imposed standard or political goal but a sense subjectively derived from an unconscious memory of being whole. More like a sense of tradition or an intra-subjective mechanism of transference, this historical sense invests the mind first of all with the body before it reflects its link with a universal political-historical idea. Originating in nature and representing universal history, genius unites the subjective with the cultural, a power that Kant finally had to relate to the notion of supersensible.

In both Lyotard and Benjamin, it is evident that Kant is interpreted in such a way that something affective (enthusiasm as outer limit of the sublime, the aesthetic idea that overflows its concept) is always in excess of conceptualization. No doubt, Kant himself develops a theological conception of the aesthetic in his critique of teleological judgment as yet another expression of this Hegelian tendency to overflow the borders of thought. Most importantly for us, in light of Kant's reference to the supersensible, both genius and taste (which is but an inchoate, passive genius) can no longer even be conceived of as a faculty.

That is, genius constitutes the nature of the subject in whose power it is (1) to reflect upon his/her experiences, and (2) to represent to itself and others through art the ontological difference between being and Being, that is, between experience and purposiveness. This difference engenders the possibility of signification, or the signifiability of nature as experience and affect. To become aware of purposiveness in the beautiful means to realize that meaning and signification of nature depend upon the subject's experience and memory. Access to past experiences is not direct but rather is available only in a reflection on the play of imagination in which they are preserved. The state of mind in this reflection, according to Kant, is determined by a harmony of the cognitive faculties. Yet he states that the reason why these faculties are in harmony is because they do not have to perform according to a concept. Their attention may be entirely directed by imagination which itself takes its course from a historic place of connecting with an other in pleasure. Through the power of imagination, the past engages the present as a represented cognitive expression. Because the unconscious already knows, this knowledge supplies the ground for the representability (*Zweckmässigkeit*) of the present experience. Genius is what establishes the power of translating this knowledge into aesthetical ideas, a knowledge that takes on the form of language in signification.

Kant shifts the phenomenon of the intelligible to the theological plane as signification by postulating a supersensible ground for all human faculties. This provides not only the basis for the "intelligible of our nature" but, in the special case of the aesthetic, its purpose. For Kant the meaning of experience as well as the experience of meaning, or purposiveness, must be a transcendental if not a religious idea of what the human mind is capable of beyond rational cognition. The relational consistency of mind and language in the production of signification marks the "faculty" of genius invoked in the power of judgment. Genius provides for the possibility of meaning through which the sign is interpreted and the other appropriated into the psyche. Connecting with an other in the absence of the mediation of concepts informs the capacity of *re-ligio* in aesthetic experience, and this explains why Kant invokes a theological determinacy for the power of judgment.[21]

The alternative to this theological recourse to genius has been articulated in a theory of the sign by Novalis. By focusing on the function of signs, Novalis overcomes a systemic relationship between the other and the self, the body and the mind, the transcendental and cognitive. By foregrounding the mutual constitution of psyche and sign, Novalis interprets the notion of genius in close proximity to a conception of *Bildung* that I will adapt as a hermeneutic faculty, or hermeneutic sense. I want to expand this to a mnemonic sense of tradition, since it is a faculty conditioned by literature that can translate experience into meaning. In remembering wholeness, the subject is driven to represent his/her experiences in language. Hence art as language renders these experiences effective, a "history of effects" (*Wirkungsgeschichte*), that the Romantics emphasized in the formation of the individual. Engaging in a semiotic process of interpreting signs, the subject partakes of the genius of history, the "miracle of signification," as Novalis would say. The individual thus enacts and activates tradition in the hermeneutical activity of the mind. This activity of *Bildung* is a creative process of what Freud calls *Umbildung*, of translating life into history, a meaningful story.

Part III

The Hermeneutics of Tradition

9

Tradition: A Matter of *Bildung* in Novalis

WHEREAS KANT GAVE A SYSTEMIC ACCOUNT OF THE MENTAL FACULTIES and processes involved in the formation of meaning, Novalis, on the other hand, adds a speculation on the dynamics of language to this account. In particular, Novalis sees a historical dimension that shapes the faculty of imagination in language and the power of the sign. What Kant attributed to the faculty of genius, the capability of causing mental representations other than mere concepts by using language, Novalis expanded into his conception of *Bildung*. And by foregrounding the idea of *Bildung* (formation or education), Novalis inadvertently laid the groundwork for a hermeneutics of reading. He was concerned with the question of what makes a historic text readable and how signs, in general, figure in the dynamic of the psyche. Novalis introduced the notion of the hieroglyph in order to show how the faculty of genius enables an individual to create figures of reading, that is, reading the (seemingly unreadable) text "figuratively." The hieroglyph will be relevant to Benjamin and his theory of interpreting history.

A bygone Greek mythology alerted the Romantic philosophers to the need of a transcendental other, for example, a community or idea/ideal of being, that could endow the self with meaning. If the self is no longer guaranteed an essence through a higher other, then it is thrown back on its material existence, on the one hand, and on its imagination, on the other. The idea of being or becoming like someone or something other, an image or ideal, lost its validity for the Romantic concept of the individual. Instead, the Romantics celebrated the life force, creativity, and genius in the individual. Instead of a static form, an ongoing formative process, or individual experimentation with life history gave a new conception of cultivation its shape. Resisting to grow into a static *Bild* or picture of the self, the individual is supposed to enhance the capacity for relating to an other through education or *Bildung*. But, as Novalis states, it is the synthesis of biographical and world history that shapes a human being: "Was anderes bildet den Menschen als seine Lebensgeschichte? Und so bildet den großartigen Menschen nichts als die Weltgeschichte." [What else forms a human being than its life history? And thus nothing other than world history forms the magnificent human being.][1] Here we should distinguish between formation or education and the idea of culture and cultivation. Because of the inherent and infinitely temporal structure of the formative process, *Bildung* knows no end (*Zweck*) or goal. As a result, self-formation is not a matter of cultivating given talents and capacities, since practice of a talent is only a means to an end, the end of imitating a given ideal. *Bildung*, on the other hand, has no end.

Even though the process of *Bildung* also involves the appropriation of an other, (history or language or someone else's experience), this "other" never becomes assimilated to the self, since this other has a certain materiality that cannot be abstracted into a formal quality. The materiality of the other does not simply perform a function but initially affects us as something strange. This contrasts with an "assimilated" other that never loses its own quality within even a changing self. The preservation of this immutable otherness depends on the art of translating that Benjamin has defined as an "assimilating," *sich anbilden* of the original's language into one's own. The difference between the original language and one's mother tongue prompts a construction, an activity of building a new linguistic structure from the material of the two languages at hand. Similar to an (architectural) building, this new linguistic structure has physical qualities which incorporate stylistic features from both the original and the translator's language. For instance, a new idea may be created by keeping the syntax of the original style while translating the words into their equivalents in the target language. These alien linguistic properties accepted by the translator effect the way the translator's text is read. Similarly, if the self adopts properties of an other (self), they effect a change in the make-up of the self. Most importantly, however, is that the other is never really "assimilated," never made into an image of the self but either adds to the self or changes the structure of the self.

The difference between the English word *assimilation* and Benjamin's original *sich anbilden* is striking since the form of the broken vessel (the Jewish metaphor for the divine) is no longer available; in Romantic terms, the image of the self is not given. In whose image is the other then to be made? The feeling of an indefinite image adheres to the expression of *sich anbilden*. The image is at best only in the making, for which the "other," its different material, becomes significant once it is incorporated in a contin-

uously changing organism of growth, which is how the Romantics conceived of the self. In his influential treatise on formation, Hans-Georg
Gadamer compares *Bildung* to *physis*: "Formation knows as little as nature
about goals situated outside of itself."[2] Nature in this sense is not an a
priori substance or a stasis but a dynamis of continual change and development. This kind of development lies at the heart of Romantic conceptions of both the individual and the work of art. At least the Romantics
saw this capacity for change as vital for the expression of genius in the formation of individuality. It no longer depended on the identification with a
transcendental and hence ahistorical, genial Other. In fact, Novalis uses the
very same expression of *sich anbilden* to form what he calls "the voice" of
the individual: "Um die Stimme zu bilden, muß der Mensch mehrere
Stimmen sich anbilden; dadurch wird sein Organ substantieller. So, um
seine Individualität auszubilden, muß er immer mehrere Individualitäten
anzunehmen und sich zu assimilieren wissen, dadurch wird er zum sub-
stantiellen Individuum, Genius." [In order to build his voice, a person has
to acquire several voices; through this effort his organ will become more
substantial. Likewise, in order to develop his individuality, he has to always
adopt several individualities and know how to assimilate, and through this
effort he will become a substantial individual, a genius.][3]

Gadamer's study of Romantic hermeneutics also leads him to insist on
the historical formation of such "genius" in contrast to the idea of genius as
"gift": "*Bildung* is an authentic historical notion, and it is this historical
character of preservation which is of concern to the humanities and to the
concept of knowledge in the humanities."[4] If the other is preserved in and
for the self, then the other or rather the experience of the other constitutes
a history insofar as nature is turned into sense. The individual's task is to
translate the other into a conscious sense if he wants to gain a historical
sense for his existence. What Benjamin in the *Task of the Translator* insinu-
ated by a "feeling for the language" we might equally apply to history:
developing a feeling for the historical determinants that help create a new
sense of being. The concept of a historical knowledge must include a
notion of feeling, a feeling for history as human experience. The emotive
quality of language supports this concept of an affective knowledge. This
may be what Novalis "felt" but could not explain in so many words when
he attributed to language a magic power of creating sense.

Like Benjamin, Novalis tried to find out the mechanism of signification
in language. And, like Benjamin, he called the signifying mechanism a
"magic" or mystical grammar because this grammar resembled more an art
form and, therefore, a different kind of knowledge than a systematic philosophy or science. He expressed the magical quality of meaning formation

as a "Sympathie des Zeichens mit dem Bezeichneten" [sympathy of the sign with the signified].[5] Such *Sympathie* in German does not refer, as in English, to a sense of pity or compassion but expresses a likeability, an attraction of the sign to the signified. This (positive) tension between sign—this is always a cultural sign—and signified (*Bezeichnete*) indicates that there exists a space between the cultural-historical semantics of signs, on the one hand, and the signified (*Bezeichnete*) produced by the text, on the other hand. We might rephrase this "sympathetic" relationship between sign and signified with a question: Why does a writer select a certain word, or combination of words, for representing an experience? But here we should qualify the notion of representation in Novalis's terms, which suggest a presencing of truth rather than an imitation of an objective reality. Novalis explicitly names the sense of representation as a calling into presence (*vergegenwärtigen*), that he specifies "in the active, productive sense."[6] By means of this "sense" Novalis points to the individual's imagination, free in its association of ideas. Hence it is in the association of other ideas that the truth of an experience is presented. In fact, Novalis has expanded Kant's "aesthetical idea" and changed Kant's transcendental notion of truth, by adding the dimension of experience.

In writing and working with the signs of a historical language (the verbal icons of words), the poet will not be confined to that historical idiom. His associations, which certain parts of the idiom may prompt, motivate his choice of very different signs that he then mixes with the idiomatic language. Writing in this constructive way creates an unintentional linkage of words, a "coincidental catenation" which establishes metonymic relations among seemingly unrelated and unidiomatic signs: "Der Poet braucht die Dinge und Worte wie Tasten, und die ganze Poesie beruht auf tätiger Ideenassoziation, auf selbsttätiger, absichtlicher, idealischer Zufallproduktion (zufällige—freie Katenation)" [The poet uses things and words like "keys" and all of poesy rests on an active association of ideas—on an autonomous, intentional, ideal 'production of chance' (coincidental—free catenation.)][7]

The coincidental conjunction of two or more signs produces the effect of a third one in the mind. From a psychoanalytically informed linguistic point of view, Jacques Lacan has considered such effects in terms of a "discourse of the Other,"[8] given that the subject concatenates things and words whose originary locus of production comes from elsewhere. For Lacan, the Other refers both to the unconscious and to language; moreover, this language of the unconscious expresses itself both metaphorically and metonymically. However, this movement between semantically motivated locations takes place in the individual's cultured, that is, (in)formed mind.

The metaphorically created image is the result of the person's historical being and of his engagement in tradition (the Lacanian "symbolic"), which manifests itself in the transformation of experiences into nonmimetic images, or intuitions, as distinguished in Kant from intellectual images or forms.

Before the discovery of an unconscious, such mental transformation in the history of the mind has been circumscribed by the notion of *Geist* or spirit, which represented a metaphysical instance of meaning formation traditionally associated with divine in*spiration*. Concerned with the problem of representation, especially the representation of feelings, Romantic philosophy demystified the concept of spirit and reestablished it as the capacity of the metaphorical mind that could form historical matter into conscious presentations. No longer representing the discourse of God, *Geist* nonetheless harbored the idea of the infinity of thought. Linked to expressing fantasy, *Geist* became the faculty that could suspend logical connections, a capability necessary for access to the absolute.

As linguistic representations, the texts of the past (the literary tradition) present an unfamiliar other with which the reader-subject has to come to terms. But coming to terms—whose terms?—implies that the subject must negotiate between the terms of the text and his own. This negotiation forces the subject, first of all, to become aware of his own "terms," his language and concepts, and, in a second step, to trade terms with the text or the tradition which will then change the composition of his original set. Finally, from this change-in-terms the subject gains a sense of himself as other in language.

These steps comprise the act of interpretation, or, rather of reading, a distinction to which I will come back later. It is an act through which the reader-subject participates in the linguistic nature of the text which raises his consciousness in relation to his own linguistically conditioned identity. In any case, the subject experiences himself as other through the intervention of language. But this other always has a certain human feature derived from experience; it is always a historical other. Recall that even Hegel's argument for the historical nature of the spirit that connects the individual with a cultural past starts from the position of tradition as other.[9] The self has to go through this linguistic otherness of tradition in order to connect with the cultural history that precedes it. Through cultural history, the self is able to relate to itself as a representational consciousness. Representation splits the self; it cannot be at one with itself, but only with history. But deriving a sense of oneself from history requires the passage through tradition.

Not only Novalis and Schlegel lamented the loss of the immediacy of a unifying sense, as they confronted the materiality of texts which resembled corpses of meaning or unreadable "hieroglyphs." Hegel, too, suggested that the world and language of the old masters, the ancestors, are alien to us; but the tolerance and utilization of these historic others in the recreation of their structure, the metonymic relations of their signifiers, could create a historical insight into one's own representations.[10] This is essentially an understanding of how our psyche works, how the "hieroglyphic power" of imagination organizes our mind as it deals with our history. For Novalis this informs *Bildung*:

> Geistige Bildungslehre: Man studiert fremde Systeme, um sein eigenes System zu finden. Ein fremdes System ist der Reiz zu einem eignen. Ich werde mir meiner eigenen Philosophie, Physik etc. bewußt, indem ich von einer fremden affiziert werde—versteht sich, wenn ich selbsttätig genug bin.

> [Spiritual/mental grammar of formation: One studies foreign systems in order to find one's own system. A foreign system stimulates the development of one's own. I am becoming aware of my own philosophy [i.e., way of thinking], physics [i.e., body experiences], etc. by being affected by the other [way of thinking or by his body]—but it is self-understood that this happens only if I am active enough [i.e., by using my "productive imagination."]

In contrast to the productive imagination that informs *Bildung*, Novalis considers mechanical thinking: "Aus Trägheit verlangt der Mensch bloßen Mechanism oder bloße Magie. Er will nicht tätig sein, seine produktive Einbildungskraft brauchen." [Out of lethargy a person demands mere mechanism [of thought] or mere magic. He does not want to be active and use his productive imagination.][12]

In Novalis's reflections on language and meaning, the concept of grammar and sign replaces the concept of image. In his other fragments, a "mystical grammar" corresponds to the spiritual or mental grammar. There is a mystical connection between signs that invokes the power of "spirits" and "magic". The stated "sympathy" between the sign and its signified also implies an erotic relation in which the "spirits are at work" and create a "contemplative life" (*ein beschauliches Leben*).[13] The grammatical relations between the signs constitute a "Logik der Empfindung und Phantasie. Logik ist schlechtweg Grammatik" [Logic of sensation and fantasy. Logic is simply grammar.][14] Novalis dissolves the borders between rational and intuitive thought by separating the dynamics of language from the principles of logic. Logic, rather than supporting the edifice of rationality, is subjected to the principles of language established in grammar. The application of grammatical rules to the order of things establishes correspondences between different registers of experience. The forms of human experience can then be read, rather than interpreted symbolically, like a text. Since the hieroglyphs of the past no longer represent a specific meaning or symbolic sense, their historical truth is lost to the modern reader. They are enigmatic signs that stimulate the fantasy and the desire to know what they *could* mean; curiosity fosters invention, and in language inventive creations produce new intuitions. "Hang zum Wunderbaren und Geheimnisvollen ist nichts als Streben nach unsinnlichem-geistigem Reiz. Geheimnisse sind Nahrungsmittel, inzitierende Potenzen." [The tendency toward the miraculous and mysterious is nothing but a striving toward nonsensual-spiritual stimulation. Mysteries are food for thought, inciting potencies.][15]

Since the potential for new thought and representation inheres in fantasy, the stimuli (*Reize*) are of extreme importance. Stimulus and its effect on the subject as irritation or stirring belong to the realm of the senses. In Novalis's elaborations on *Bildung* and thought, fantasy and imagination can only depart from a refined sensitivity toward nature. The sensuous realm cannot be split off from the formation of concepts. "Alles Objekt wird Reiz (und Formel) einer neuen Objektion. Es ist die unterste Reihe; das nächste Subjekt ist die Differenzenreihe. . . . Es ist eine beständige Größe, das Subjekt eine veränderliche." [Every object becomes stimulus (and formula) for a new objectivity (or idea). It is the base line; the next subject is the differential line. . . . It [the object] is a constant entity, the subject is a variable entity.][16] The subject changes by virtue of being affected; and he lets himself be affected in order to exercise his imagination in representation. Life, for Novalis, consists in this exercise and in being constantly stimulated. It describes an analogy to the living body and (potentially meaningful) life: "Der eine Faktor ist ein Lebendiges (Erregbares)—der andere Leben (Reiz)." [One factor is a living being (which can be excited), the other factor is life [itself] (the stimulator).][17]

If language participates in this constant excitation as part of life, then language itself provides an environment of constant stimulation. This is especially true in the case of historic forms of poetry, because "historic" means far removed and unfamiliar, hence an allegorical reading along the lines of the hieroglyphic (figural) composition of the text is required. Constant stimulation—through unfamiliar or strange forms—is absolutely necessary for a formative education. Humanity cannot be improved without developing a high degree of sensibility which would lead not only to tolerance but also to adaptations of different expressions of life: "Vermehrung der Sinne und Ausbildung der Sinne gehört mit zu der Hauptaufgabe der Verbesserung des Menschengeschlechts. . . . es kommt nun vorzüglich auf die Vermehrung und Bildung der Sensibilität ... an." [Multiplication of our senses and training of the senses equally belongs to the main task of improving humanity. . . . It is above all a question of increasing and educating one's sensibility.][18] For Novalis *Bildung* starts with the senses, and, unlike Kant, the body figures foremost in the training of the discerning mind and the receptivity for what is other than the self. "Je mehr sich unsere Sinne verfeinern, desto fähiger werden sie zur Unterscheidung der Individuen. Der höchste Sinn wäre die höchste Empfänglichkeit für eigentümliche Natur." [The more our senses become refined, the more capable will they be for differentiating among individuals. The highest sense would consist in the greatest receptivity for what is singular in nature.][19]

If a new sense for the enigmatic, singular historic signs can be created with the help of fantasy, then fantasy performs this creative task by dredging up intuitive material from the individual's past. Although these enigmatic signs are not representative of any meaning, they nonetheless indicate the existence of a cultural past. This formed past now serves as sign material for representing the individual's own past. Interlocking the cultural and biographical past, the reader uses the material sign as a stimulator for fantasy and as a projection screen for intuitions of previous experiences. But the materiality of language renders the sign an objective, viable, and communicable frame for one's own imagination. In the reading subject the linguistic sign develops, if not produces, consciousness. With the aid of the sign, a conscious grasp of subjective history will transform the human being from merely "being thrown into existence" to assuming the role of a historical agent who is able to reject socially imposed standards of thought and behavior. Indeed, the mere idea of individual self-formation is incompatible with a social or transcendental ideal, and is not compatible with a cultural training that thinks according to prescribed rules. In Novalis, the emancipating idea is the conditioning of thought by one's own senses. Giving credence to the "feel of things" prevents the subordination of the thing; in contrast, the thing or the other person has equal status with the subject if it can influence the latter with its "feel."

More generally speaking, Novalis has the emancipation of nature in mind, not in and of itself, but in us as thinkers, since nature as the (evil) other was expunged in the Enlightenment concept of instrumental reason. Novalis advocates a reading and thinking subject that no longer has to be afraid of the other, of being affected by nature, because he can reflect upon it as a fantasy that is triggered only by a linguistic sign. To reflect upon the relationship between affect, fantasy, and language is to become both a philosopher and poet, that is, to combine *Vorstellung* with *Darstellung*, which for Kant characterized "genius."

Mit der Bildung und Fertigkeit des Denkers wächst die Freiheit. Freiheit und Liebe ist eins. (Grade der Freiheit.) Die Mannigfaltigkeit der Methoden nimmt zu; am Ende weiß der Denker aus jedem alles zu machen. Der Philosoph wird zum Denker. Dichter ist nur der höchste Grad des Denkers oder Empfinders etc. (Grade des Dichters).

[With the formation and skill of the thinker freedom grows. Freedom and love are one. (Degrees of freedom.) The multiplicity of methods increases; in the end, the thinker knows how to make something out of anything. The philosopher becomes a poet. The poet is only the highest degree of the sensitive thinker etc. (Degrees of the poet)][20]

Articulating a feeling in language, the thinking person automatically turns into a poet. It is a matter of reconnecting the signs *within* the hieroglyph of literary tradition according to one's fantasy that mixes the spheres of life; thoughts become feelings and vice versa. Since these historic signs are, however, remnants of a certain culture, they historicize and transmit the subject's experience as cultivated signs. Language as literature thus provides a historical inventory for contemporary stagings of experience. Benjamin illustrates this same kind of meaning formation in the allegorical representations of the German tragic drama.

Benjamin's theory of history grew out of a minute study of the philosophical and aesthetic fragments of both Novalis and Schlegel, but especially Novalis who is far less conspicuous in Benjamin's acknowledged sources.[21] Assembling the "ruins of history" and recycling the hieroglyphs in a new configuration constitutes the poetic task of the historian. The historian effects a commemoration of the past in the guise of an allegorical construction of meaning. As an object of knowledge the hieroglyphic sign and its signifying tradition need to be worked through. Benjamin, like Novalis, established this kind of historical work as a shift from the representational to the allegorical, which unleashes the individual fantasy without suppressing history. This led to a philosophy of hermeneutical understanding which produces not the object of history but a historicity of understanding, a moment or phase in the process of formation when the subject gets hold of his feelings by recognizing them in the "spirit" of the text as a memory of his own past.

The manner of meaning, the poet's art, expresses the linguistic genius, the passions (from *pathein*) in language which produce a sympathy (*sympathein*) of the sign with the signified. Allegory may be ultimately said to be an emotional writing that transforms the signs into a mentality or spirit in the effect of the historic remnants on the individual mind. But as Benjamin summarizes his theory of allegory:

> For something can take on allegorical form only for the man who has knowledge . . . [though] the intention which underlies allegory is so opposed to that which is concerned with the discovery of truth that it reveals . . . the identity of the pure curiosity which is aimed at mere knowledge with the proud isolation of man.[22]

What the allegorical intends is not the static knowledge of things but the productive imagination of the individual which can associate and create new ideas about a different and better historical setting. The impact of allegory on cognition causes a constant transformation of attitudes and thoughts about reality.

In terms of the individual's formation, Novalis juxtaposes an Ego to the Non-ego of the sign. The "hieroglyphic power" of the Ego uses the sign of history, the text, and so on, so that the Ego can establish itself as its self. "Das Ich hat eine hieroglyphistische (?) Kraft. Es muß ein Nicht-Ich sein, damit Ich sich als Ich setzen kann. These, Antithese. Synthese." [The Ego has a hieroglyphistic (?) power. There has to be a Non-ego for the Ego to posit itself as an Ego. Thesis, antithesis. Synthesis.][23] This power pertains to none other than the spirit or phantom of history that motivates a fantasy ostensibly emanating from the sign, but in actuality emerging from the memory of which the fantasy retroactively recreates a (lost) meaning for the hieroglyph. This historically contingent fantasy encompasses what Novalis calls both the sign's "synthesis" and "sympathy" with an allegorically produced signified. Whereas the old mythology emanated from a symbolic and stable view of the natural world, the "new mythology" according to Friedrich Schlegel, "has to be formed out of the deepest depth of the spirit;" he alludes to the unconscious memory of the spirit when he continues, "[w]hy should what has already been not become anew? In another fashion of course; and why not in a more beautiful and magnificent fashion?"[24]

Language was no longer seen as an arbitrary system of signs whose signifying qualities came into being by social consensus; in Novalis's terms language was a "magic" or "unconscious" device that inextricably links the subject not only with its personal past but also with the cultural past. Awareness of language as constitutive for being in the world ultimately led to a different method of reading and to a recognition of the transitoriness of absolute meanings. Hence, the genre of the fragment did not merely represent a literary form of writing but also expressed the philosophical insight of the non-being of absolutes.

This insight had a great bearing on a reconceived nature of myth, and ultimately of art as well. A new (way of) reading—rather than a "new" mythology expressed in positive terms—turned myth and art into allegorical texts whose truth or meaning was always in a state of becoming, rather than a complete representation. In fact, the incompleteness or imperfection of human nature became an accepted standard in Romantic philosophy of history. It even found its expression in the writing strategy of romantic irony that was aimed at disrupting the illusion of perfection and fulfillment in aesthetic experience. The desire for perfection and wholeness was not meant to be satisfied by art. However, art—with its enlightening and liberating potential—was to make the subject aware of the ontological nature of desire, that is, of its inherent unfulfillability. It is this insight and this didactic mission of art that places Romantic aesthetic philosophy in a precursory line of a psychoanalytic hermeneutic. The lesson for living a life in reality, that is, in history, demands that one assume the fragmented and contradictory emotional structure of one's self.

Novalis occupies a revolutionary position in German Idealism, because he took for granted the possibility of change and defined it as a possibility that depends on flexible relations among the faculties of the mind. This flexibility can be trained through criticism. Not a self-identical being, the self is already the principle of highest diversity and therefore the ground of all knowledge. Exhaustion of this ground is not possible since the process of self-critique, of a dialogue between self and the world, takes place in time which leaves the dialogue open-ended. In this dialogue, with its linguistic base of understanding, tradition engages the self in its transformation of the world into a meaningful space of communal or social being.

Rather than cherishing the illusion of narcissistic self-completion through identifications with an other (an image), a Romantic philosophy of hermeneutics temporizes and thus displaces the wish for identification with a concept of formation, *Bildung*. *Bildung* propels the activity of criticism, or *Kritik*. Criticism and critical distance assures the noncompletion of the image of an ideal and idealized mythologized human being. As an approach to art and other vestiges of tradition, criticism prevents the fetishization of images, and of art in general, which otherwise transforms the aesthetic realm into a realm of compensation. After all, the illusion of the fetish excises all potential power of art to affect the individual in its capacity for change. Also, the fetish value ensures that both art and political history remain in separate realms. In defending against this threat of historical stagnation and fragmentation of life, the Romantics uncovered the dynamic character of individual growth in the process of education. Though still deriving from the anticipation of an ideal state of being and from the desire for happiness, the idea and value of *Bildung* required a learning from the past and a renewal of tradition through critique and commentary.

This practice of critique consists of translating history and the past into a signifying example for the struggles of the present, a struggle that is at the same time one of representing and hence understanding the present in order to "imagine" a way out. Thus, the critic's task is precisely not to represent the past once and for all but to use it in its materiality and create a representation of the present. Given this historical representation, which is but a translation of the past into the present, tradition lives on as the "formed" (*gebildet*) power of imagination that acts *on* as well as *through* language. History can then no longer be considered merely an object of some sort, because history is the ground and support of sense in language. Within language, history connects individuals to their cultural past and is relevant to their desire to find meaning in linguistic representations. This is what motivates us to read books, which not only affects our imagination, but incites our potential for change.

10

The Hieroglyphic Nature of Tradition

AT THIS POINT I TURN TO NOVALIS'S CONCEPTION OF THE HIEROGLYPH IN order to demonstrate a pre-representational notion of language that is foundational to Romantic understandings of consciousness and signification. Of special importance is that the hieroglyph, according to Novalis, takes to the side of the corporeal and the sensuous. In that way, the hieroglyph pertains to a semiotic expression of affect that relates directly to my prior discussion of feeling and the maternal body in Kant. Unlike Kant, Novalis developed a language theory that accounted for the origination of signification in terms of the difference between the intuitive, which is pre-representational, and the conceptual, which is itself representational. More explicitly than Kant, Novalis sees the imagination as the faculty that mediates the pre-representational and the representational. How the faculty of imagination relates to Novalis's understanding of signification in terms of the hieroglyph is a central concern for me, especially since this relation directly bears on the work of Walter Benjamin which borrows quite freely from Novalis with hardly any direct attribution.

Readers of German Romanticism are aware that the notion of the hieroglyph surfaces frequently in both Novalis and Friedrich Schlegel for whom it represented the loss of a mythology that spiritually connected the generations of past and present. Given the demise of mythology, a new understanding of history was needed, an understanding that was to rest on the immanence of signs—the materiality of a language that confronts human beings with a self-conscious process of signification if not the possibility of sense in general. In its nonreferential or pre-representational function, language exposes its material literariness, or "literary absolute." Since Romanticism, this literary absolute has not been generally considered in philosophical definitions of literature, because, as Philippe Lacoue-Labarthe and Jean-Luc Nancy point out, "the literary Absolute aggravates and radicalizes the thinking of totality and the Subject."[1] That is, the literary absolute threatens conceptions of subjecthood and totality that are fundamental to pragmatic (i.e., Lockean) notions of communication and meaning production.

It appears that only Walter Benjamin was willing to take the literary absolute seriously in the earlier part of this century, and this is one of the reasons, certainly, why Benjamin placed such importance on re-theorizing Novalis's conception of the hieroglyph. If Benjamin grasps the connection between human experience and language in terms of tradition and the unconscious, the Romantics themselves started with the idea of tradition as linguistic production, shifting the focus away from poetry, the linguistic-artistic product full of symbolic references, and toward "poiesy," the production of sense (meaning and feeling).[2] The productivity or "generativity" of language implies that poetry is in a constant state of change. As Novalis says, the poet is controlled by words, and, being is patterned after language:[3] "Wie, wenn ... [die] Wirksamkeit der Sprache in mir wäre? ... so wär' ich ein berufener Schriftsteller, denn ein Schriftsteller ist wohl nur ein Sprachbegeisterter?" [What if the effects of language were operative inside me? ... My calling would then be to be a writer, for a writer is probably only someone who is enthusiastic about language (i.e., someone who is taken over by the spirit of language).][4] The poet is affected by the "spirit" of language which is none other than the whole of history of human imagination from which he draws his linguistic ideas.

The appearance of the letter, its mere form, bespeaks a lost or unavailable content or referent. An event or experience is no longer associated with and hence intuited by such a sign; instead, a feeling of loss of meaning is generated. This loss not withstanding, the hieroglyph stands as a witness to a past without representing it to us and without signalling a meaning for us. The connection to a tradition existing in the form of texts is lost together with a reference to the transcendental realm of God. The connection between transcendental and immanent sense is rendered by Novalis as an "intuition" whose support is the letter: "Die Zeit ist nicht mehr, wo der Geist Gottes verständlich war. Der Sinn der Welt ist verloren gegangen. Wir sind beim Buchstaben stehngeblieben. Wir haben das Erscheinende über der Erscheinung verloren. Formularwesen." [The time is no more when the spirit of God was comprehensible. The meaning of the world has been lost. We are left with the letter. We lost the intuition over the appearance. Merely a formula.][5] The mediating realm between appearance and intuition would be a communal sense that no longer emanates from the letter. But by having isolated the letter from the meaning that is now lost, Novalis actually has performed a linguistic analysis. He has cracked open the structure of the sign, juxtaposing the image of the hieroglyph to the referential structure, since the former no longer functions in the service of imagining history.

The hieroglyph, therefore, stands outside the model of representation. In other words, Novalis opens a space between signifier and signified which for the time being can only be a temporal space, an interspace between an empty form and a new content or significance. Not only that, but in the search for a new mythology—a new communal sense that would not refer the individual to a defined transcendental realm—the Romantics valorized the power of imagination that could link individual experiences and desires with language. In short, it is impossible to consider the hieroglyph in Novalis without taking imagination into account as well.

In fantasy, the Romantics understood that the convention of exercising rational control over meaning had to be lifted in favor of exploring the subject's life of the mind. Shunning the myth of light and reason, the Romantics rendered the night and the dream as motifs for creative meanings so that in his poem, *Hymnen an die Nacht,* Novalis attests to such a shift in focus within the mind. It is in the subject's unconscious mind (*Gemüt*), or emotional states, that new meanings find their source:

> Ins tiefre Heiligtum, in des Gemüts höhern Raum zog mit ihren Mächten die Seele der Welt—zu walten dort bis zum Anbruch der tagenden Weltherrlichkeit. Nicht mehr war das Licht der Götter Aufenthalt und himmlisches Zeichen—den Schleier der Nacht warfen sie über sich. Die Nacht ward der Offenbarungen mächtiger Schoß—in ihn kehrten die Götter zurück—schlummerten ein, um in neuen herrlichern Gestalten auszugehn über die veränderte Welt.

> [Into deeper sacredness, into the mind's higher realm, the soul of the world moved with its powers—in order to reign there until the daybreak of the miraculous world. No longer should the light [of the day] be the sojourn of the gods nor should it be their heavenly sign—they threw the veil of night over themselves. The night became the powerful womb of revelations—into it the gods returned and fell asleep only to rise, in new and more wondrous shapes, over a transformed world.][6]

The envisioned new mythology, which needs to be understood not as a new inventory of myths but as a new form of meaning and of knowledge, is created from the self's desire, as opposed to the old mythology that referred humans to an ahistorical and nonphysical, hence divine realm of being. This anticipates Freud who brought to philosophical understanding the idea that fantasies and dreams are representations of feelings and un-worked-through experiences. Such fantasies are metonyms, experiential parts of the subject's unconscious past that in the dream work are assembled into rebus images. The specter of the past is visible in creations that stem from the unconscious mind. In bypassing the power of reason, which rules during the day, the "nightly mind" offers another world in which the things are miraculously transformed into imaginary signs that lose their referential character. They no longer point to a rational world of conscious perception and sensation but become pre-representational hieroglyphs whose meaning needs first to be created in a hermeneutic situation, presumably in the free associations of the subject or, in the context of psycho-analysis, the analysand.[7]

It is through random associations that the internal interaction of a person's feelings are exposed. The particularity of that person's emotional and unconscious text has to be retraced and each contiguity and condensation of affective signifiers has to be illuminated by the construction of an imaginary event, an imaginative scenario of the inferred experience. Within this psychoanalytic context so reminiscent of Freud, Novalis's distinction between representation (*Vorstellung*) and intuition (*Anschauung*) becomes extremely relevant: "Unterschied zwischen Stoff und Materie. Letztere ist Substrat der Anschauung—Ersterer der Vorstellung." [Difference between substance and matter. The latter is the substrate of intuition—the former that of representation.][8] The analysand's feelings, the "substance" (*Stoff*), are to be made into representations of historical events; they are to be understood in remembering. Whereas intuition already harbors a certain image or fantasy quality derived from previous non-or semi-conscious perceptions, Novalis bases intuition on (sensuous) matter (*Materie*). Intuition might in fact be the perception of an object or scene linked only marginally with the forgotten experience. But it is this kind of associated images that help to stage the feeling in imagination.

At one point, Novalis suggests that space belongs to the sphere of intuition; indeed, a spatial scene is necessary for the formation of a representation which allows the feeling to be reflected in consciousness. Both spheres, intuition and representation, are joined in the "sphere of time" which constitutes consciousness: "Bewußtsein—Sphäre der Vorstellung. Raum—Sphäre der Anschauung. Zeit—gemeinschaftliche Sphäre." [Consciousness—sphere of representation. Space—sphere of intuition. Time—communal sphere.][9] However, as Heidegger has shown for Kant's postulation of time as an a priori category, time itself is only an intuition of imagination. In other words, what unites both spheres is the power of imagination. Still, language is crucial if representation and intuition are to interact, if not intersect, in communicative discourse, say, to recall psycho-analysis, that between analyst and analysand. As one scene is described (in-tuitively) by the patient, reliance on linguistic images and the automatic use of turns-of-phrases may, through unconscious attention to the literal meanings of these idioms, prompt another memory, another intuition, which shifts the analyst's awareness to an allegorical representation of the patient's feelings. Language, Novalis says, in regard to intuition and repre-sentation, is "Verknüpfung des besondern sinnlichen Gedankenstoffs mit sinnlichen Zeichen. Zeichen ist eine hypothetische Anschauung, bedingt durch eine Vorstellung" [the connecting of a particular sensuous substance of thought with sensible signs. A sign is a hypothetical intuition contingent on a mental representation.][10] Indeed, the relation of language to intuition consists in developing the power of thought and imagination to transform intuitions into concepts. The analysand's feelings are to be objectivized, that is, finally understood as (imagined) childhood events. Without a de-veloped power of imagination, the subject cannot understand feeling in terms of his or her own history, a point that is crucial not only for Novalis but for Freud as well. Hence for Novalis, "[v]orgestellte Anschauung und angeschaute Vorstellung machen also das Wesen der Einbildungskraft aus" [represented intuition and intuited representation constitute the essence of imagination.][11] The educated imagination is a prerequisite for construct-ing representations around seemingly irrelevant signs (hieroglyphs).

Given such a condition for self-understanding, I differ with Gezá von Molnár who defines imagination in Novalis as a "free agency." Imagination is precisely not "but another term for the self, which emphatically conveys its true nature as free activity" since imagination is, in fact, conditioned by language and history.[12] In imagination the self shares with culture the matter of intuition, the substrate of historic signs. Adhering to the tran-scendental scheme of German Idealism which insists on a divine center of self-identity and meaning, von Molnár misconstrues Novalis when he reads Novalis's statement "Practical reason is pure power of imagination" as producing an equivalence between self, imagination, and freedom.[13] Practical reason, we remember from Kant, is an ability to judge from expe-rience. In other words, practical reason proceeds in an *unconscious* com-parison between the past and the present in terms of reflecting on the affective state at hand. Practical reason, because it is imaginative, is related to the pure power of history as it shapes (*bildet*) the subject in its percep-tions of the present. Since Novalis also makes representation a constitutive part of the essence of imagination, language influences the power of imag-ination, for its literary absolute ties the imagination to the substance of affect. Hence, imagination is never a neutral power of the mind, but always proceeds under the motivation of a past experience, following the memory traces of feeling.

Crucial to Novalis is the idea that signs are sensuous entities through which we represent the other to ourselves. This relates quite directly to the fact that in German the notion of concept (*Begriff*) suggests the sensation of touching an object, a sensation that can only be truncated by a representational imagination that directly and crudely associates thing and idea—that apprehends existing objects as material for constructing a representation of the concept. Novalis differs from a Lockean understanding of language in which ideas are merely conceptual envelopes for pre-existing things by arguing that material associations are different for everybody and cannot be consciously intended because they are determined by an intersection of biographic and cultural history which gives associations an affective intent. Stored in specific signs of language, affect directs the individual's representations in an effort to understand the world.

Language puts us in touch with the world because the concepts attached to the signs send us on a detour through our life history when we first were, literally, in touch with the objects associated in the concept. That this relation is non-totalizable is crucial to Novalis and to Romanticism in general. As Jochen Hörisch has rightly pointed out, in Romanticism totality loses its hold over philosophical thought.[14] Since knowing the world only proceeds through the creation of immanent signs, knowledge is necessarily fragmentary in the experience of finite beings. The whole is only an idea which lacks representation; it can no longer be grasped in poetry because it is itself only a fragment in the formation of the individual. It can only be constructed in an open-ended process of tradition.

The *desire* for wholeness would, however, connect individuals in their finite existence. Therefore, when Novalis makes reference to the absolute that "can be only negatively acknowledged," he also implies the importance of becoming aware of this desire, so as not submit to a false consciousness. The synthetic Ego, in which feeling (desire) and reflection (imagination) combine, is without consciousness anyway.[15] Since desire refers the subject to a blissful relation with the (m)other, it can act as social motivation for community. But a consciousness of this has to be achieved through language, for it is also through language that we judge and connect with the other. We get a handle on our own desire that otherwise confronts us as an unruly other. Language turns desire into intution; hence, the task of poetry: "Kunst ist Ausbildung unserer Wirksamkeit—*Wollen auf eine bestimmte Art*—einer Idee gemäß—Wirken und Wollen sind hier eins." [Art is the training of our effectiveness—*desiring in a certain manner*—according to an idea—having an effect [on the other] and desiring are here one.][16]

Language provides the tool for change and self-determination. But it is only in the crafted objectivized language of poetry that we become aware of this tool. In aesthetic discourse, we might say that the pre-representational desire for an affective ground— what in Kant I associated with *Mutterwitz* or the (m)other—is transferred or transposed to the letter of representationality that compensates for the Ego's loss of its own affective ground—the maternal bond.

Given Novalis's sensitivity to the pre-representational, it is not surprising that Novalis speaks of "categories" of the self which seem to exist prior to reflection. "Die Kategorien müssen *freie* Handlungsweisen oder Denkformen sein." [Categories have to be free ways of acting, or forms of thinking][17] In other words, they have to be habits and patterns of thought. These categories derive from material experiences. At least I interpret Novalis in this vein when he defines them as "[n]otwendig freie Wirkungen des Lebens auf das *Was* im Ich" [necessary free effects of life on the *what* in the Ego.][18] Reflection finds a form, an image for the as yet unformed experience, which is remembered only as a feeling. In a mental or metaphorical exchange (*Wechselrepräsentation*) of (preconscious) word-representations and (unconscious) thing representations, the act of reflection constitutes experience as a conscious first time of a hermeneutic event. Yet, the completion of experience is never just a question of reflecting on a feeling, for it always needs an object that will, for ever anew, initiate an interpretative process at stake in the historical completion of experience. With the creation of an image, the remembered past experience is transformed into a meaningful category, an intuition, for interpreting the present. The conceptual difficulty seems to lie in the fact that Novalis did not have recourse to a psychoanalytic theory of the mind or a worked out concept of the unconscious.

However, the notion of "hieroglyphic power" suggests a sense in which the unconscious and imagination are combined. Benjamin, who does not mention Novalis, sheds more light on this "hieroglyphic power" when he anchors the capacity for images, which he calls the "mimetic faculty," in linguistic tradition. *Thus, in language, imagination does not proceed according to a principle of similarity between object and individual sign but according to a configuration of signifiers that mimick the scenario of an unconscious experience.* In the triggered fantasy of the Non-ego, representing the complementing other, the mother, God or a transcendental self, the link to this past unconscious scenario is manifest in an over-cathexis or *Überbesetzung* that results from translating the fantasy into a textual image. In the attempt to imagine an ideal Ego (as Non-ego), the Ego makes use of a cultural past; its hieroglyphic power recycles the linguistic figures of previous texts for

the creation of a new text. Textual language, then, is not a synchronic structure of conventional signs but a historically and unconsciously motivated
configuration of signs whose metonymic relations recreate a history of
human experiences. Through this textual grammar, knowledge is preserved in a language that supports and is supported by our capacity for
association, the "productive power of imagination." Novalis states, "[d]ie
erste Kunst ist Hieroglyphistik. Mitteilungs-, Besinnungskunst oder
Sprache und Darstellungs-, Bildungskunst oder Poesie sind noch *eins*" [the
first art is hieroglyphistics. Communicative or reflective art or language
and representation, formative art or poetry are still *one*.][19] The mind is generally artistic; it creates a textual assemblage of experiences that composes
and represents the self to itself. Artistic mental activity and self-formation
concur. "Alle unsre Erinnerungen und Begebenheiten reihen sich an eine
mystische Einheit, die wir Ich nennen. Indem wir uns in der Welt umsehn,
finden wir eine Menge Sensationen aller Art, wunderbar gewählt, gemischt,
geordnet und zusammenhängend." [All our remembrances and occurrences attach themselves to the mystical unity which we call the self. In
looking around in the world we find a quantity of sensations of all kinds,
miraculously selected, mixed, ordered and interrelated.][20] The unity of the
self expands and is transformed into a textual structure or life history created from an ongoing interpretation of one's own experiences, of what the
Romantics understood as the concept of *Bildung* which forms the individual like a work of art. The "hieroglyphic power" of the subject turns nature
into historical signs. Nature receives the allegorical gaze of the artist. The
artist, who is but the prototype of a self-forming individual, transforms
nature into fantastic, allegorical images.

> Genialische, edle, divinatorische, wundertätige, kluge, dumme Pflanzen,
> Tiere, Steine, Elemente etc. Unendliche Individualität dieser Wesen. Ihr
> musikalischer und ihr Individualsinn, ihr Charakter, ihre Neigungen etc. Es
> sind vergangene, geschichtliche Wesen. Die Natur ist eine versteinerte
> Zauberstadt.

> [Ingenious, noble, divinatory, miracle-performing, shrewd, dumb plants,
> animals, stones, elements etc. Infinite individuality of these beings. Their
> musical and their singular sense, their character, their inclinations etc.
> These are bygone, historical beings. Nature is a petrified magic cityscape.][21]

Novalis interprets nature as a "Raum als Niederschlag aus der Zeit—als
notwendige Folge der Zeit" [space as the condensation of time—as a necessary consequence of time.][22] Benjamin establishes the same connection
between nature and history in the melancholy gaze of the allegorical poet

which devoids the natural object of any inherent or symbolic meaning and endows it—by virtue of his hieroglyphic power, as Novalis suggested—with an allegorical, hence constructed, meaning.[23] Melancholy here expresses the poet's awareness of the lost meaningful context, the lost myth of a totality of experience in which the Ego is the same as its ideal Non-ego. Thus, in the subject's mental context, nature's objects become metonyms, ruins of the subject's past experiences. In the metaphorical exchange between language and memory, the genius of the mimetic or allegorical faculty becomes "the facies hippocratica of history [which in the allegory] lies before the eyes of the contemplator as a petrified primeval landscape."[24] Remnants of the past, the metonyms of unconscious experiences are connected with other signifiers in the hieroglyph. The hieroglyph is then animated in an allegorical (poetic) reading of the unconsciously created text, which is the Ego's antithesis in its position vis-à-vis the objects of nature. The synthesis or interpretation finally provides the self with a sense of historical being, of his standing in a tradition of cultural signs which he continually assimilates to his self.

The work of imagination produces hieroglyphic constellations from historical/cultural material and incorporates the additional "effects which life has on the substance (*Stoff*) of the subject" (Novalis), that is, the new experiences of the meantime into constructed images. Making sense out of life involves the subject in a continuous translation or mimetic exchange "between being and non-being" (Novalis). In this imaginative sphere of exchange, representations continuously change as more of life is formed into signs through the historical mediation of language. The Ego's consciousness is, finally, constituted by the form of images that function as signs, as nonbeing. Novalis establishes a connection between knowledge, consciousness, signs, and life in terms of being and non-being:

Das Bewußtsein ist die Sphäre des Wissens. (. . .) Was für eine Beziehung ist das Wissen? Es ist ein Sein außer dem Sein, das doch im Sein ist. (. . .) Das außer dem Sein muß kein rechtes Sein sein. Ein unrechtes Sein außer dem Sein ist ein Bild. Also muß jenes außer dem Sein ein Bild des Seins im Sein sein. Das Bewußtsein ist folglich ein Bild des Seins im Sein. Nähere Erklärung des Bildes. (Zeichen.) Theorie des Zeichens. (Theorie der Darstellung oder des Nichtseins im Sein, um das Sein für sich auf gewisse Weise dasein zu lassen.)

[Consciousness is the sphere of knowledge. (. . .) What kind of relation is knowledge? It is a being outside of being which is nonetheless in(side of) being. (. . .) The being outside of being need not be a real being. A nonreal being outside of being is an image. Therefore this 'outside of being' must be an image of being. Consequently, consciousness is an image of being in(side of) being. More exact explanation of the image. (Sign.) Theory of the sign. (Theory of representation or the nonbeing in being, in order to let being be present in a certain way.)][25]

Life, as such, cannot be comprehended, only signified in the subjective and linguistic sphere of the self, the sphere of being and nonbeing which corresponds to an unconscious sphere of the mind—the historical sphere as it were—between Ego and Non-ego, the sphere ruled by imagination. In this sphere a reciprocal relationship produces first and foremost the opposed poles of signifier and signified. As constituents of a sign, they emerge at the same time as thesis and antithesis. In his critique of Romantic metaphor, Winfried Menninghaus focuses on this reciprocal effect of signifier and signified in signification: "Their unity is not a process in time, but always a momentary fact;"[26] the creation of the meaningful sign (synthesis) originates in the hovering movement of imagination. Imagination selects from the unconscious the state (*Zustand*) that matches the respective object (*Gegenstand*) at hand. Novalis presumably proposed such a simultaneous emergence of sign, signifier, and signified in order to negate the pre-Romantic idea of a pure spirit that preexists language. The spirit "does not emerge until its magical contact with the letter, the magic wand that sets up a mutually constitutive relation."[27] Without the spirit, no path could be marked by signs; for as Menninghaus notes, "there exists instead of the spirit's plenitude only nothingness . . . the void of a *nihil privativum*."[28] Spirit does not exist outside of language. To know the spirit would mean to be in control of language. But as long as imagination remains a hovering power, resisting permanent positions, language will equally be just as flexible in its historical eruption of signs. Signs are not metaphors for being, but signs present the originary difference to being which motivates interpretation. In Novalis' injunction of "to let being be present in a *certain way*," we are reminded of Benjamin's theory of translation that insists on preserving the "way of meaning," the mode of signification in the original text, so as to reconnect the pieces of a broken totality in the awareness of a lost meaning.

Tradition weaves the meaning of human experiences (i.e., history) into language in the act of reading as translation, with an impetus toward writing down the experience one has with the original text. The loss of an absolute meaning or "spirit" reduces the signs, for Novalis, to the status of hieroglyphs: "Ehemals war alles Geistererscheinung. Jetzt sehn wir nichts als tote Wiederholung, die wir nicht verstehn. Die Bedeutung der Hieroglyphe fehlt. Wir leben noch von der Frucht besserer Zeiten." [Formerly everything was an appearance of spirits. Now we only see a dead repetition which we don't understand. The meaning of the hieroglyph is missing. We still live on the fruits of better times.][29] But, the loss of the spirit(s) also lays the signs open to a hermeneutical interpretation that Benjamin further qualified as an act of allegorically constructive reading. The connections made by the reader in this contextualizing of hieroglyphic signifiers may be compared to weaving a story that, in its final significance, supercedes the semantic valence of individual signs. Gadamer's theory of hermeneutic understanding again comes to mind, since it suggests that understanding is not a method but a *mode* of positioning the subject in tradition. In fact, Novalis calls the Ego a drive to represent itself, which it can only do by positioning itself in relation to an other. Novalis exposed this drive as a basic drive for self-representation that fuels the power of imagination. Imagination uses the other as image material or as sign value with the aim of representing and exteriorizing experience so that the subject can reflect his own past, incorporating the other into his biographic text.

> Das Subjekt ist aber nur Subjekt in Beziehung auf ein Objekt—das Subjekt kann sich, wie es doch sein muß, nichts entgegensetzen als das Objekt—für das Subjekt ist also das Objekt, was ihm das reine Ich für den Beobachter ist. Es überträgt aufs Objekt alles, was es vom reinen Ich weiß—das reine Ich hingegen aufs Objekt alles, was es vom Subjekt weiß—das Objekt ist Träger beider Akzidenzen, insofern das *eine* Substanz ist. Das Objekt ist aber an sich nichts als eine wechselseitige absolute und identische Beziehung des reinen Ichs und des Subjekts.

> [But the subject is only subject in relation to an object—the subject cannot oppose anything to itself, as it however must, but an object—to the subject the object is what the pure Ego is to the observer. It transfers everything to the object that it knows about the pure Ego—the pure Ego, on the other hand, transfers everything to the object that it knows about the subject— the object is carrier of both cases insofar as it is *one* substance. The object is nothing but a mutual, absolute and identical relation between the pure Ego and the subject.][30]

The "Pure Ego" (*das reine Ich*) refers to the imaginary possibility of sameness between Ego and the image the subject forms of her ideal Ego which, in Novalis's definition, is always a Non-ego. In the object, this image is nothing but a representation of feeling, and, qua object, it then *stands against*, in op-position to the subject as alienated self. Thus for the subject to "get a hold" of her feelings, that is, to reflect upon them, she must posit her self as an other. This creates the structural split between Ego and Non-ego, delimiting the subjective "sphere." But *in* imagination, as a fantasy, the sphere represents a unified space of pure Ego, whose existence can be felt as longing. It is the longing for a lost symbiosis or identification with an other, a (ful)filled sphere of being that could achieve the status of ideal Ego; but it is, at once, the death of the "real" subject. From this imaginary, pure Ego stems the "drive" to overcome the split between the (empirical/ historical) Ego and the imagined Non-ego. The Non-ego is projected on an object that absorbs all of the former's imaginary qualities. The task of the drive is to support the signifying exchange between subject and object, between feeling and thought. Motivation for this task comes from the self's desire to be one with the projected Non-ego. Novalis comprehends this relation between drive and desire in the "drive to be me" (*der Trieb Ich zu sein*) which is but the subject's desire to complement herself in the imaginary realm. Because of this need for the imaginary, the subject is never a stable position. "Alles Objekt wird Reiz (und Formel) einer neuen Objektion. . . . Es ist ein Geronnenes und das Subjekt ein flüssiges, eine Atmosphäre. Es ist eine beständige Größe, das Subjekt eine veränderliche—beide in einer Funktion." [Every object becomes the stimulus (and formula) of a new objectification. . . . It is something coagulated and the subject something fluid, an atmosphere. It is a constant entity, the subject a variable—both in one function.][31] The subject's self-experience is contingent on the object, as substance for her feelings. The object stabilizes the subject's identity because it initiates the process of remembrance through which the Ego connects with the Non-ego projected into the object. These are imaginative connections which overcome the initial dualism between self and other. Imagination mediates between self and other by positing them as opposite poles between which it "hovers" (*schweben*). This hovering activity fills out the opened up space between the internal and external pole of reflection with material from the past, memories, and intuitions. Representing this sphere amounts to creating it as a text that precludes the immediacy and impression of a unified image. The text as form presents a figural image or hieroglyph, and within this linguistic image a kind of musical relation prevails instead of semantic structures. *Musical* designates the constant displacement of the signifying poles and their properties in the hovering movement of imagination. Musical notation seems to be Novalis's analogy for the notion of textual grammar. I presume, that Novalis associates with it the rhythmic mobility of imagination to hover between signifiers, marking out a path of signifying relations in various repetitions.

Because of the mobility of imagination, the subject can, indeed, never take a firm stand vis-à-vis an object; imagination will always be distracted

by another object or another feature of the object at hand. As different elements of the past are remembered in the object, the Ego's imagination has
to reestablish the constellation self and other. Setting up such constellations, imagination is the creator of the subject's experiential or historical
reality:

> Ichheit oder produktive Imaginationskraft, das Schweben bestimmt, pro-
> duziert die Extreme, das wozwischen geschwebt wird. Dieses ist eine
> Täuschung, aber nur im Gebiete des gemeinen Verstandes. Sonst ist es etwas
> durchaus Reales; denn das Schweben, seine Ursache, ist der Quell, die Mater
> aller Realität, die Realität selbst.

> [Selfhood or productive power of imagination; hovering determines, pro-
> duces the extreme positions between which the hovering takes place. This is
> a deception, but only in the realm of common sense. Beyond that it is some-
> thing thoroughly real, because hovering, the cause of the real, is the source,
> the mother/matter of all reality, reality itself.][32]

The state of abeyance in reflective imagination was immensely valued by
the Romantics. They deemed it as an ideal state of being because in it the
individual resists any fixation of intellectual positions or dispositions. It is
the facilitator of personal and historical change. The insight into the possibility of change made the concept of *Bildung* inseparable from reflections
on the conditions of meaning formation. The productive power of imagination virtually guaranteed the continuous suspension of a final frame for
representation leading to the idea of art and history being an open-ended
text. *Bildung* was not to be guided by a norm or historical telos, that is, a
human being and its history should not become *form* or *image* which
would only objectify life and repress experience. Instead, *Bildung* processes
the history of human experience in the self's attitude, its sensitive stance
vis-à-vis the world.

Novalis describes this hovering state of the imaginative with a metaphor
of the creative mother, "*mater* of all reality." Once again, this kind of connection between imagination and being invokes the psychoanalytic ground
of sense and sensibility: the original experience of being self-same with the
(m)other. Freud's analysis of the representational process, as one that repeats the memory of the mother's body in the production of perceptual
identities, enables what Novalis has anticipated in his model of the sphere
between Ego and Non-ego. In the imaginary identity of Ego and Non-ego,
the relationship between self and mother is reproduced. The feeling of
pleasure, associated with the unconsciously triggered fantasy of the mother,
represents a mental movement in which the subject overcomes his/her

distinct position vis-à-vis the object, just as in infancy when the child could not yet perceive itself as a being separate from the mother's body. In this relational state of being, the child has not yet taken a position vis-à-vis the (m)other. The process of reading and writing is conditioned by a repetition of relational being. Concretely, imagination and its hovering signifying movements between elements in the text recreates a constellation between self and libidinal other. In the relation-forming activity of reading, the text itself presents the subject with a hieroglyph of his own unconscious mind, his personalized canon of non-mimetic representations. The subject's imagination then acts like a grammar of fantasy, creating metonymic relations among the signs in the text which, at the same time, remember fragments of forgotten experiences and perceptions in these signs. In the text, metonymic signs function as signifiers for the subject's memories.

What substitutes for the (historically) lost intuition of a transcendental signified is the power of the unconscious self to construct signifying relationships among discarded material from the past by doubling the text's figuration. The *matter*—if not also the *mater*—of textual figures prevails over the semantic and symbolic value of the unrecognizable signs, that is, the hieroglyphs. The very notion of hieroglyph and hieroglyphics precludes recognition. Meaning becomes a matter of style, or linguistic architecture.

If Novalis's intuition determined the meaning effect of language as a mystical, even mysterious power, he nonetheless links this power to the existence of a cultural past. Novalis derives the notion of a mystical grammar from the cabbalah, and we might keep in mind that *cabbalah* itself means literally *tradition*. This kind of tradition is grounded in the medium of signs where it effects "permutations and constantly new combinations of the letters in God's *name*."[33] A comparison of Benjamin's treatise on language and Novalis's conception of a mystical or magical quality of language shows that "god's name" is not simply a word but *names* the whole of language and its mystery of representability. The idea of a divinity of language expresses the very possibility of sense, of human or historical sense. Any human artifact in history has the status of sign; as such it is or can be part of a language. In the case of texts, these artifacts build a collective linguistic unconscious which the educated reader draws on in his unconscious reconstruction of a primary experience that makes a text readable to him. But it is the work of the historian-critic that makes this unconscious tradition conscious:

> Auch die Gegenwart ist gar nicht verständlich ohne die Vergangenheit und ohne ein hohes Maß von Bildung—eine Sättigung mit den höchsten Produkten, mit dem gediegensten Geist des Zeitalters und der Vorzeit, und

eine Verdauung, woraus der menschlich prophetische Blick entsteht, dessen der Historiker, der tätige, idealistische Bearbeiter der Geschichtsdaten nicht so entbehren kann wie der grammatische und rhetorische Erzähler. (. . .) Bücher sind eine moderne Gattung historischer Wesen, aber eine höchst bedeutende. Sie sind vielleicht an die Stelle der Traditionen getreten.

[And the present is not at all comprehensible without the past and without a high level of education—a saturation with the highest artifacts, with the formed spirit of the contemporary epoch and of the past, and a digestion that engenders human prophetic vision. This vision the historian, in his idealistic activity of working over historic dates, cannot do without as can, for instance, the grammatical or rhetorical narrator. (. . .) Books are a modern genre of historical fantasms but nonetheless a highly significant one. They may have replaced the traditions.][34]

Because in modernity the commemorative and communal rituals, which enacted the traditions of people, are gone, books take on the function of tradition. But without the historian and the critic these books may nonetheless be unreadable. It is their social and political task to train our imagination in order to return the spirit to the letter, to be able to grasp the ideas afresh that others before us have already thought. Ideas are but the memory of mankind which is shared and passed on in reading and in the knowledge of language. The understanding of language also provides a historical consciousness, and it is through such an informed consciousness that people develop a vision of the future. Contrary to our use of the word "ideas," they are, in essence, not abstract entities but derived from the historical existence (experiences) of human beings. Humans guide other humans; remembrance and memorability provide the inspiration for conducting and interpreting one's life. For Novalis tradition has the same "spiritual" meaning as it has for Benjamin:

Der Mensch lebt, wirkt nur in der Idee fort, durch die Erinnerung an sein Dasein. Vorderhand gibts kein anderes Mittel der Geisterwirkungen auf dieser Welt. Daher ist es die Pflicht an die Verstorbenen zu denken. Es ist der einzige Weg in Gemeinschaft mit ihnen zu bleiben."

[A human being lives, and lives on only in the idea, as a remembered being. Immediately, there is no other medium of operative spirit(s) in this world. Therefore, it is our duty to remember the dead. It is the only way to stay in communion with them.][35]

And similar to Benjamin's notion of the Now or *Jetztzeit*, that is, the moment of recognizing the meaning of the present by virtue of the past,

Novalis says, "[a]lle Erinnerung ist Gegenwart. Im reinern Element wird alle Erinnerung uns wie notwendige Vordichtung erscheinen." [All remembrance is presence. In their purer state, all memories will seem to us like a necessary pre-poetic poetry.][36] Without the knowledge of a cultural past, the linguistic genius—a faculty in everyone—cannot be stimulated, and meaning would no longer be something that humans create. The critic sets an example for individual creativity; he prepares the linguistic ground for change. By dissolving worn or petrified semantic structures, and by creating new tropes and rhetorical figures, he provides the conditions of freedom. In the critic Novalis sees a facilitator of social and political change. "The physical state of critique is the element of freedom."[37] Moreover, for the Romantics, critique was an integral part of poesy and the theory of literary production; for them, the critic also had to be a poet because he himself had to be able to produce what he criticized:

> Wer keine Gedichte machen kann, wird sie auch nur negativ beurteilen. Zur echten Kritik gehört die Fähigkeit, das zu kritisierende Produkt selbst hervorzubringen. Der Geschmack allein beurteilt nur negativ.

> [He who cannot write poetry will also judge poems only negatively. Genuine critique demands the capability to produce oneself the work to be critiqued. Mere taste judges only negatively.][38]

In the Romantics' concern for a new society based on the freedom of creativity, "poesy is the basis for society as virtue is the basis of the state."[39] Ultimately, freedom's substance was seen to be in language, that is, in language use. Without language and its interpretation, the faculty of imagination would not be trained to produce new and different representations. Language is the material of *Bildung*, and, as such, it is the *absolutum* of ideas-in-formation. Language manifests the tradition of human imagination which the Romantics considered for a theory of knowledge under the name of "philosophy":

> Auch die Sprache ist ein Produkt des organischen Bildungstriebes. So wie nun dieser überall dasselbe unter den verschiedensten Umständen bildet, so bildet sich auch hier durch Kultur, durch steigende Ausbildung und Belebung die Sprache zum tiefsinnigen Ausdruck der Idee der Organisation, zum System der Philosophie.

> [Language, too, is the product of the organic drive towards formation. Like this formative drive which, in the most different circumstances, creates everywhere the same thing, language, too, transforms itself through cul-

ture, through increased training and animation [of the hieroglyph], into the profound expression of the idea of an organization, into the system of philosophy.][40]

Novalis's definition of philosophy is, however, not a matter of transcendental ideas—as it was for Kant—because "[p]hilosophy is originarily a feeling," and "[t]he limits of feeling are the limits of philosophy. Feeling cannot feel itself."[41] Feeling returns philosophy to the body, to the immanence of human existence and experience which influence the subject's ideas about his place in a world full of historical signs. He must organize these signs if he is to achieve the sense of context for his conscious life. Language creates the necessary (affective) familiarity in a context by transforming objects into figural forms of thought. "It is entirely comprehensible why, in the end, everything turns into poesy. Doesn't the world, in the end, become all mood and mind [*Gemüt*]."[42] For Novalis a philosophical understanding of the world is its poetizisation. The world should no longer be an empirical object of study but become part of our being, a being we are aware of. In the power of figure, language reveals its human intention of tradition, of transmitting a feeling about the world. In bygone mythological times, this intention of language was understood as the spirit of God that is shared among people, and the world was nothing but a (readable) sign of God. All of Novalis's ideas about a new mythology that would bring about an ideal state of existence were based on the figural potential of language that would stimulate people's imagination to perceive the world through the lens of aesthetic representations.

> Die Wortfiguren sind die Idealfiguren der anderen Figuren.—Alle Figuren etc. sollen Wort oder Sprachfiguren werden—so wie die *Figurenworte*—die innern Bilder etc. die IdealWorte der übrigen Gedancken oder Worte sind— indem sie alle innre Bilder werden sollen.

> Der Fantasie, die die *Figurenworte* bildet, kommt daher das Praedicat Genie vorzüglich zu.

> Das wird die goldne Zeit seyn, wenn alle Worte—*Figurenworte*—Mythen— und alle Figuren—Sprachfiguren—Hieroglyfen seyn werden—wenn man Figuren sprechen und schreiben—und die Worte vollkommen plastisiren, und Musiciren lernt.

> [The word figures are the ideal figures of all other figures. All figures etc. should become word or rhetorical figures—just as the figural words are the internal images etc., the ideal words of all other thoughts or words—by transforming themselves into internal images.

Fantasy, which creates the figural words, well deserves the label "genius."

It will be the golden age when all words will be figural words—myths—, and all figures will be figures of speech—hieroglyphs—, when people learn to speak and write in figures and know how to sculpt with words as well as to make music.][43]

What in olden times was called a divine spirit in language, Novalis preserves in the idea that language (still) has a "magical" power, linking the unconscious mind with the faculty of imagination. Novalis expropriated the idea of magic from the mystics by employing it in his sign theory as an analogy to the creation of sense: "Magic is the art of using the sensuous world arbitrarily [i.e., like figures]."[44] Magic therefore expresses the freedom to combine and merge signs into new imaginative representations. The subject's capability of transforming the world into a language, a meaningful system of signs, coordinates his intuitions and experiences. Through the creation of a new language, one in which the body's sensorium would come to mean, a new sense of community could be installed. Society is no longer formed according to an idea or moral ideal, but rather in terms of a mutual understanding attuned to the other's feelings and fantasies expressed in words. Literature and art become a new way of communicating and developing a common spirit or horizon, that is, a tradition of conscious fantasies and desires. The literary spirit of language relates people to their perceptual worlds. Without it, the world would not be memorable in its appearances and would not have what Benjamin, too, defines as "those magic correspondences and analogies"[45] which had once connected people's imaginations and actions to occurrences in nature. We will explore this somewhat further in the next chapter where the hermeneutical understanding of a reading community and horizon of meaning becomes of relevance for an understanding of tradition.

11

Building the Memory from Signs

IN HAVING CONSIDERED HOW TRADITION IS CENTRAL TO PROCESSES OF cognition in Kant and Novalis, I wish to turn to both contemporary hermeneutics and psychoanalysis in order to show how tradition continues to be of central importance to recent understandings of language, cognition, and *Bildung*. In particular, I will be concerned with the work of Hans-Georg Gadamer and Jacques Lacan, two figures who, despite their marked differences, are also surprisingly more compatible than one might at first assume. But more importantly, it is in the complementarity of their structuralism and hermeneutics that a more complete picture emerges of how tradition is actually transmitted. Gadamer has no theory of the unconscious, nor of the sign, but he does contribute a theory of intersubjectivity to the question of transmission, a theory of intersubjectivity which he calls application: the application of a text's language to the reader's horizon. Lacan lacks a theory of Gadamerian sociality, that is, of handing a meaning or an experience over to an other person. But Lacan's distinction between signifier and sign—between an unconsciously motivated word or turn of phrase and the referential function of a sign—illuminates what determines the reader's application of the text to his own mind, or, unconsciously, to his experience. In my attempt to wed both thinkers I hope that the reader will see how a certain epistemology of transmission is advanced.

We recall that *Bildung* speaks to a developmental process in people that develops various horizons of signification. Although both Kant and Novalis were aware that language played an important role in *Bildung*, they lacked the kind of theoretical grasp that has become characteristic of the so-called "linguistic turn" in the twentieth century. Both Gadamer and Lacan have been very sensitive to this linguistic turn and have postulated that the development of mind has to be grasped primarily in terms of what

Edmund Husserl called a horizon that pertains to language. By horizon, Husserl meant an interpretive construction without which something could not be known to consciousness as some thing in particular. Unlike Husserl, who did away with the notions of mental faculties and *Bildung*, both Gadamer and Lacan have been sensitive to how the construction of linguistic horizons is inseparable from the acquisition of cultural tradition that is transmitted by way of the written text.

In contrast to a passive acquisition of textual meaning, from a hermeneutical and psychological point of view, *Bildung* thematizes the individual's own history and agency in and as the process of understanding. This grasp of personal history suggests that the subject operates within horizons or limits that conform to those interpretive textual constructions that are of meaning to the subject. It is in this sense that a historic text posits the horizonality of where subject and text overlap without collapsing into a singular entity. Essentially, the reader-subject is dealing with the text as an other before finding or rather constructing a common ground of meaning.

The recognition of a horizon of possible meanings delineates itself when the reader becomes conscious of the fact that one's own representations are posited or situated in response to a text and that, far from being universal, these representations are grounded in personal experience. It is when personal constructions clash with textual constructions that the reader is jolted into suspending or resisting judgment, perhaps in anticipation of the construction of new meanings that will alter aspects of the reader's intellectual formation. When the reader identifies with representations that are brought to the text, assumptions about the self are naturally at stake, since the linguistic dynamics of the text challenge preconceived horizons within which the reader is already comfortably situated.

Such dynamics, of course, need not be purely ideational. From a materialist point of view, the text may well produce, say, a metonymic movement of signification that subverts, distorts, and engages metaphorical representations that the reader may already have in mind. In his essay, "Agency of the Letter," Lacan has talked about this at length in a commentary on Freud's *Interpretation of Dreams* in which Lacan strategically reverses the usual way in which we take Freud's definition of condensation and displacement. Lacan links condensation to metaphor and displacement to metonymy, something that reverses the orthodox Freudian definitions. Mental representations are subjected to logical configurations of the signifier. The figure in the text transforms the reader's habitual images and expectations. Such alteration of the reader's horizon of imagination opens him or her to a new historical experience.

In being challenged by the figures of the text, preconceived representations, or what Gadamer calls prejudices, not only demonstrate changeability but also their susceptibility to the transforming power of language. The structure of language thus proves more powerful in the effect of meaning than do static representations (i.e., pictures), since it is through language's temporal movement that the subject's horizon of meaning can be changed. Therefore insofar as consciousness is representational, the subject can only represent to itself what language offers in relation to its desire for being whole, a desire that, as we have seen earlier in Kant and Novalis, is sublimated in language into a desire for meaning.[1]

Bildung, then, describes a linguistic process in which the subject acquires a sense of being through the formation of meaning with which it then identifies in order to gain a horizonal image (*Bild*) of itself. This horizonal image is susceptible to change in the subject's flexible horizon of signification. That is, the horizon has to be capable of reformation whenever the encounter with linguistic formations challenges the dogmatic configuration of the horizon. Given the change of horizon and self-image, the limits of understanding are constantly transgressed and *Bildung* can be said to have taken place. I would like to emphasize that it is not the new information in the text that may change the subject; rather, the text's language, allegories, idioms, and rhetorical structures affect the subject by rousing unconscious memories.

Of course, given the horizon and its objectification, the limits of understanding can be said to be not only transgressed, but submitted to the literality of a text that reflects the position of an other who challenges prejudice since the other introduces the presence of a tradition that is transpersonal. The effect of tradition takes the form of an appeal to the self's desire for being (whole) in language. That is, the appeal's impact emanates from the linguistic nature of tradition which, as figure, duplicates a text of desire that is already inscribed in the subject's unconscious.

In short, we are now in a better position to see to what extent the unconscious is involved in the figurality of language. It invests signs along the lines of their surreptitious recurrence as signifiers for the self's desire for narcissistic completion. Such completion takes place in the other (text, image, history) that the subject consciously wants to know, and unconsciously has already known in fantasy. This unconscious knowledge of the other is indicated by the power of the appeal, when the text addresses and captivates the reader as belonging to the text's tradition, or history of transference. The text, in this dynamic or activating sense, expresses a desire of its own that nonetheless takes hold of the reader. Expression of the text's desire depends on the subject's reconstituting itself, his *Umbildung*, through the meaning effects of language. In other words, knowledge of the text's desire must traverse the affective and conceptual history of the subject.

The motivation to formulate questions not only demonstrates an appeal but also implies that there already exists an interpellative relationship, a common ground, between self and other (especially if the other is the other of the self) in which the question and answer game can take place. Gadamer has posited this ground as tradition, namely, as that text which is appropriated in the process of interpretation and thus transferred into the present. In the form of the interpretive text as translation of a historic text, tradition exercises a powerful linguistic drive. It is this linguistic drive toward verbal articulation that provides the common ground for our understanding a past that asserts itself in the horizon of signification.

Gadamer is self-evidently correct when he says that a hermeneutical understanding of history is based on a dialogue in which language plays out its signifying drive as a transferential structure wherein elements of tradition are carried over from one subject to the next. Thus Gadamer is opposed to those approaches of understanding which attempt to statically reconstruct a merely factual historical frame of reference within which what the text says is to be comprehended without being interpreted. In contrast, the hermeneutical condition for an understanding of the text of the past incorporates one's present situation into the interpretation of the text insofar as the present imposes certain conditions of receptivity that are in and of themselves hermeneutically predicated on a personal history of development. As a process of understanding, interpretation advances itself through a displacement of the meaning of the text into our own particular horizons of signification, which is not merely a movement between heterogeneous realms, but one that takes place within the commonality of language itself. Participating in this movement of language, the subject, who is itself constituted by language, necessarily experiences itself as dis-placed (*ver-standen*) and yet also understood. It is here, of course, that Gadamer and Lacan are not so far apart insofar as Lacanian analysis also concerns the interrelation between displacement and understanding: displacement of the *sujet* compensated for by the logic of the unconscious signifier.

In Gadamer the subject is inherently displaced, given that it is in transit between places and, hence, reflects what one might compare to the structure of metaphor, the *meta-phora*. For what is transferred (*überliefert*) is actually not as much the content meaning of a text as an awareness of our relation to tradition. We are made aware of how we are situated in relation to tradition. In this way, tradition already determines if not understands us as potential readers who interpret or construct meanings. If the reader were not always in another place than the tradition that is being transferred or handed over, the text would not be in a dialogical relation and could not speak. It would not be, as Lacan puts it in his famous "Rome Discourse," a *parole pleine*. To quote Gadamer:

> Hermeneutics must depart from the assumption that he who wants to understand is [already] connected with the matter which, with the work, comes to language through transmission (*Überlieferung*), and that he also connects or achieves a connection with the tradition from which literature (*die Überlieferung*) speaks.[2]

According to Gadamer, the moment of tradition establishes itself for the subject as a sense of belonging to the same ground as the subject matter of the text. The reader is forced to take a historical stance toward the work. The "same matter" in the text and in the reader-subject is primarily language in which the encounter of self and other takes place. Language as its own matter occupies the place of the Other where tradition speaks in the form of signifiers. But these signifiers of tradition become readable signs with the help of the reader's (historical) imagination. Imagination must then relate to Gadamer's *wirkungsgeschichtliches Bewußtsein*, because this attests to the fact that the past operates by way of language effects on representation (*Vorstellung*), and it is through this interaction of language and imagination that a consciousness of one's historicity may be achieved. History, which influences imagination, takes the form of a human memory that unfurls in figures of representation.[3] Hence in reading, memory is activated as the signifiers of the past are repeated in the language of the present.

Here the hermeneutical and psychoanalytic perspectives overlap, since they both consider representations (or prejudices) to be solely determined by past experiences. The psychoanalytic dialogue, particularly as developed by Lacan, establishes a transference between the subject and the analyst as other through language. Language provides the stage (as Other) on which the past is acted out in narrative figurations. *A similar transference, or passage, is reflected in a hermeneutical understanding, for it is always an understanding of the self in the other by means of a common language.* In the medium of common language, the self cathects the other with the desire to be a complete and perfect self. Language is the place where the other person or object triggers an unconscious memory of feeling whole. In textual hermeneutics, this memory appears as the desire to construe meaning with the sign (i.e., the appearance) of the other. But in this process, the other is no longer just the unfamiliar text but also language as a historical material that carries the cultural remainders or hieroglyphs of human experience in general. It is here that a cultural history of signification merges with the personal history that is unconscious for the subject.

In and through language, tradition manifests itself for the subject who, in the hermeneutical experience, becomes aware of meaning formations, pre-judgments, and a horizon of signification that has, until now, confined the subject's interpretation. As in the analytic situation, the effects of the past are thematized in the attention paid to the figuration of language in narration. The consciousness that is achieved through such attention allows for a hermeneutical awareness that is open to new interpretations. Although he does not distinguish between interpretation and experience in the sense elaborated above, Gadamer does speak of "hermeneutical experiences" that are based on the ability to question one's horizon. This includes tradition.

> Hermeneutical experience has to do with tradition (*Überlieferung*) which is supposed to become the object of experience. Tradition is, however, not simply an event which one recognizes in experience and learns to master, but it is language, that is, it speaks by itself like an other. An other—the you—is not an object but relates to the self.[4]

In the psychoanalytic dialogue, the subject is brought to a quasi-hermeneutical consciousness in which one can accept the otherness of the past as one's own unconscious that determines one's horizon of meanings in and for the present; this is to say, that the present representations are not representations of the past but signifiers for the unconscious that needs to be listened to as an other in the language of tradition. The otherness of the unconscious, however, is experienced through the effects of language in the communication between the linguistic sign and its signifying value (as signifier) in the unconscious. This communication between the unconscious and consciousness evolves from the meaning that the present has for the subject. As a relation to the other, this communication transfers an unconscious representation to a sign and thus transforms the sign into a signifier for what is absent; yet, through the support of the signifier, this absent being determines, nonetheless, the particular pattern of signification in the present discourse. The original *sign* is in effect overdetermined in this transference, and this means that reading contains the power of transference that intensifies meaning through overdetermination. The intensity of meaning brought about by the subject's own past distinguishes reading from interpretation.

Psychoanalytically, transference is itself an unconscious phenomenon that takes place within the temporality of repetition which Freud saw as a manifestation of the unconscious that was not content-bound but which functioned as cause for the process of signification. Here we must assume an emotion, a surprise, that overcame the subject but which the subject is incapable of remembering, since remembrance relies on signs. This experience cannot actually be said to be repressed, for only representations can be repressed; yet experience creates the Ego's desire for such a repression, and this means experience has to first become a sign.

As primary process, this original emotion opens up the "rhythmic structure"[5] of the temporality of experience in which the lacking content of an originary experience is "made up" retroactively in the present when it is turned into a sign. The fiction of an originary event only comes into being through a secondary process of linguistic inscription in which a subjective transference mis-takes the past for the present. Since perception depends on a system of signifiers, it is conditioned by repetition which, as Lacan insists in his reading of Freud, is not a reproduction of the past—this would be its representation—but a perceptive path which writing has cut through language. Writing engages the subject in tradition, in the transference of an emotion onto the plane of representation in metaphor. The "building" of metaphors, in which meaning formation coincides with the formation of an image (*Bildung*), fills the gap opened up between the unconscious emotion and the *Wahr-nehmung* in the present. The psychical apparatus reacts to the ungraspable emotion, addressed by Freud as primary process and expanded by Lacan in the notion of desire as radically other.

Lacan, for his part, saw evidence for a radical otherness of desire in the formation of symptoms because symptoms manage to repress the threat of otherness by maintaining the ground of pleasure for the Ego's representations. For the neurotic subject, symptoms are compromise formations that allow the self to stay connected with the abject other in the past; the other is at bottom the desired object but this desire is disavowed by the Ego in a pathological symptom. Therefore, Lacan defines metaphor as symptom formation; metaphor is an attempt to satisfy the Ego's desire to be intact, in touch with the other, as it were, in an image of self-completeness. Whereas metaphor then represents a sublimation of desire as "Other" in the other as image or meaning, the subject's affliction with emotion cannot be eradicated on the level of representation.

Heterogeneity in the psychical economy of the "categories" of affect and sign led Freud to assume an unconscious without "*Vorstellungs-Repräsentanz*." The assumption of an ungraspable unconscious facilitated the idea of a radically other that is at work in the subject's repetition of symptom formation, that is, in its repetition of *Wahrnehmungen*, hence mistaking the appearance for the thing-in-itself. It might be said that

Freud considered perceptions on the level of metaphor, uncovering their basis in a refusal of the Ego to understand (*ver-stehen*), of standing in the place of the other, whereas Lacan transcended the categories of such an opposition between the I and the other.

Lacan replaced the positions of I and other with a movement of semiosis that corresponds to desire and the impossibility of representing the other as Other. Although not calling it semiosis, he analyzed the process of signification linguistically in its mechanism of metonymy, for metonymy produces infinite combinations of signifiers resulting in new signs, new metaphors, and new symptoms. This move allowed him to think desire in terms of language, a metonymic desire that promotes an unconscious temporal structure of meaning expressed in a text, and that beckons reading instead of interpretation.[6]

That which resists meaning as representation raises questions for us and challenges our understanding as to why this is not part of our horizon of understanding. At the same time, this insight into our limited knowledge of the particular situation of the encounter with the foreign text leads to an awareness of the historical delimitation of this horizon. The emerging question is thus not merely directed at the other but also to the self in that it tries to find an answer within the conditions of understanding that cannot include this potentially significant but still foreign object. Otherness, nevertheless, is experienced as what constitutes the knowledge of identity. The support of identity is given in the symbolic order which transforms our experiences into a stock of recollections that we can call up at will as meanings. Otherness does not have the status of a symbol with respect to our experiences; it does not represent us and our background.[7] To the extent that our background, the horizon, is symbolized in our use of language, what is also addressed by the hermeneutical question is the symbolic capacity of language as such.[8] Coming to terms with this symbolic Other involves the recognition of one's hermeneutical situation that is equally constituted by language and which, according to Gadamer, is characterized by prejudgments. We might now interpret these as a "pre-symbolized structure" of our capacity of understanding with which the subject approaches the other as in an unfamiliar text.

Given the theory of a tropological consciousness expressed in language, Gadamer's pre-symbolized structure can be considered a tropological screen. Structured by prejudices, our understanding affects the text of the past as a repertoire of tropes that exist in metonymic relation to each other. The Other consists of linguistic structures that assume their semiotic function through correspondence to these prejudgments by means of which the subject already knows itself as being different from the other. Such prejudgments are not prejudicial in the objectionable sense because they are symbolic structures through which understanding operates. Indeed they provide the basis or potential point of departure for (another) understanding to take place, or to fail. As such, they perform the duty of *mneme*, preserving the subject's past. This allows the subject to project itself on the other and, in a second step, become aware of the past in this projection. This procedure of understanding is what Gadamer means by his formula: "fusion of horizons." Hence it is not a fusion of two distinct entities, but rather a mediation of one's judgments and preconceptions in the interpretation of what is said in the text. Nonetheless, prejudgments are evoked by the otherness of how the text says what it says. The prejudgments defend the reader's Ego against a past memory he does not want to know. For, the text's signifiers actually turn the reader back upon himself with the appeal of applying appropriate questions to the text's mimesis. This effect directs the subject away from dealing directly with the unfamiliar other but instead with the figural structure of the text as symbolic Other.

Also, the question needs to be asked, how does the text symbolize the other, the world to which it refers? The answer does not lie with the subject, and his projections, but is immanent in the textual figuration that allows the reader to follow the turn of phrases and syntactic patterns. This manner of (figural) reading prevents the subject from merely recognizing signs located in the text. Such a "recognition approach" to the text would imply that the subject has power over the text and is able to remain positioned outside it. In contrast, an understanding which results from an "overpowered" reading takes on the form of an event, the event of an effect which could not be predicted prior to the reading act; thus, the *reading effect* that causes a (new) understanding or meaning did not previously exist in the horizon of the subject. An understanding that derives meaning from reading must yield to the temporal structure of a happening in the psyche. The figural or tropological structure of textual signifiers is translated into the memory structure of the reader's unconscious. A forgotten experience gets revitalized and becomes conceptualizable through the imagination of the text. Meaning is thus created in the event of remembering what was unconscious and never occupied a place in the imaginary which the reading of a story now provides. Hence this event of a reading effect or the happening of understanding shapes the horizon of the subject's present by also effecting a form of historical consciousness, the remembrance of a past through the (historic) language of an other.

If different meaning formations are indeed only more prejudgments, then the enlargement of the horizon consists either in the accumulation of more tropes or in a metonymic change in their connections. Arresting the continuous acquisition of such linguistic features and verbal thoughts in order for the self to differentiate itself from these linguistic tropes would mean breaking these tropes apart. Insofar as the subject is also a language user and a linguistically constituted self, his sense of himself depends on the acquisition of historical insight through language. Tropes are essential for the self's composition, the containment and meaning and communicability of his emotions. As W.R. Bion has shown in his analyses of psychotics, the capacity to transform sense data—comparable to Gadamer's preconceptions—into verbal thoughts is necessary to facilitate (1) the conjunction of one set of sense impressions with another, and (2) the introjection of feelings.[9] If tropes were to be broken apart, the subject's experiences would either never make sense to him or else he would not be able to remember, judge, and interpret them in a historical existence for which tradition is the vehicle of meaning. Both Gadamer and Bion point to the abstraction and rigidity of a scientific discourse—in contrast to narrative or figural language—that inhibits the self's capacity for tolerating its own psychical realities and hence the mental representation of the subject's past experiences.

If understanding acquires the nature and structure of language, then language must determine understanding in a process of translating an unconscious signifier into a conscious signified. In Gadamer's elaboration of tradition as both transmission and transformation of the message from the past into the linguistic horizon of the present, the process of translating the subject's own past into the representational frame of the present seems to be linked to the process of transmission in interpretation. Gadamer, who does not have a marked theory of subjectivity, implies a subject in hermeneutical understanding, which he posits as a happening, a surprising event effected by an encounter with the language of the text of the past (*Überlieferung*). In this encounter, he neglects the fact that the language of the unconscious, created by the traces if not tropes of the subject's past, is itself interpreted in the larger interpretation of the past as a textual configuration.

At this point a brief clarification of Gadamer's use of the words *tradition* and *transmission* is warranted. Gadamer calls the text an *Überlieferung,* which is, however, not transmitted (*überliefert*) until the reader interprets it. Thus his concept of tradition in reference to a concrete text differs from mine in that I have tried to focus on the transmitting of tradition. This is a process in which effects of meaning occur in language as a result of an unconscious transference of libidinal energy, a deliverance of emotion to the signifiers of a text in which a cathexis thereby occurs. By not differentiating the text of the past from the process of tradition, Gadamer opens himself to criticism, for he gives the impression of being caught in a circle that maintains that tradition as text is language, and, that what is transmitted in the event of understanding is also language because the reader herself is only a body of language. This circularity reduces all textuality to the transmission of tradition. The subject in this interpretative process, therefore, would be merely a transmitter rather than an entity of *Bildung*, a subject formed by the process of tradition.

Psychoanalytic theory also deals with the process of understanding from the viewpoint of the construction of history and the formation of the subject and can correct some inconsistencies in Gadamer's project of hermeneutical understanding. The subject's past experiences are preserved in unconscious memory in the form of signifiers which, according to Lacan, behave like a language and thus prestructure our understanding in language along the synchronic and diachronic axes of signification. On this temporal axis, Lacan has mapped the signifying process onto the structure of metaphor and metonymy. His analysis demonstrates that metaphor can even be collapsed into the overall signifying structure of metonymy as well, a point underscored by Lacan's well-known student and interpreter, Serge Leclaire.[10]

If metaphor implies a movement of meaning from one signifier to another without a relationship of resemblance at work, it is only possible because of the metonymic connection between signs in a text.[11] Above, I have referred to this meaningful connection as the text's grammar. But even more basically, it is the grammatical relation between signifiers within a syntax that brings different signs into association. By bringing such signs into contact with one another, syntax may well annihilate the delimited signified of each word. This is a semiotic view also held by Julia Kristeva in her book, *The Revolution of Poetic Language,* wherein she discusses how the meaning of each word can be sublated, enhanced, and transformed by the emergence of a third and quite unexpected meaning or attribute to the original meanings of the words. This attribute or new meaning is produced in the reader's imagination by the clash of original verbal meanings. The signifying power of syntax therefore can be said to override the semantic features of conventional signs. Without syntax, the metaphoric process could not be controlled by the representational structure of signs. *Metaphora* would run amok in the reader's fantasies and psychologically end up in a state of hallucination rather than being directed and contained by the signifying process at work in the concrete text. Both Gadamer and Lacan agree that the signifying status of syntax supplants the structure of words as signs and turns them into signifiers that submit to the grammatical features of the text. These features participate in the construction of the text's tropology which then superimposes its rhetorical structure—traditionally analyzed as style—onto the semantic context, thereby transforming it.

In contrast to Lacan, Gadamer's argument is based on the idea of a traditional dichotomy between subject and object: the subject vis-à-vis tradition as objective text. This is true even if he admits that both subject and object positions are displaced in hermeneutical understanding. Again, Gadamer's concept of *begreifen* and *Begrifflichkeit,* understanding in language as grasping and thus imagining something, is supposed to capture the essential nature of interpretation. But in comparison with Lacan's insistence on the metonymical basis of meaning creation, Gadamer's *begreifen* seems to employ a strict dichotomy between understanding (*ver-stehen*) the text and determining its content by referring to objects outside the text. What underlies understanding is a constructive-conceptual thinking as opposed to a referential-representational thinking.[12] Understanding—the German word does associate a mobility of standpoint—is tied to an acceptance of the possibility of the signified to detach itself from the sign's position in a sentence and impose itself on another sign whose signified is thereby eclipsed.

Gadamer's choice of words for his hermeneutical concepts are misleading here, because they cover up the hermeneutical basis of understanding in the text's rhetorical features. It is therefore important to carefully register the few passages that Gadamer devoted to an unconscious process of signification, for it is in those passages that he tries to approach a theory of the interpretation of tradition in and as language. The decisive feature of language for a hermeneutical experience is the ability to posit understanding as an event (*Geschehenscharakter der Sprache*):

> Not only is language use and the developmental formation of verbal means a process such as no individual consciousness can knowingly and selectively correspond to it—with this respect it is literally more correct to say that language speaks us than we speak it.[13]

Gadamer starts from the thesis that tradition as language already determines our understanding of the text when we try to interpret it. Meaning occurs as a suddenly-becoming-conscious of a connection between previously unassociated "things." By seeing now how things relate (*Sach-verhalt*) or *can* relate to one another, a new insight into the reality of the subject matter has been made. The effect of a recognized relationship between "things" is elaborated by Gadamer as the hermeneutical experience that has its motivation in the effects of language on what he calls consciousness, even though he qualifies it as a "consciousness of operative effects" (*wirkungs-geschichtliches Bewußtsein*).

It is the subject's imagination that puts its "own" history into a textual *mise-en-scène*. By inserting the scene of imagination into the picture of understanding, I will expand on Gadamer's point that "in the coming to language of what is said in the text of tradition, language concludes (*ausmacht*) the actual hermeneutical event which is at the same time appropriation and interpretation."[14] The "actual hermeneutical event" takes place in the scenarios of our representations, though Gadamer continually asserts that hermeneutical understanding of the language of tradition is an understanding "for me" and not of tradition itself. He underlines this property of the "for me" with the notion of application: the language of tradition has to be applied to *my* horizon. By this he means "my historical situation." But this concept of horizon also includes those unconscious experiences of the past that left their traces as an emotional structure of signifiers that are remembered and therefore sutured in the signifying connections of the text that is tradition. The figure of the text that is assembled by linking signifiers in reading provides the reader with an imaginary scene for his or her re-membered emotions. Gadamer's variant, *Sinnhorizont* or horizon of "significance," as distinguished from horizon of "signification" or meaning, has to include this unconscious anticipation of sense in the subject's language as it encounters the language of the text. Since the application of the text's language to my own (unconscious) use of language determines the hermeneutical experience of tradition, I must be able to imagine a situation in which I would have a sensuous experience of what is said in the text. This experience is *in potentia*, because it involves a sensuous contingency. It enacts a repetition of an experience in my past with the difference that the representational scene has changed; but the scenario, the structure of the scene, the figure of the image in the text, is the same as in the past that is preserved in the unconscious. The sensuous component of understanding tradition in response to language can only be an imaginative one.

> The truth of tradition (*Überlieferung*) is like (!) the present which lies open to the senses. Tradition's mode of being is, of course, not an immediate sensuous one. It is language; and the listening which hears [and understands] it includes its truth into a[n ap]propriated linguistic relationship with the world by interpreting the texts. The linguistic communication between the present and tradition (*Überlieferung*) is, as we have shown, the event (*Geschehen*) which in every understanding rifts a trace.[15]

Imagination appears to represent the link between two signifying structures, the language in the text, and the language of the unconscious. Both structures are involved in reading the text of tradition, especially when the text resists the reader's tendency to recognize objects in the mirror of written or spoken words. When the recognition of meanings no longer makes sense in the context of the text, then Gadamer's approach of a hermeneutical understanding overlaps with a psychoanalytic theory of reading that pays attention to the figural function of language. Psychoanalysis uses signs as signifiers whose meaning is only anticipated or deferred until those signifiers have established a relation to other textual signifiers. This is analogous to the interpretation of dreams in which the psychoanalyst awaits the dreamer's associations to details in the dream. The textual relation is repeated in the subject's unconscious—the unconscious also reads—where the signifiers of experience are actualized and cathected in terms of the Freudian drive. These cathected signifiers now motivate imagination for a representation; in the dream narration this would be the association which is always a concrete memory. But this memory already harbors a fantasy around a strong affect which has been staged in the dream. The unconscious fantasy and the scenes in the dream correspond to one another. This fantasy is what the analyst tries to make conscious in the patient so as to understand a primary experience from the scenario of the dream. For a better psychoanalytic understanding, such primary scenarios of experience might be the oedipal triangle, the mother-child symbiosis in feeding, or the scene of castration, which, as figures of experience, structure the imaginary scenes or situations that the subject ultimately constructs in his mind when he reads the text on the level of its rhetorical structure.

This reading of the text's figurality sidesteps the verbal appeal to positive representation (*Darstellung*) by taking, in its place, the route of an emotive appeal. Only in a secondary processing of the emotion does this appeal lead to a representation (*Vorstellung*) which is no longer immediately that of the word's referent, since it is motivated and moved by the affect. In the unconscious, affect has its own signifiers that are transposed by fantasy into representations. In this transformative process, those representations do not try to mirror the meaning of the text but help in apprehending the figurality of the text's language.

If the signifier causes a self-estrangement in the reader who has become aware of his self as other in interpretation, then this awareness grounds the experiential aspect of hermeneutical understanding. In experience, *Erfahr-ung*, the subject travels the path between the unconscious past and the present. In interpretation (exegesis), which in German literally means to "place outside" (*Auslegung*), the reader externalizes and estranges his own past by means of the text's language. The reader "ex-plains"[16] an unconscious past from the "plane" of the text *(explanare)*. Like the subject matter, the reader is figured and hence displaced. Indeed, this displacement even extends to tradition, given that tradition is transmitted through language in which we inscribe our experiences.

For me, the difference between language and signification necessarily requires the concept of tradition as I have elaborated it. In this I differ from Gadamer who reduces the subject, as well as the subject matter (*Sachverhalt*), to language alone. No doubt, a conflation of the text and its subject matter would be consistent with the view that tradition is language, except that the historical basis for tradition as an object of the text has been dropped out. Tradition supports the production of meaning in language, but there is no meaning or horizon of sense without the temporal delay of experience that language (dis-)places into history. (In analogy to Gadamer, experience *comes* to language.) But this translation, as we can see with the help of Freud and Lacan, is possible only if experience is already prestructured by the language of the unconscious. The linguistic unconscious preserves experience in the form of signifiers which have correlates in the verbal language of the text. The text that cannot be understood in itself is turned into a *pretext* for the subject's past that is staged on its linguistic plane.

Despite the impossibility of understanding the text as totally other, there exists a mutually constitutive relationship between the text as other and the self in the *mnemotechnique* of the text's figuration. What the text preserves for successive readers is inscribed as a claim on these readers, as "being intended by the past," as Benjamin would say. This call of the past on us in the form of the representability of the text's meaning makes us aware that we are limited in our capacity of representation by our historical existence. In interpreting the text, we engage in a tradition that performs the function of the text's re-membrance and connects what has been split off—the loss of an other that had originally rendered a sense of being whole. After the subject's insertion into the symbolic order in Lacan's sense, the originary physical sense of being was displaced onto the meaning of language. With the advent of language in the subject's psychical economy, desire for meaning was born in a capacity of the linguistic signifier to stand in for the loss of the (self-sustaining) other.

Language has the figurative capacity of saying something else than it means because its affective structure of metonymy and metaphor duplicates the (experiential) structure of the mind. This mind is not neutral. Instead, the mind is a motivated structure in which signifiers are determined by the unconscious memory of feelings. Feelings are part of the mind and act as the vehicle for an experience, and when the time comes that experience finds its conscious expression in meaning. But for meaning to occur, experience has to be first translated into meaning and this happens when a textual arrangement of signifiers refigures the original scenario of that hitherto unconscious experience. The text's memory hinges on the figurality of language which serves as a vehicle, a *mnemonic* device, by which the subject is figuratively transposed into his own past, in the representations which occur to him when he reads the text. As feelings are a sign of memory and refer us, unconsciously, to the past, we can say that understanding is motivated by the past preserved in imagination and enacted in the signification of a text, in how the text signifies something for us. The efficacy of language in the text, owing to the desire of tradition for articulation, is reflected in the understanding of tradition's "message." This message is to experience oneself as determined by a past that can only come into being as meaning.

The fact that tradition is transmitted in language and articulated in the words of an interpreter means that if we are displaced by being interpellated within tradition, that tradition is also itself displaced. Although the "subject matter" of tradition is conditioned by language, it is like understanding, "never merely object but comprises everything that can ever become object [of tradition, i.e., interpretation]."[17] Gadamer points to Greek ontology—where the word names being—when he argues that tradition is the ground for the mutual dependency of language and thought, given that the Greeks were not able to distinguish conceptually between language as form and content of thought. The Greek *logos* may be invoked by comparison with the hypothesis that thought implies acts of interpretation, since these are based on the latent content of tradition in language.

Gadamer's allusion to logos is analogous, of course, with the German Romantic notion of *Geist* in language. In the representation of aesthetic ideas, Kant has already demonstrated that *Geist* is an ambivalent faculty that bridges mind and language. The concept of spirit contains the interpreter's creative mind. As such, it is no longer determined by the meaning of the word for which the word is only a sign. Instead, it expresses a relation between the word and the power of imagination, and this relation causes a conceptual understanding that constructs representations according to the subject's own experiences. For logos to assert the truth of the word, it would have to find its signifying support in the subject's experience, accessed in imagination. Hence the logos would merely be an imposture if it did not refer to the subject's horizon of significance. Logos implies the perspective and standpoint of the language user for whom the word expresses truth. Its truth claim is held in check by history. It cannot speak the truth of tradition until it has been subjected to a process of transference, the *meta-phora* in language. Only in its capacity to surrender to metaphor, and thus to be flexible instead of absolute, can the logos intend us and relate us to tradition.

Metaphoricity of language involves the psyche. That is, the subject's unconscious overdetermines the words and turns them into signifiers for his experience. Without the unconscious, the signifying power exercised through libidinal cathexis in language could not be used to translate experiences into representations. Without the potential of words to become signifiers for the subject's past, tradition would have no meaning and would not allow the recognition of history, since experience would remain unconscious and could not be redeemed. *The redemption of experience signifies tradition as meaning which, in Benjamin's sense of tradition, constitutes history as* Jetztzeit, *as a significant Now.* The mnemotechnique of a text exploits the unconscious memory of signs and uses them as signifiers for an experience through a rhetorical association of affect. The rhetorical or linguistic connection between several signifiers may be an amplified affective connection installed through libidinal cathexis.

With respect to the relation between thought and word, Gadamer uses the term *Zuordnung,* attribution or application, to stress the discriminating work involved in logos. Application, which is logos, is thus much more than mere correspondence of words and things—as presupposed in theories of mimesis. Precisely because the inherent truth of logos is not that of merely noticing (the *noein*), not simply of allowing being to appear, but of positioning *being* under a point of view and thus attributing something to it in its cognition, the support of truth (and of course of non-truth) is not the word (*onoma*) but the logos. What is usually misrecognized, is "that the truth of the matter lies in discourse [the *usage* of words], that is, it lies in its last instance in the intention toward a common opinion about the matter and it does not lie in the particularity of words—it does not even lie in the entire inventory of words of a language."[18] It is a going beyond referentiality that Gadamer associates with the concept of logos in its opposition to *onoma*. In essence, Gadamer here names the difference between the figurative and literal use of language. But his point about the difference between logos and *onoma* is more specific, because he tries to show that with the applicability inherent in logos, it is the mind that interferes between word and thing and creates a relationship between the two. Logos, part mind, part word, is determined by experience. Only experience can apply the word to things in a meaningful way. And this meaning must also represent the subject's attitude toward the thing, a matter of feeling or memory that is applied to the present. This memory or feeling, then, positions the subject vis-à-vis his being as he understands it in every meaningful event.

If the function of logos in understanding was not conscious for the Greeks and even for most of Western metaphysics, as, for instance, Martin Heidegger asserts in invoking a "forgetfulness of Being," the signifiability of language in relation to being seems nonetheless grounded in the logos. Heidegger refers to this signifiability as Being without which being could not become meaning. This ontological difference of being and Being, of existence and reflection on one's existence, opens up the realm or method of a different kind of knowledge that is not the knowledge of history as facts or things; it is, rather, a hermeneutical knowledge of understanding one's position or relation to things. This relationality of the subject's mind determines logos as the unconsciousness of language, that is, it predisposes the subject to the object through language.

The object of hermeneutics is what Gadamer calls the "conceptuality of all understanding," an object that leads to a gross misunderstanding of Gadamer's project if the German *Begrifflichkeit* is translated as "abstractness," as is the case in the English edition of *Truth and Method*. Precisely because the German verb *begreifen*, which also means to understand, implies the physical, tangible notion of grasping, it does not employ an abstraction from concrete and thus historical reality, as for instance in abstract mathematical or logistic thought. This conceptuality must rather be associated with the function of representation in imagination, that is, with content rather than with a formal reduction by the Kantian faculty of understanding. It is tied to the figurality of language and not to the sign function of words or objects. The interpreter is usually not conscious of the signifying power of figurality in speech. Hermeneutics attempts to interpret the influence this power exercises in textual interpretation; hermeneutics isolates this signifying power to demonstrate that history works as tradition:

> The interpreter does not know that he invests himself and his own representations (*Begriffe*) in the interpretation. The verbal nature of his formulation inheres in the intended meaning [what he wants to say] so completely that it can in no way become a [separate] object for him. Thus it is understandable that this [linguistic] side of the hermeneutical procedure remains totally ignored.[19]

Insofar as the interpreter-subject "does not know" the conceptions (*Begriffe*) of his own discourse, the created meaning is less a conscious sense wrested from the text than an unconscious meaning effect. The reader is not conscious of how his or her conceptions interact with the figure of the text; but it is in this psycholinguistic interaction that meaning is produced. Although Gadamer does not acknowledge an unconscious meaning mechanism in language, he does sense that interpretation is not an intentional act but, as he says, a happening. Because "understanding proves to be kind of an effect" as a result of applying the potential significance of a text to the historical situation of the interpreter, this application cannot, I conclude, be entirely conscious.[20]

Gadamer's formulation of an "effective-historical consciousness" might be better understood as the power of a historically conditioned imagination that is able to build scenes from memory through the combination of present signifiers. Understanding, Gadamer asserts, is always motivated, but the motivation has its roots in the interpreter's past and, as psychoanalysis has taught us, this is hardly ever conscious in the act of interpreting the text. The role of language in this motivated understanding is that understanding occurs as language, what Gadamer calls the *Sprachlichkeit des Verstehens*. But far from having verbal signifiers in our head, we understand what is said by drawing on images from our present circumstance. Hence we understand a situation not because words have meanings, but because these words also function as signifiers that evoke a representation, or a feeling, to which we associate an image. To not grasp (*begreifen*) the meaning of a text is to be unable to *imagine* what the text says, even though one recognizes each verbal icon.

What then determines the implied double reading process in which the language of the text takes hold of our imagination? If imagination is merely a faculty of representation, that is, of images, how does it decipher and read signs other than in their representative value of the signified objects? The answer must lie in the fact that imagination is not an autonomous mental faculty; to the contrary, its image production is already a secondary process of an agency that first transfers the signifiers of the text to another signifying structure onto which they are grafted. This agency not only deals with language but also acts within language by means of its capacity to move signifiers around; thus, it reveals itself as a meta-phoric instance.

Lacan has developed the structure of the unconscious based on his translation of Freud's "considerations of representability" as "the role of the possibility of figurative expression."[21] This rendition of representability foregrounds an understanding of the figural rather than the representational force of the unconscious with which it articulates and transforms the material of perception and sensation. Precisely because of this difference between the figural and representational form of expression, Freud distinguished between a "dynamic unconscious" in which the signifiers combine to build a signifying structure and a "descriptive unconscious" in which censored representations are repressed. In the dynamic unconscious, the structure of the signifier is realized by the mobility of desire, operating in the drive for repetition. Only in the recurrence of a particular signifier can a figure or context be recognized as a potential form, that is, as a structure of meaning. What ultimately constitutes the figure of the text depends upon the relational features of that unconscious signifier. The power of combining signifiers to form such figures as *Gebilde* distinguishes them from images. We have tried to address above, in the chapter on Kant, the *Bilder* of imagination as wit. And, by stressing their belonging to the unconscious dynamism, we have found that it was the capacity of "mother wit" that could account for the formative faculty of recognizing signifying patterns.

To return to a key concept related to the unconscious as language, it has to be said that the drive in the dynamic unconscious does not refer to a physical instinct but rather exerts the changing dynamics of investment itself. This does not rule out the body from signification since it is the body's original satisfaction that gave the child the feeling of being whole. It is only after the encounter with language that the experience of wholeness is lost and satisfaction is broken down into the functional units of needs which are articulated in language as demands for objects. "Precisely because by and through language needs are diversified and reduced to a point at which their scope appears to be of a quite different order, whether in relation to the subject or to politics"[22] can they be manipulated into being satisfied in the realm of the imaginary which the signifying strategies of language serve. Because language inserts itself and creates the difference between imaginary and physical experience, it blocks the body's possession of itself because, as much as reference to one's body wants to be a conscious effort, it is nonetheless dependent on a mediation in representation. The subject thus responds to an image of his body-self and not to the source of his need.

In the gap between bodily experience and language, desire emerges as a mode of being frustrated by the experience of an other who is not the satisfying mother. On the significance of that symbolic *Other*, Lacan writes:

> Demand in itself bears on something other than the satisfactions it calls for. It is demand of a presence or of an absence—which is what is manifested in the primordial relation to the mother, pregnant with that Other to be situated *within* the needs that it can satisfy. Demand constitutes the Other as already possessing the "privilege" of satisfying needs, that is to say, the power of depriving them of that alone by which they are satisfied. The privilege of the Other thus outlines the radical form of the gift which the Other does not have, namely, its love.[23]

What the Other offers is a false presence constituted by the signifiers of language that simulate the experience of an appeal for identification with the (m)other. Identification requires the repression of otherness and as such the subject has to repress the mother because she alienates his needs at the moment these needs are transformed into signified constructs. This is what constitutes a primal repression that can never be lifted, because it supports the capacity of language to function in the place of the mother where identification can take place by way of a representation. Indeed, the very fact of identification is prepared by the physical need for the mother when the child was not able to distinguish between its and the other's body. Unconsciously, the subject is still linked with the mother, a linkage which on the conscious level is demonstrated by identification with an other. Lacan attributes this capacity for identification to a *méconnaissance* that constitutes the (conscious) Ego-function of the subject when it gives in to the illusion of *being* that language offers. The syntactical structure built on the copula "be" defines the subject: "I am that."[24]

The nature of the demand that estranges the subject's needs is determined by language. Thus linguistic "proofs of love" are only representations of not-being. The difference between language, the signifier, and being, engenders desire for being which splits the subject into a conscious and an unconscious signifying function. Lacan insists that the subject cannot know its desire but can only mis-take the demand of love with reference to the Other on which both are contingent. In the order of language, the sign is thus not a sign of love but a signifier for desire, inscribed by Lacan in a theory of the unconscious as

> *"discours de l'Autre'"* (discourse of the Other), in which the *de* is to be understood in the sense of the Latin *de* (objective determination): *de Alio in oratione* (completed by: *tua res agitur*).[25]

A nonlinguistic example for the significance of a signifying relation between desire and the unconscious is the transitional object, the security blanket or the nappie, which, for the child, serves the need to relieve the negative effects (anxiety) of detaching from the security of the mother-child symbiosis. This transitional object also serves as a signifier for an unconscious fantasy of being loved that Lacan identifies as the condition of the unconscious, since it means something other than it represents: "The representative of representation in the absolute condition is at home in the unconscious, where it causes desire according to the structure of the phantasy."[26]

This definition is comparable to Freud's drive that cannot have its own representation but can only attach itself to one. Thus the representation (perception) is only representative of the drive (memory), *Vorstellungs-Repräsentanz*. The memory that the drive enacts in the place of the Other, as the repetitive "force" of memory, endows the signifier with a representation that unconsciously satisfies the drive in a vicarious way. The drive experienced in the child's need to avoid anxiety enacts the remembrance of the mother by way of the nappie that stands for the fantasy of being whole. Thus the place of the Other, which is occupied by the pillow, serviced by the drive, keeps the presence of the memory trace in the unconscious mind.

Transposed into language where the subject operates on a double level, in conscious and unconscious signification, the function of the signifier is "to represent a subject for another signifier."[27] For Lacan, the subject is merely an effect of language, and we might add, of language that makes sense to a mind, or of a language that has the quality of affect, of an affect expressed. Invested with the drive, the signifier acts merely as a metaphor for the subject's demand for love, a demand that is addressed only to himself. Thus the metaphor is read on another level as a displacement of desire because the subject has to recognize that the proofs of love are his own investments in the Other as opposed to merely himself. The displacement of the signifier of the drive articulates another signifier that is read by the unconscious as a "signifier of a lack in the Other."[28] Language cannot give love.

This displacement of the signifier of the drive takes place across the whole signifying chain as a metonymic movement whose operation of combining signifiers achieves the power of designing and designating a figure that is recognized by the subject's unconscious as the original scenario of desire. Since no one word in its object representation expresses the experience that desire is after, it takes a series of words that, in their contiguity, render at least a figure or a figurative context for that desire. Hence the drive contributes to signification on the level of substitution by attaching itself to a word other than the one that might cause the representation of the desired "object." Meaning is then effected by a temporary satisfaction through an overdetermination of a sign while the cathexis is transferred from the desired but censured representation to a word-representation affected by the word's signified. Language becomes the necessary psychological interface between desire and meaning.

Whereas desire aims at an imaginary, unrepresentable object (and can thus only be articulated but not satisfied in language precisely because it is articulated there in the place of the Other)[29] the drive, on the contrary, can invest a signifier and use it as an ersatz object of satisfaction in a metaphor-like fashion. The drive can thus represent itself in a representation which indicates that the mental representation does not represent the drive, but that it functions as a signifier for another representation that is repressed.

Of course the signifiers of representation can vary. The exchangeability of representations for the drive links the drive with the desire that cannot be arrested in one signifier. In relation to desire, the drive acts out its temporal force of repetition by cathecting various signifiers. This aids in bringing words into contact with one another, thereby creating a signifying chain that is not ordered by its individual signifieds but by the metonymy of contiguity. In the unconscious, the movement of the drive likewise traces a path in an unstructured field of simultaneous memory traces and differentiates them along a diachronic line drawing the outline of a figure (Kant calls this hypotyposis) that is activated in the encounter with the text. As repetition of cathexis, this elaboration of the drive acts rhythmically in spacing the signifiers and allowing a potentially significant pattern or form to occur. It is through figuration that the rhetoric of the unconscious comes to speak in the order of the Other. Yet the rhetoric of unconscious signifiers is nonetheless not established out of its own accord but through the "fall of the subject into language." Hence the scenario of being is not created by the subject but by the Other, by means of cathected signifiers. The desire for being is the desire for the Other.

> Man's desire is also the *désir de l'Autre* (the desire of the Other) in which the *de* provides what grammarians call the "subjective determination," namely that it is *qua* Other that he desires (which provides for the true compass of human passion).[30]

In returning to our theme of the text of tradition, we can see that tradition is associated with the unconscious Other of language that speaks the subject. As language would not have meanings without tradition, tradition would not be passed on in the desire for meaning if the logos could not name being as desire in language. Thus logos is hardly impassionate, for it supports the human condition of suffering in history that it asserts as a signifier.

In line with the Gadamerian passion for understanding language as tradition, Lacan has drawn a similar conclusion:

> This passion of the signifier now becomes a new dimension of the human condition in that it is not only man who speaks, but in man and through man *it* speaks (*ça parle*), that his nature is woven by effects in which is to be found the structure of language, of which he becomes the material, and that therefore resounds in him, beyond what could be conceived of by a psychology of ideas, the relation [in the figure] of speech.[31]

What else is the "relation of speech that resounds in man" if not tradition, the words that originally belong to transmitted texts, forgotten in our everyday use of speech. But what is important to add to both Lacan and Gadamer's theories is that tradition conditions the subject's imagination. Tradition is neither just language nor imagination, it is the relationship between the two. Language as tradition is part of our unconscious where the transference, the translation of the past into the meaning of the present, that is, the meaning for us, takes place. This unconscious translation is itself only possible because the unconscious is constituted by marked signs that, according to Lacan, interact with one another like a language. These signs become meaningful and hence conscious for the subject once they are interpreted by an other, the text or another person, in any case in a dialogue, because it is in this intersubjectivity between the I and the other that a translation of unconscious and ununderstood experience into meaning begins. What happens in this translation, unfolding in the dialogue, is the fusion between the existential desire for meaning and the desire for being. The words are animated by the subject's conscious feeling of being alive. This is the core of the hermeneutical experience, when life makes sense to a person. Assuming that the life force is always a force toward expression, it is through this force that we cathect what is culturally available to us with a sense of our own. We appropriate tradition through affective attachments to cultural signifiers. In our transferential relationships to the world we incorporate the history of this world and fuse it with our own life history.

If we are spoken by language, in the sense that the logos speaks through us, then the logos must be a manifestation of tradition. Logos transforms words into historically determined representations of our imagination. What speaks through us is not then another voice but a mimetic power that is not conscious of its meaning effects because it presents itself only in the form of *ver-stehen*, of standing in another place than from which we speak when we traverse the world with the help of our imagination.

Part IV

Redemption of the Past in Allegory

12

Woman as the Allegory of Modernity

Die Sprache hat es
unmißverständlich bedeutet, daß das
Gedächtnis nicht ein Instrument zur
Erkundung der Vergangenheit ist,
sondern deren Schauplatz.

[Language has unmistakably
indicated that memory is not an
instrument for the exploration of the
past but its stage.]
—Benjamin, *"Berliner Chronik"*

THE TOPIC OF WOMAN AND MODERNITY, FROM THE VIEWPOINT OF WALTER Benjamin's theory of culture, has raised the following questions for my treatment of experience and its structure of remembrance as mapped on the body of the mother: if modernity is defined by a loss of experience, and if woman can indeed be viewed as an allegory of modernity, can one also detect a corresponding loss of femininity along with the loss of historical experience?

In connection with this question, woman and her femininity are related to the experience of history. The so-called historical avant-garde of the turn of the century aimed to break with a tradition of mimesis that has its roots in the Renaissance and was still alive in the latter half of the nineteenth century. With this break, the artists of the avant-garde meant to reveal how works of art exploited the psychological mechanism of *appearance* (illusion), a mechanism that previously had never effectively been made conscious but was unconsciously at work in the subject's constitution of his reality. Especially in the realm of the aesthetic, experience is always only an illusion, and hence not authentic, but artificially mediated.

However, if one considers the development of the status of art since the eighteenth century, a process in which art separated more and more from everyday reality as well as differentiated itself from this reality by developing an autonomous, compensatory realm of the aesthetic in which the subject tried to experience himself, then the argument of illusory experience with respect to the experience of reality loses its urgency. Art no longer claims to mediate between the individual and his circumstances or "objective" reality. Instead, what prevails is the experience of subjectivity. Since the subject-object dialectic is eliminated in the autonomous realm of art, given that art is increasingly cut off from life, this subjective experience is also not authentic in the sense of being a reliable source for the constitution of the self. Rather, it is a fantasy experience. The realm of art becomes a place for unconsciously projecting one's desires. From this angle, the avant-garde sees itself as reflecting an Enlightenment project which is no longer merely content-oriented but which puts the status of art and the aesthetic realm in society in question. It does so by confronting the individual with his wishful fantasies of wholeness and an experience of happiness. If one accepts Freud's theory that these wishful fantasies have their origin in a happily experienced past, then art offers an illusory connection to history and suppresses the (historical) experience of the Now. The danger lurking in this aesthetic submission to appearance is the loss of both a historical consciousness and a historical agency that could change the practice of life.

In the aesthetico-historical polemics opened up by the avant-garde, the usurpation of women for the mechanism of representation in the history of aesthetics is exposed and made conscious. In the avant-garde unmasking of the illusionary character of a traditional system of representation (*Darstellung*), femininity becomes a cultural sign. The concept of femininity, then, is not derived from historically extant women, their life contexts and their psychological make-up; rather, femininity is part of the definition of the aesthetic per se.

Whenever aesthetic representation has aimed to express what cannot be expressed by rational semantics (as, for instance, the transcendental, God, infinity, nature, and beauty), these ideas are often conveyed in the history of art through the representation of woman. The representation of woman in the aesthetic realm did not, as stated above, intend to produce knowledge of woman herself but, rather, the experience of these non-rational, nonquotidian areas of metaphysical being. Hence, women have had the same cultural status as art objects. They have participated in the same "aura" as works of art by appearing to have a transhistorical value and by embodying imaginary desires. Having defined the important function of tradition for culture in the context of the aura, Benjamin shows how art, through its aura, essentially contributes to the self-understanding and self-experience of the individual when his "free-floating contemplation" has been triggered by the art object.[1] The self experienced in the realm of art is, of course, that of the male subject, while the auratic woman is its necessary object. As subject, the male invests the object with his libidinal wishful fantasies, such as the desire to be whole and immortal. Woman mediates such unilateral experiences of wholeness, thus serving as the medium for the male subject's projections.

Woman in the context of aesthetics can be said to be the sublimated representation of male desire. For it is a criterion of the auratic woman, and consequently of the worship of woman as the ideal of humanity, to be asexual herself, which means her body and her sexuality are either repressed or sublated and displaced into a nonphysical value. Feminist scholarship has thematized this aesthetic tradition as bearing the historical conditions for the "anorganic" body of woman.[2] A body without organs is a corpse. This has led to the notion of the absence of women in history. The dead body of woman only functions as an image, a projection surface (Freud) for male fantasies. If the aesthetic object triggers a "disinterested pleasure" that is to be defined as beautiful in the Kantian sense, it also triggers a pleasurable feeling of life by exciting the imagination. The (male) subject gains a subjective experience of his self through the feeling of pleasure stimulated by the aesthetic object, in this case, woman. To summarize somewhat provocatively: the privilege of the aesthetic to convey a consciousness of life and self is based on woman and her physical death. For, as Kant formulates it, the actual existence of the aesthetic object should be of no interest to the observer.

The significance of the dead body in the representational system of aesthetics has been elaborated by Benjamin in his work on modernity and allegory, both in his *Ursprung des deutschen Trauerspiels* and the *Passagenwerk*. While in traditional aesthetics the subject was not aware of a dead body within the mediating structure of the aesthetic system of meaning, in avant-garde art, the subject is confronted with the illusionary quality of his experience in the aesthetic realm. The failure of a coherent (and concealed) structure of meaning is experienced as shock, a shock that ruptures aesthetic immanence. The representational system no longer *refers* to an experiential outside, be it transcendental or real, but is itself the reality that is experienced. What becomes visible in an avant-garde art constructed of fragments is the surface of the aesthetic sign and its economy of exchange. In the case of woman as aesthetic sign—consider the paintings of René Magritte—the female body is disfigured by emphasizing the body's *parts* in order to focus attention on the female body as a matrix of the production of meaning. Woman in the avant-garde, of course, is still in the object position and figures as the ruin of the aesthetic tradition. As corporeal ruin, she assumes a twofold role: one, she refers to the representational system in which she figures as dead body; and, two, she serves as a reminder of the myths of wholeness and transcendence that characterize aesthetic subjectivity. That is to say, the female ruin evokes the idealization of woman from the past.

Since a relationship to the absolute, to infinity, and to God, cannot be established through woman, the subject loses a transcendental anchor in the aesthetic. Yet, a new anchor, that of sexuality, will be established. Insofar as this anchoring is essential to the constitution of the subject and self-understanding, it is concomitant to the loss of experience as a loss of identity that results in the psychological dissolution of the unified self.

Benjamin sees the expression of this loss of experience in and as melancholia. He correlates the psychological state of melancholia with the notion of the souvenir (*Andenken*), which in German also incorporates the idea of always thinking about the lost object and thus being fixated on a specific stage in life. This fixation, elaborated by Freud in *Mourning and Melancholia* as introjection of the other, prevents the subject from experiencing his present circumstance, causing him to feel more and more estranged from his current (historical) context. Melancholic perception is tainted by the death of the loved object, which is always remembered and in this way preserved and idealized in *Andenken*, the souvenir-like mental idol. As a "dead" object, the remembered image of the lost object is entirely open for projections of the subject's narcissistic needs.[3]

Benjamin identifies the loss of authentic experience with the repetition compulsion of the Ego that, in its imaginary obsession of seeing the lost love object in everything, is fixated on the past. The subject experiences outside reality only phantasmagorically. In their phenomenal status, objects and surroundings are reduced to mere signs that trigger subjective fantasies. These are not reflected experiences, or *Erfahrungen*, that in the Benjaminian sense would lead to cognitions of history and to a change in historical practice. Rather, these imaginary experiences are passive experiences (*Erlebnisse*) of self-indulgence. In these experiences the unconscious intent is the imaginary reestablishment of a lost world. The individual's psychological adaptation to a fragmented world of the spleen (the subject's mental obsession) proceeds by libidinally investing the various broken pieces of the past and treating them as souvenirs of a blissful experience of wholeness. Meaning in this modern world of fragments is now formed by the subject's conception of these fragmentary pieces as fetishes, as a means for a substitute experience of bliss.

The significance of the fetish is tied primarily to woman and sexual experience. In the prostitute, the fetish assumes the illusion (appearance) of an authentic experience that recalls the image and feeling of a happy past in the male subject. Through the fragmentation of the female body and the semiotization of the prostitute's genitals, woman represents the fragmented experience of modern reality, and, in the construction of her sex, supports the appearance of nostalgia, that "once upon a time it was beautiful." In the prostitute's body an original relationship between woman and the aesthetic is preserved. She is the *Andenken*, the reminder of happier times. Her sexual appeal evokes the longing for a past experience of bliss which historically has been mediated by the aesthetic ideal of woman.

In this context, woman in modernity can be considered a symbol of the past, especially with respect to the perception of projections by the melancholic psyche. In the role of prostitute, woman exhibits her body for the male subject's wishful projections and feelings of nostalgia. Exciting male fantasy by veiling and garnishing her sexuality, woman replaces the authentic experience of love that is tied to a mythical past of feeling wholeness with a sexual experience heightened by the fantasy of a "real" experience of the past and the lost object of love. The attraction of woman's body lies precisely in this promise of bliss that is connected to the history of art as well as to the individual's libidinal past—the mother-child symbiosis. This remains, however, unconscious to the subject. "Here [on the streets of the metropolis] bliss winks at him from every woman's body as the chimera of sexuality, as his type."[4] Fetishization of woman is part of the novel experience of metropolitan space which, shifted to the imaginary, amounts to an experience of exaltation. The modern environment is perceived through an aesthetic filter.

If a feeling of life was once triggered in the subject by an aesthetic object that gave the subject a sense of self, in modernity this feeling is triggered by sexuality. In the prostitute, sexuality alludes to the feigned possibility of overcoming "fate," that is, overcoming the force of the modern environment in the pleasure of sexually charged images. Benjamin elaborates the elevated function of sexuality as more than merely the satisfaction of a drive, since attached to it is now a value of hallucination that can be compared to a bodiless woman's mediation of transcendental values. Sexuality *seems* to be something else or other. In the whore Benjamin sees the "superstition that defeats the figures of fate."[5]

Finally, the prostitute embodies the phantasm of infantile fantasies of omnipotence. To surrender to the lure of the prostitute and the ocean of images in the metropolis is the same as experiencing and enacting one's wishful fantasies by investing the cityscape with libidinal energy, and the body of the whore as part of the urban space. The stimulating effect of the city on the individual compounds libidinal investments and fantasies into an intoxicating experience that is the modern equivalent of aesthetic experience. As the modern representative of sexuality, the prostitute represents an intersection of time and space where this stimulating experience of the city can no longer be distinguished from a sense of being—from ontic experience. This explains why Benjamin, along with artists of the avant-garde, insisted on the experience of shock in order to awaken nineteenth-century society from its dream state induced by the allurement of the world of prostituted commodities.

Inspired by their forms of appearance—their exhibitory, representational quality (*Ausstellungs-wert*)—phantasmagorias have semiotized the world of objects.[6] The aesthetic disguising of the object turns it into a commodity form that demands consumption. Since individual objects in modernity are no longer positioned within a uniform context of meaning, they seem like hieroglyphs whose meaning has become enigmatic because of the loss of authentic experience and the loss of connection between generations.

Benjamin has described this assemblage of hieroglyphs as "facia hippo-cratica." Without there being a relationship to the past that could throw light on its significance for the present, the death mask of history is admonishing us of the past and the transitory nature of things. In the *Trauerspiel* Benjamin explains that the history that animated these things ran like lifeblood out of their bodies, leaving behind corpses. The corpse figures as the allegory of history, as the sign of its decline. In contrast to the momentary mystical experience of the symbol that is tied to the aesthetic realm, allegory does not reveal any absolute meaning.[7] An allegorical way of seeing raises questions about man's existence; the death's-head raises to consciousness man's subjection to nature and throws a doubtful light on the individual's biographical historicity. "Everything about history that, from the very beginning, has been untimely, sorrowful, unsuccessful, is expressed in a face—or rather in a death's-head."[8] In the place of a historical meaning that would elicit an awareness of the historical testimony that these things might portray, the appearance of a novelty that feigns progress takes its hold. Since progress in the nineteenth century signified the most important idea of history, on the social level fashion corresponded to the appearance of novelty governed by the law of perpetual, progressive change.

Since fashion in Benjamin is a species of allegory that needs a host, it requires a willing but dead body, a thing it can dress up and disguise. The ideal physical support for fashion is therefore the mannequin. Unlike the organic body that could ruin the image character of fashion, thus destroying the *appearance,* or illusion, the mannequin has no life of its own. Hence, fashion becomes the accomplice of death: death of the organic, of history, of experience. "Each [fashion] stands in contrast to the organic. Each one sells the living body to the anorganic world. Fashion exercises the rights of the corpse over the living."[9] Benjamin adds that fashion's efficacy, or rather, people's addiction to fashion, stems from its appeal to repressed libidinal needs and desires: "Underlying the sex appeal of the anorganic, fetishism is its life blood."[10] Fashion uses woman just as art had used her before, as an image surface behind which the body disappears or dies. This death is, however, equally the result of the dominance of the look in modernity. Look(ing) compensates for the loss of experience and the debilitation of agency in an industrialized environment. And by extension, fetishism signifies the atrophy of sensuous experience even in the sexual realm, where experience is reduced to scopophilia (pleasure gained by looking only). When feminist criticism today takes issue with the predominance of the women's look and men's gaze exploited by the media, and then blames it for reducing woman to an image, it should also deal with the history of the loss of experience and the dethroning of the subject in modernity. Luce Irigaray intimates this when she says, "the moment the look dominates, the body loses its materiality."[11]

Authentic experience can only be one of materiality, for example, that of the body; otherwise, it is a phantasmagoria, void of any social efficacy. An apathetic subject is thus the consequence. Allegorical disguises and optic changes are of sole importance. The object, the thing, *appears* to be something that it is not. The power of appearance to constantly change forms inspires the fantasy of the observer. He actually deceives himself in the appearance of the object, perceiving in it only his own projections propelled by the animation of his unconscious drives which trigger a visual (mental) representation, a *Vorstellungs-Repräsentanz,* as Freud calls it.[12]

As Benjamin claims, the substitution of fashion for art in modernity is predicated on the aesthetic appearance that both fashion and art have in common. Fashion temporally unites people in a newly visible ideal, keeping a traditionless society artificially in place which would otherwise disintegrate. Fashion makes the individual contemporaneous with a social system whose defects and historically heterogeneous fragments fashion covers up. In supporting a historical consciousness based on the uninterrupted remembrance of tradition, Benjamin attributes the decline of culture to fashion: "Fashions [and fads] are medication that is supposed to compensate, collectively, for the catastrophical effects of forgetting. The more shortlived an era, the more it is oriented toward fashion."[13] Here fashion seems to be the vehicle of ideology. But in the prostitute, fashion as disguise and commodified desire/pleasure are interrelated. Thus woman, while representing a social ideal for humanity in the eighteenth century, turns, in the role of prostitute, into a caricature of her own history. In the allegorical form of physical pleasure, the whore sells her *appearance* of femininity as well as the implicit illusion of bliss.

Attached to the prostitute *qua* woman is the aesthetic illusion of a value from the past—a value that can be identified with the feeling of nostalgia. At the same time, this illusion is demystified and unmasked as an article when exchanged for money. Since the status of woman as prostitute is not only that of a commodity, but also that of a mass produced article, woman actually gains a deconstructive power that destroys the aura of projected femininity, revealing its mere function as image. In this context I am thinking of the avant-garde art of Andy Warhol, specifically of his multiple repetitions of Marilyn Monroe's face, which has had the effect of demystifying the feminine, sexual aura of woman by exposing how the media creates such aesthetic effects. Like the prostitute, Marilyn Monroe exists in the numerous repetitions of her social function—what is repeated is the exhibition of her sex as fragment.

If it is true that modernity is determined by the commodity character of history, and Benjamin, by analyzing fashion, has already allegorized the world of commodities as the corpse of history, then woman as prostitute represents the allegory of aesthetic history. Different from the mimetic-symbolic system of representation, allegory deconstructs the production of appearance and of an illusionary totality: "In the field of allegorical intuition the image is a fragment, a rune [ruin]. Its beauty as a symbol evaporates when the light of divine learning falls upon it. The false appearance of totality is extinguished. For the *eidos* disappears, the simile ceases to exist, and the cosmos it contained shrivels up. The dry rebuses which remain contain an insight, which is still available to the confused investigator."[14] As modern allegory, femininity in the prostitute is this "rebus," the enigmatic image whose meaning is not present; yet, as hieroglyph, it testifies to a past significance that is lost for the present. Allegory is an alternative way of reading that assembles fragmentary pieces in a collage that consists of various, if only once meaningful, representational elements. "What is singled out by allegorical intention is sequestered from the contexts of life: it is destroyed and preserved at the same time. Allegory holds fast to the ruins."[15] In the commodified female body of the prostitute, the appearance of a feminine aura—mediating the transcendental—is destroyed. Still, the whore's exhibition of the body points to the former significance of the aura. Although woman "died" in the corpse of the commodity, she dissimulates that death by disguise and make-up. "Displacement into the allegor-

ical resists the treacherous [radiant] appearance of the world of commodities. The commodity wants to look into its own face. It celebrates its
incarnation in the prostitute."[16] In modernity the commodity character has
created a new "life" principal whose allegorical figure is 'woman as
commodity.' Interpreting the status of woman in Baudelaire, Benjamin
describes her as "the most precious loot in the 'triumph of allegory'—life
that means death. This quality irretrievably adheres to the prostitute. It is
the only thing that one cannot negotiate with her."[17] The stress on the body
of the prostitute inevitably also makes visible the body's mortality, thus
undermining illusions of eternal life, forcing acknowledgment that beauty
is a myth of femininity.

13

Benjamin's Hieroglyphs

As we have seen, the figure of the prostitute is a complex embodiment of the hieroglyph as *facies hippocratica*, the death mask of history that survives in the metropolitan landscape awaiting a new meaning in modernity. In the *Trauerspiel*, Benjamin argued that in literary texts, too, one can find hieroglyphs that not only occur as defunct word clusters, but that like the commodity fetish of the prostitute are mystified or enigmatic. For Benjamin, the literary hieroglyphs first appear to be meaningless signs or pictographs with which we cannot immediately associate a referent; the original referent is no longer accessible or meaningful in present cultural horizons. Assuming, nonetheless, a signifying potential in a historical sense—that once upon a time these dead signs were readable—these word clusters still suggest or even signify a temporality, the temporality of meaning. Something of significance existed before. That is, they stem from a past context of meaning that is no longer accessible to the reader in the here and now. Given this awareness of the temporality of textual figures and hence of meaning, Benjamin has turned to allegory as a model to represent the historical moment in terms of how a text affects us as readers even though we cannot determine its meaning. I would even go further and posit that Benjamin established a theory of language on the model of allegory precisely because he wanted to salvage a historical sensibility that would ultimately depend on literary language and its redemptive or memorial capacity in rhetorical structures.

For Benjamin, the theatricality of the sign's transformation in baroque drama helps viscerally demonstrate the seventeenth century critique of theology and of an illusory transcendental signified in the symbol. The lesson of these plays (a lesson akin to that of the prostitute) is that nature and with it a certain myth has been lost and that being has fallen into the immanence of history without any hope for transcendental redemption. The *Trauerspiel* is a play on how nature (not transcendence) is redeemed in history, a *nature morte* that stays with us in the form of symbolic re-minders of the finitude of our lives. Yet, this transformation of nature into history and the play of symbols that are now only mere signs of the past prevents those originally religious symbols from taking hold over the subject's mind. What traditionally has signified and symbolized a tran-scendental being and human salvation in an afterlife is now emptied of such a redemptive meaning. All symbols are rendered nil when they are juxtaposed within the allegorical structure of requisites on a stage that also presents the play of death, with corpses and body parts littering the stage. The awareness of mortality counteracts any nostalgia for a once possible transcendence or unification of body and spirit (and mythos) in infinity.

In the baroque tragic drama Benjamin uncovered the allegorical pre-sentation of symbolic meaning, by showing how the allegorical stage un-dermines the meaning of symbols and the presence of a redeeming God. What concerns Benjamin is the transformation of a mythic consciousness into a historical consciousness. A reading of the baroque stage facilitates a reflection on the illusion of what is performed on stage. The *things* on stage as it were do not harmonize with the people and their acts on stage. This jarring between object world and subjectivity points the way for allegory to perform an intellectual distance to what is experienced. Allegory therefore resists the seduction of an image, or the imaginary scene of the stage, with which one can easily identify. Instead, the onlooker or reader is challenged into taking an intellectual stance where s/he has to construct a context for the now allegorical arrangement of signs on stage in his or her mind. The meaning of this new allegorical view of things is, unlike that of the symbol or image, not immediately clear. Benjamin suggests that only through an allegorical reading or an allegorical eye can the remnants of history make sense in the present.

Paul de Man analyzed the distinction between the symbol and the alle-gory in terms of the self's renunciation of its desire to coincide with its non-self. The self's recognition of a non-self is painful.[1] In psychoanalytic terms, the mother has to finally be recognized as an other and not part of the self. In allegory, the imaginary nature of the other, as mother, reveals itself as myth, a myth that is nonetheless cited in allegorical figures of woman. In its historical/temporal structure of signification, allegory always incorporates a no longer meaningful sign of the past as myth, visible for in-stance in seventeenth century art and its depiction of antiquity in ruins. In the following I try to examine how this transformation from a symbolic (transcendental) conception of signs into the allegorical representability of nature and experience takes place in language.

Since allegory is not a fixed or referential sign but a combination of a historical image and a sign whose signification is in flux, it performs its meaning through a combinatory structure. The allegorical synthesis of several signs, no longer meaningful on their own, I suggest, is achieved through the metonymic relations between the emptied-out signs in the word complexes that make up the hieroglyphic structure. In allegory, this initially obscure architecture of signs superimposes itself on the still visible *forms* or skeletons of symbolic meanings. If we call these metonymic concatenations of signs or words "writing" per se, then writing (as a different signifying process) appropriates the convention of word meanings as its own signifying device by treating the signifieds themselves already as metaphors and not as referents. Writing, which sustains the allegorical nature of language, performs as a force of its own; it subverts the metaphoric structure of language by metonymically interconnecting the now metaphoric signifiers (no longer verbal meanings) in a text. This subversive realignment of words and senses occurs over time, of going from one to the other and associatively doubling back on what came before in the text. Unlike interpretation, reading produces a new sense that depends upon a temporal space in which this new sense or meaning is deferred. The new sense has to be postponed because a double displacement is actually taking place; first, in terms of the metaphoric substitution of profane words for transcendental concepts, and second, in terms of the metonymic exchange of a metaphorically charged word by another one in the grammar of the text. Thus, the primary meaning of a word remains eclipsed in the substitution produced by both metaphor and metonymy.

In the conversion of a metaphoric into a metonymic structure of language, the loss of a static or fixed symbol can be said to set the stage for belated signification. With the loss of a fixed, primary symbol, new meanings are created over time. The text's signifying structure then lends itself to a reading in terms of an allegory of the loss of that symbol which affirms being. Such a reading has been suggested by Joel Fineman[2] who applied a structuralist insight to the poetics of allegory that draws from Roman Jakobson's definition of the diachronic and synchronic principle of language in speech. For the structure of allegory to be meaningful, he posits an originary scene of loss—loss of the originary scene of the symbol.[3] This supports my argument that desire in language compels an allegorical reading of the text, if the text is to be understood from within tradition in the Gadamerian sense: "Understanding is not a method but a standing within an event of tradition."[4] Although this historical effect of desire in the structure of allegory is closer to Gadamer than Fineman, Gadamer nevertheless lacks a theory of language as *signifiance*. Benjamin himself was able to synthesize a structural and historical approach to language and illuminate the dynamics of signification. He was concerned most of all with a historically effective consciousness that is primarily conditioned by language.

By relating allegory to consciousness, Benjamin succeeded in using an allegorical linguistic matrix wherein the shift from history (nature) to tradition (culture) is performed. Benjamin's theory of allegory demonstrates a signifying model for history as tradition. Ultimately, allegory goes against mimetic imitation of being and shows that history is precisely not a representation of nature. As representations of the prostitute taught us, history is always already a transformation of nature according to our experience of it. And experience cannot be thought independently of the body's affects that respond to nature as other.

Precisely because allegory has traditionally opposed the symbol—in its conventional power of simulating instantaneous presence—it reveals an affinity with modernist and psychoanalytic theories of signification that try to resist the narcissistic, ideological pitfalls of logocentrism, assuming a one-to-one correspondence between sign and referent. In splitting being off from language, theories of language presuppose that representation no longer represents an essence but only an illusion of totality. Representation in the age of post-allegorical Enlightenment presumes its medium to be the logos of divine being.[5]

Benjamin's insistence on reanimating the dead signs of seventeenth century history, or *nature morte*, in an allegorical intuition or reading will make more sense once we gain insight into how allegorical signification works on a psychodynamic level. For instance, Lacan's analysis of the mechanics of the signifier, for which another signifier is always substituted both in metaphor and metonymy, assumes that signification can only work when connections between various signifiers are formed. Juxtaposing the findings of Fineman with Lacan's, I posit that allegorical figurations are mapped on the slippage of meanings in metonymy. These signifying connections are not arbitrary, but motivated by the subject's mental scene of a mutual reference which then lends the signifiers the value of signifieds. Only on the grounds of such internally associated meanings can the words on the page be compared and subsequently connected with one another. This other (mental) scene of reference, which always stages a loss of being, is covered up for the eyes of the conscious Ego by the substitution or displacement of textual signifiers. In light of Benjamin's theory of allegory, adapted from the genre of the *Trauerspiel*, I suggest that this "other scene of reference" is not primarily the subject's unconscious past, but the cultural past, as an archaic history which has become the reference point for tradition and readability of texts and has shaped the rhetorical dimension of language up to the present. A reading by the tradition as defined by the subject's literary as well as biographical background both articulates and covers up the network of meanings in texts. As we have seen in earlier chapters, tradition intervenes in reading as an unconscious Other that is always already there. Tradition already reads the text before the subject has become aware of what he is reading.

This Other that is tradition and assists the self in reading has a twofold role with respect to meaning in language. It reflects both the subject's split into an Ego that offers its support in the imaginary identification with verbal meanings, and an unconscious Ego function that carries out the displacements and transferences of specific signifiers because it is driven to remember the past and repeat the subject's fantasy of being one with his self. But the conscious Ego's desire to be "one" encounters the loss of being and the fall into history on the level of the unconscious. This is a moment of castration where the self is cut off from the supportive physical (m)other of the presymbolic stage of the subject's development.

Let's keep in mind that Benjamin is concerned with the materiality of language and history; hence, on a psychological level, the mother is the affective ground of meaning or what Lacan calls *lalangue*. Once this loss from nature is made conscious, say, in the aesthetic experience of reading, a place for tradition to intervene between psyche and language is opened up. Within this space of tradition, the memory of the fall is kept alive in and through an awareness of language and its effects on the psyche. Hence, the whole human past is redeemed within this space and the moment of tradition can come forth because the temporal instance of reading and the epiphanic experience of bliss in the reading process provide a meaningful "meantime," what Benjamin calls "messianic splinters of a *Jetztzeit*," in which sense and therefore a reconciliation between the past and present is achieved. Philosophically speaking, these splinters of a fulfilled Now represent the singular moments of hermeneutical understanding, moments that animate tradition in the reading effects of language on the psyche. These animating and emotive effects emanate from a figurative power of imagination that constructs the equivalent of an allegorical image that then confuses the past with the present. The Romantics designated fantasy as the actual mental power to produce such a happy state of confusion, one in which a multitude of sign qualities and textual features are translated into states of physical experience. What they, like Freud, tried to valorize is the importance and awareness of psychical realities that can only be communicated to someone with an allegorical eye (or ear) to their hieroglyphic structure of signs by which they are expressed.

In allegory the subversion of metaphor by metonymy occurs. In metaphor, the intended likeness between the subject's own past and the language of another cultural text is brought about by a transposition of the reader's feelings onto the text's fictional scene. The word clusters in a literary text become a symptom for the subject's past. Words in relation to other words undergo semantic change in terms of the reader's past experience. In metonymy, this symptomatic process is thwarted since the desire for meaning is subjected to a different kind of desire that does not attach itself to an object but is only operative in the movement of reading and writing in language. Lacan calls this the desire of the Other, of language itself. The Other here is no longer the supporting (m)other object.

With respect to the meaning of language engendered by tradition, the Other is not simply the structurality of language as an autocratic symbolic order, as Lacan would maintain, but the tradition itself. Metonymy expresses the grammar of such linguistic desire in a text by forming non-mimetic correspondences among words; in contrast, metaphor operates through a mimetic relationship between words and things outside the text. Significant correlations between words are established in the unconscious where all previous encounters with words and texts (i.e., with a literary tradition) are stored as qualities of experience, for example, as feelings attached to these words. Bear in mind that all words were once embedded in a living, affective situation when we learned or heard them spoken or written by others. These forgotten affects reappear in the proximity of verbal meanings that tap an unconscious fantasy surrounding those repressed affects. Thus, what metonymy adds to the semiotic function of textual language is a resistance roused in us to identify with the intended, conventional meaning of words. Rather, their semantic intentions are suspended in a web of phantasmatic correspondences between words on the basis of their emotional connections within the subject's unconscious past.

To clarify the correspondence between metonymy and fantasy, I will draw on an example described by Jean Laplanche and Serge Leclaire. In their essay "The Unconscious: A Psycho-analytic Study,"[6] a dream analysis is advanced in which a particular dream about a unicorn has a close affinity with the Benjaminian understanding of the hieroglyph. In an obsessional neurotic's recounting of a dream about a unicorn, we are introduced to a deserted square of a small town in which the dreamer meets a woman, Liliane, who says, "it's been a long time since I've seen such fine sand." Suddenly the dreamer is in a brightly colored forest that he imagines is filled with fauna when suddenly a unicorn crosses his path. Leclaire, the patient's analyst, notices that the dream embeds at least three childhood memories. There is a childhood memory of a square with a unicorn fountain, the same fountain that is missing in the dream; there is a walk in the mountains where the patient remembers bright colored heather; and there is the memory of a time when the patient had been on a beach by the Baltic Sea and had noticed the fine sand. There he is also introduced to salty herring. A relative, Lili, had mocked the patient for repeating the phrase "j'ai soif" (I'm thirsty) and dubs the boy, "Philippe-j'ai-soif." In the very recent past, the day previous to the dream, the patient had been in the woods with his niece, Anne, and had tracked some deer to a place where they had stopped for a drink. The unicorn is evidently a metaphor for these deer. In considering the dream, Leclaire asks, "Why is it precisely under the sign of the unicorn that the memory of a gesture, performed no doubt for neither the first nor the last time, is engraved?" This gesture, which is the cupping of hands in order to drink, signifies a desire to satisfy an oral drive that is also emblematized by the unicorn. Furthermore, we know from the patient's childhood memory that the unicorn is associated with a fountain. For the patient it therefore emblematizes the opportunity to drink.

Leclaire will say that the patient's thirst is to be associated with an oral drive that receives the caption "J'ai soif," a phrase uttered by the patient but singled out as an insignia by Lili. Moreover, Leclaire notices that the word for unicorn—in French, *licorne* —carries a signifier, "li," that sutures the licorne to Lili, to Philippe, as well as to the word *lit* (bed). Leclaire suggests therefore that the licorne, in addition to being an emblem or metaphor that stands for various referents, is also the metonymy of Phi*li*ppe's desire. Speaking of the unicorn, Leclaire says,

> The unicorn appears in the dream as a marvelous metonymy, harking back to the fountain, but also to its own legend and, indeed, to a whole circuit whose structure still remains to be determined in detail. . . . The unicorn is a metonymy in the sense that everything in it, in the effigy as in the word, indicates not only condensation, of course, but also the displacement and the interval that separates the terms it joins. For the li(t) in Lili to the horny callous (*corne*) that Philippe would like to have on his feet, the licorne maintains in the interval between its two first syllables the intermediate elements of the unconscious chain. On another level, it refers more simply to the fountain it overlooks, to the water that springs from it.[7]

When Leclaire and Laplanche ask themselves what motivates this thirst in terms of need and demand, they argue that as oral drive the need to drink is most likely associated with the mother's breast that for Philippe never satisfied his thirst. Only much later does this unsatisfaction manifest itself in relation to Lili who points out that Philippe is always thirsty. Leclaire and Laplanche conclude that the metonymical slippage of the "li"-sounds manifests "the capture of drive energy in the web of the signifier."[8] This means that the signifier "li" is emotionally motivated by the drive in its archaic relation to the mother. Yet, the emblem within which this slippage of the signifier occurs is, as the authors say, merely an effigy. That the fixated if not effigy-like emblem of the unicorn subsumes the drive in its archaic relation to the mother is quite reminiscent of Benjamin's hieroglyph, in that Laplanche and Leclaire are saying the metonymy is drive related and therefore always expresses an affect that has its roots and (unconscious) representation in the past.

In another essay—though less successful than Laplanche and Leclaire's—on Benjamin's concept of the nonsensuous likeness of words in the mimetic (phantasmatic) faculty, Werner Hamacher develops a critique of metaphor by showing how the allegorical correspondences between texts and words detach the desire for experience (i.e., the desire for the mother) from the word in a process of reading that disrupts the possibility of conscious images for the desired (m)other. In this detachment, allegory calls attention to the power of language as it repeats a feeling for words that refer the subject to an undefined past. The allegorical power of language, whose detachment I have construed as metonymy, prevents a metaphoric process of enduring images. Hamacher alludes to this as follows: "No text and none of its words can have a likeness to another from its own repertoire or from that of its interpretations, except as a piece broken from it, and that makes every one of its correspondences allegorical: they intend a likeness that they are constitutively incapable of reaching."[9]

I disagree, however, with Hamacher's analysis of the "word" in Benjamin's text since it is grounded in non-mimetic representability of language, in the singularity of the word itself.[10] For instance, Hamacher uses the semantics of the word "cloud" (*Wolke*) for representing the phenomenon of "likeness" as a nebulous mixture of various words in one. As I have tried to show with the help of Lacan, Fineman, and Laplanche/Leclaire, the crucial signifying mechanism in language exists in the connections *between* words, that is, in their alignment or figurality and in their syntactical relationships that establish associations based on their contiguity. Hamacher ignores this by rigidly adhering to mere semantics, which he associates phonetically. If from the perspective of a child Benjamin's narrator associates words by means of phonemes (*Childhood in Berlin around 1900*), then Hamacher succumbs to this seduction and, like the child dreamer in Benjamin's text, lets himself be pulled into the "text's womb." What should happen instead is an attempt to refrain from duplicating Benjamin's syntactic moves, something Hamacher does not do. Indeed, I have the impression that Hamacher ignores Benjamin's theories of allegory and history when he touches upon the issues of historicity, experience, subjectivity, or textuality. His critique, in fact, does not so much create a historicity for his reader as it stays *werk-immanent* or rather "word" -immanent, clouding over any possible subject position or subjective, readerly experience with semantic homophony (*viol . . . , Walter, vol, Gewalt,* and so on).

No doubt, these phonic combinations do not establish or illuminate the allegorical power of language that Benjamin reveals in non-mimetic representation. In language Benjamin sees a relationship between human emotional experience and the figural design of natural occurrences. (Language preserves a dead nature as history!) This is repeated in figural language. Because Hamacher does not refer to the "syntactical gestures" that work in Benjamin's text, he is a good example for showing the difference between *reading* and *interpreting* words at hand. Hamacher interprets but does not read in the sense of creating an allegorical structure between the words in their verbal context. For my argument concerning the nature of hieroglyph, it is crucial to understand that hieroglyphs cannot be interpreted, especially since as pictograms they belong to a different, no longer accessible historical context in which they were immediately recognizable as meaningful signs. In the present, hieroglyphs have to be *read* or reinvented, that is, reconstructed into a new meaning they might have for the reader's own experiences.

Rather than working through the textual gestures and then paying attention to, for instance, the allegorical form of the female body in Benjamin's story, Hamacher digresses from sexuality and death—the injured or dismembered body—as a fertile ground for an experience in reading.[11] This obviates the fact that Benjamin's text is also a psychoanalytic means of staging the mother's body for a scenario that deals with signs. In Benjamin's allegorical view of reading, the experience of a text waiting to be read is compared to the threat of death.[12] Attached to experiences with books are sexual features—intimacy, getting inside of a womb, anticipation of unknown feelings—which turn the act of reading into a sensuous and affective experience. Such physical and affective events in language are what allegorical structures are all about. Allegories reinsert the (subject's) body in reading, and, as a reading strategy, they animate the dead body (*nature morte*) of an other, the text, through a combination of subjective memory and historical allusions in the text.

It is important to note that there is always the presence of a body, like the body of the reader. It is this body that senses what is expressed in language, a body for whom the color violet may be a sensual experience. In other words, it is the memory of perceiving the color violet and not the *word* violet that causes sensation. Words are here merely signifiers or triggers for recollecting the synaesthetic, sensual part of experience. The agency of sensation does not lie in the word but in the subject's body. And in those allegorical correspondences, it is not the author's words that as Hamacher claims "intend a likeness that they are constitutively incapable of reaching" but the reader's mind, his imagination and desire, that finds a likeness between the figural assembly of words and his previously lived scenario of an emotional experience. With an unconsciously melancholic eye for this scenario, the reading subject reconstructs his history from words and reads them as signs for an old but still significant experience of nature. With Benjamin we can say that the subject reads those words as remnants of a nature from which the reading subject has so far been detached. There is an undoing of repression at work here which makes reading the hieroglyph significant for a psychological analysis of reading literature. Hamacher, however, never asks the question of what motivates "the relationship of likeness itself" which he attributes to the principle of a synthesis expressed merely in the word itself. If he were to have engaged the question of motivation and emotion, it would have certainly put him back on the track of the subject and subjectivity. As we learn from Benjamin, the omission of subjectivity and the body eliminates tradition and dehumanizes literature. This seems to be a major problem in a non-historical grounding of deconstruction to which critics like Hamacher subscribe.

In a recent article on mass culture as anaesthetics and social control, Susan Buck-Morss has also reemphasized that "Benjamin is demanding of art a task . . . to *undo* the alienation of the corporeal sensorium, to *restore the instinctual power of the human bodily senses for the sake of humanity's self-preservation.*"[13] For an experience to integrate itself, the imagination has to be stimulated by an other, for instance, by the words in a text. Experience is dependent on the "synaesthetic system [a sense consciousness] . . . wherein external sense-perceptions come together with the internal images of memory and anticipation."[14] Buck-Morss contends that it is this synaesthetic system that has atrophied in the brain operating in a technologically controlled social environment. Benjamin derived from Romanticism a more philosophical explanation for this body-mind system: "mimetic genius." This mimetic faculty cannot operate when memory is blocked by simulacra of sensation.

What Benjamin claims for language is a mimetic genius in analogy to an archaic power evolved from cultic rituals in which people tried to imitate processes in nature. To this power he attributes the quality of life; it is a life determining power (*lebensbestimmende Kraft*).[15] Departing from an inborn sense for imitation, Benjamin suggests that this sense becomes transformed by language as the latter inserts itself between the body and nature and takes on the power of mimetic genius without itself representing their similarities. In its mediating function, language is non-mimetic; it does not produce similarities to nature but translations. The similarity is produced in the interaction of unconscious and conscious mind, between the memory of sense perceptions and the conscious perception of linguistic signs. The mimetic element does not lie in words but makes itself felt in the "sense context of words or sentences" which Benjamin calls the semiotic support of similarity, a similarity produced by the subject and through his perceptions.[16]

In language, mimesis has become a matter of connecting, not representing different things, something that is key to Benjamin's own style of writing. In collections or clusters of different things in differential forms, language can be said to be an archive of nonsensuous similarities, because arbitrary connections can coopt dissimilar things in their mental essence and produce a similarity to the scenic constituents of an experience now apprehended by the mind in an allegorical image. That Benjamin has already assumed an allegorical type of representability when he refers to language as a canon of *unsinnliche Ähnlichkeiten,* I have tried to preempt with my translation as "non-mimetic representation" rather than "nonsensical similarities." Non-mimetic representations match the technique of allegorical representation, a representation that does not mean what it represents.

The allegorical sign refers the reader back to an anterior signifier that stands in for the loss of history, or, better, for an unconscious history; therefore it represents a conscious forgetting. The conscious subject is unable to identify with such signs since they lose their status of metaphor by referring the subject back to another sign to which he has no conscious recourse. The subject is now forced to *read,* link, and relate words instead of identify with them as icons. A friction therefore develops between the conscious function of the Ego that reads the text for identification and the unconscious Other that reads according to the figurations of desire, thus displacing the signifier in the text. Consequently, the Ego is exposed in its imaginary identity that can no longer be propped up by signification. The metaphor, which has been superimposed onto metonymy, no longer applies to something outside the text; for the text is now the temporal interval between what the signifier represents and what the subject fantasizes about his being. If it was once the subject's fantasy to be whole—a wholeness for which the metaphor was in charge—it is now the loss of this fantasy that is staged with the collapse of metaphor into allegorical, metonymic readings.

Since metonymy also acts as a metaphor for the loss of the signifier (for being whole), this signifier now represents a different desire, the desire for history or a return to the past. The original signifier for the fantasy of wholeness is now a signifier for the faculty of memory. What Fineman failed to mention is the power of memory which, given the force of desire, enacts history as the truth of signification. Again, memory is an unconscious structure in which the contiguity of signifiers produces fantasies that become manifest, like the manifest content in dreams, in the conscious correspondences of metaphors. Without history, figures of speech would have no signification, no metaphoric content or metonymic (transformative) tradition. Perhaps this is why, beyond all structuralist exegesis of language, Jacques Lacan acknowledges the importance of history for recollection which psychoanalysis facilitates by paying attention to the analysand's choice of words:

> It is the truth of what this desire has been in his history that the patient cries out through his symptom [the metaphor], as Christ said that the stones themselves would have cried out if the children of Israel had not lent them their voice. And that is why only psychoanalysis allows us to differentiate within memory the function of recollection. Rooted in the signifier, it resolves the Platonic aporias of reminiscence through the ascendancy of history.[17]

The referentiality of the signifiers is limited by the history that informs a tradition which we unconsciously use in our figures of speech to signify something other than what they actually mean. This is why I remarked above that the connections which signifiers form in signification are not arbitrary but, rather, are embedded in a tradition that symbolizes history. The words themselves have a history, reflected in their multidetermination over time. The previous meanings are not wiped out by those that follow, but put the word into a discursive relation with itself. This dialogic nature of the word, manifest in the sedimentation of its history, is articulated in the textuality of language.

Let me just cite one of numerous examples from the emblematic phrases of baroque drama to illustrate how historical/political metaphors are transmuted by the metonymical relations among words in order to turn established metaphors (the state as machine) into allegories of human suffering and emotion:

> In der Uhr der Herrschaft sind die Räthe wohl die Räder / der Fürst aber muss nicht minder Weiser und das Gewichte . . . seyn.

[The councillors may be the cogs in the clockwork of government but the prince must nonetheless be the hand (and "the wise one") and the weight (and, "the one that is burdened").][18]

Phonetically linked are the words "Räthe" (council men) and "Räder"(cog-wheels), which are in turn semantically linked with "Weiser" (wise man, here in dialogue with the intended meaning of "clock hands") and "Gewichte" (clock weights). It is important to note that these lines are uttered by the courtier, the intriguer of the court, who often comments on the loss of humanity in the state and the state's head, the prince. In other words, with his enigmatic words, the courtier retrieves the creaturely aspect of the prince, his organic nature that is crushed by the state's machine that weighs heavy on his shoulders. Since weight is here articulated as physical weights that propel the workings of a clock, what weighs down on the prince is history's temporality whose progression he must guarantee with his life. The unarticulated signifier in whose place metonymy creates the same meaning is "life", or rather it signifies the loss of (the prince's) life. The status of prince in an absolutist state is incompatible with that of a human being.

14

The Melancholia of Ideas

Having looked at the figure of woman as prostitute and Benjamin's concept of the hieroglyph, I want to turn to the question of affect associated with melancholia. Because I want to elaborate on Benjamin's notion of melancholy and its potential for historical consciousness, I would like to emphasize that Benjamin's concept differs from Freud's in a crucial way. Whereas for Freud melancholy is a pathological form of mourning over the lost object, for Benjamin it is a positive psychological disposition toward the past. Benjamin still associates melancholia with a genius theory and exhumes the creative aspects of melancholia and melancholic writers from the tradition of antiquity and the Middle Ages. At the same time, as I have shown in my chapter on Novalis, genius and historical sensibility are fused in the Romantic concept of the artist. For Benjamin and Novalis it is precisely not the point to let go of the lost object with a healthy but temporary period of mourning, as Freud suggests. Instead, to be fully in touch with the past, insofar as that is possible, is to be emotionally in contact with what has happened; it is to remember the importance of a lost origin within a perception of the present that is indebted to the past. Such remembrance, of course, involves feeling in terms of *Sehnsucht*—nostalgia or tolerated sadness.

Psychoanalytically, Julia Kristeva has demonstrated that melancholy is an attitude toward the past, a non-forgetting that is body bound and that need not necessarily lead to depression but, rather, to creative work like writing. Melancholy presents an unconscious tie with the body of the mother and recovers what Melanie Klein has called the depressive position toward the loss of the mother. A "healthy" depressive revival of the signifier (for the mother) frees up the subject by means of a phantasmatic development in which the drives are converted into signification. As a psychoanalytic concept in object relations, melancholy reveals a very different pathological structure than clinical depression as defined by psychiatrists who have adopted the diagnosis of *DMS IV*. In severe depression, thought

199

and affect are so out of alignment that they often cannot be mediated and realigned in language—the talking cure. Melancholy represents the psychodynamic structure of a link between conscious remembrance and unconscious memory, and, phenomenologically, both overlap in language to provide a crucial psychological support for the melancholic mind.

It is through affect that ideas believed to be unrepresentable by Kant are nevertheless experienced. According to Benjamin, even though these ideas are embedded in our canon of non-mimetic representations, language cannot be separated entirely from the mental faculty of representation, for imagination follows the linguistic figurations of ideas and projects them onto the external life context. And, since language achieves its figurality and rhetorical effects by incorporating previous human experiences, we could say that language projects the "passions," the sufferings, and the bodily experiences of previous generations into the subject's present realm of experience. As bodily experiences encrypted in figures of language, the affect of rhetorical figures relates the body of others to our own. The linguistic coinage of metaphors and tropes by those who came before us creates a legacy that unfolds our horizon of ideas about life and its significance. That we no longer recognize an originally physical experience in those metaphors is a function of a symbolic world view that has supplanted history with idealism. Benjamin is therefore not just a literary critic but also a philosopher that exhumes the buried *physis* underneath metaphorical language. A no longer conscious metaphoricity of language constantly seduces us to mistake the nature of language as an ideal essence rather than as the corporeal properties of human existence.

In his critique of philosophy, Derrida has associated (the death of) metaphor with philosophical discourse along similar lines: "This *end* of metaphor is not interpreted as a death or dislocation, but as an interiorizing anamnesis (*Erinnerung*), a recollection of meaning, a *relève* of living metaphoricity into a living state of properness."[1] But by philosophy Derrida only has a metaphysical project in mind, whereas Benjamin redeems philosophy not as a discourse on essences but as a critique of history that names the affect of history and the inherently retrospective and melancholic nature of our imagination. It is not that we no longer live in a metaphysical world, but that metaphysics has always repressed the physical nature of our thinking and being, supplanting it with illusions of a nonphysical and therefore transhistorical essence to ground us in the realm of (ideal) meaning or spirit rather than in the realm of life.

Insofar as metaphors function as symbolic images of life, both Benjamin and Derrida admonish us not to take these symbols for granted but to ask questions about the image value in such symbolic representations. We ought to become aware how these symbolic images discourage reflection, given their incongruence with our experience of life. The lack of such reflection may have been responsible for a death of the literary in our current era, since electronic media, in particular, have recycled the literary in terms of ready-made, dead visual metaphors stripped of historical context and hence of certain imaginary potentials. Typical would be Disney's cartoon version of *The Hunchback of Notre Dame* or *Anastasia* in which the crude caricature, garish coloration, and fast paced action deprive the viewer of the capacity to experience much revery. Everything, it seems, happens in the here and now. In contrast, melancholy would be indicative of a reflective mind that is aware of the lost or missing origin of its current thoughts. Benjamin's claim is to keep this melancholic state of awareness in mind, for it is in terms of such a psychological disposition toward the past that he hopes to rescue tradition from forgetting and to strengthen the individual's imagination against the mental take-over by technological, mass-produced images that merely simulate an active natural intelligence.

For history to survive and still be meaningful in terms of a tradition, Benjamin suggests we read allegorically, since allegory dissolves the false "sensation" of "nature [that] gives itself in metaphor."[2] Given the fact that nature is dead and that the "natural" origin of meaning is lost, all we have left is an allegorical understanding of this lost natural origin. By means of allegorical reading, we have a way of coming to terms with our own experience of loss, since we can turn this loss, and its affect, into something meaningful. If allegory inherently recognizes its distance from the things lost since the beginning of time, it also allows for a transposition whereby the disjunctions of the present and the past can be bridged by means of a psychological working through of loss that, according to Benjamin, is melancholic. As I will show, for both Walter Benjamin and Julia Kristeva, melancholy is a psychological frame that facilitates the vision of allegorical language as an expression of history and memory.

Because language is not merely a structural device for building meaning but a store of human experiences, it can shape the imagination of individuals who want to reconstruct their own experiences in an intuition of history. Encounters with others in the present would be meaningless without the physical imagery of linguistic concepts, of what Benjamin calls *Sprachbilder*. Thus, the linguistic "props" of human history indeed set the stage for an interpretation of an encounter or an event in the present. But for the human mind, if not to say for the hermeneutical mind, this event is never identical to itself and is never entirely situated in the present. Language always rebuilds such an event into a historically affective structure adapting subjective experience.

When, instead of being the symbol for a historical totality, a ruin serves as prop for the space of representation, namely, in terms of the text as stage, time as well as nature are signified in their interdependence in death. In the experience of times past, the emotive effect on the reader is melancholic, and if time is signified by a decadent nature, then the task is to make a mental connection to one's own life and recognize it as an embodiment of a history whose progression is the loss of being. The specific task for the (revolutionary) historian-subject is to bring this progression repeatedly to a standstill in a *memento mori* where remembrance can redeem the past as lives lived, in an allegorical intuition of the life world in the present. This would also achieve a didactic image of one's personal experiences in which history repeats itself. Hence a redemptive nature adheres to the life of the individual: life unfolds in a historical process that can be influenced through a recognition of this life as being conditioned by tradition, the previous lives and work of others. Such recognition harbors the possibility of change; it takes place in language, in the interpretation of the past or the archive as related to one's own experience of the past.

Only if we succumb to an experience with the materiality of language, that is, of what Benjamin calls nature-history preserved as idioms and, by extension, as ideas in language,[3] can we begin to reflect on our participation in a dialectic of signification. As we are engaged in reading we are also engaged with the other(s) of the past. In a signifying dialectic, historic texts are actually transmitted. In this transmission of even sacred texts and prophetic writing, the rhetorical figures of these texts are gradually absorbed into the natural "idiom" of language; but prior to this transformation into idioms, they were, as Derrida points out, once created in an "analogical chain of analogies."[4]

In an essay on Warburton, Derrida's analysis of the power of writing comes very close to Benjamin's notion of language as "canon of non-mimetic representations." This essay shows how, over time, a symbolic mode of representation has disguised the material, historical, that is, experiential essence of writing. Originally, ideas were not abstract or transcendental notions, but concrete concepts derived from human behavior. Both Derrida and Benjamin emphasize an original figurality of writing that mimics the gestures of the body. Derrida says that the word and its phonetic quality is always only finite and does not reach far enough; its duration is too short for an inscription in human memory: "The necessity of marks, figures, and language arose from the very beginning by reason of the (human) finitude of the word."[5] Through the idiom, we are referred to this primeval history of signification which exerts its dialectical effects only in the allegorical intention for nature's death; nature has to die for (historical) significance to enter our lives. Hence, the history of the world is compressed into a person's life. It is this person's body that suffers the experience of history as the metamorphosis of history into nature.[6] In the linguistic idiom, the relation with a historical other cannot be evaluated on the same level as an identification of the reader with the image in the text. It cannot aim at a sense of self-identity in the reader but, on the contrary, forces the reader-subject to set himself apart from this other so as to recognize its difference in language. Derrida addresses the same issue in terms of a "veiling of writing" and asks the question of why writing reached the point of veiling itself throughout history. In so doing, he cites the science of the "oneirocritics," those who consider the unconscious an agency that has recognized the veiling of writing in humanity's attempt to archive the knowledge of nature:

> It is as if a catastrophe had perverted this truth of nature: a writing made to manifest, serve, and preserve knowledge—for custody of meaning, the repository of learning, and the laying out of the archive—encrypts itself, becoming secret and reserved, diverted from common usage, esoteric.[7]

Derrida's aim is to unveil the fabrication of our knowledge by showing, along with Warburton, that, just like the original hieroglyphs, writing is purposely designed and thus "structures the content of knowledge" according to bodily shapes.[8] Derrida suggests that a veil of secrecy "befell" writing so as to veil the body and render writing abstract and authoritative in its transmission of transcendentalized ideas that have either taken on a metaphysical life of their own or have been abused by social, hegemonic powers. Writing was originally designed to preserve history and to memorialize the laws derived from deeds and thoughts of people. However as hieroglyph, that writing requires continual reinterpretation, since the laws of language are themselves never transparent and could be said to veil themselves anew for each generation of readers that comes along, given the fact that no state of past understanding can escape obliteration or loss by way of the historical attrition of common knowledges and understandings.

In reading, the subject's experiences are highlighted and shaped by adapting the historical material furnished in the idiom of language. Between the idiom and the subject's experience, language effects an infinite semiosis which, by using the past, propels us forward in the formation of meaning. Infinite semiosis is but an infinite process of historical redemption: the ruins of history are recycled in language for the transformation of subjective histories into sense and sensitivity toward an other, expanding one's horizon to incorporate the other. Alluding to Benjamin's angel of history, we could say that rather than ignoring and adding to the pile of historical debris, the historian's, and *in potentia* , every individual's task is to spread out the ruins synchronically into a configuration of readability. This suggests a subjective responsibility and response to the reminders of the past, and it requires a psychological disposition to those reminders and remainders. This disposition is melancholy.

In the figure of a text, the ruins have a chance to be redeemed in a hieroglyphic script that encrypts a secret meaning: "the secret meeting [*Verabredung*] between the past generations and ours"[9] which would support Benjamin's claim that he derived from the cabbalah, namely, that "we were expected on earth."[10] Since the material of meaning does exist already, even if in the form of ruins and chaotic debris, the picture of history and the formation of a meaningful story is not a new revelation of genius but, rather, an uncovering, an *Er-findung*, a re-finding of what was covered up in the representative mode of signification, in the symbol that represented the idea. Representation of ideas through symbols led to a forgetting of history as lived situations in analogy to which "writing," in Derrida's sense, has been "designed." The symbol with all its references to idealism also led to a repression in the subject of his sense of being disconnected from the other(s) of the past. Figurative (associative) usages of words are, however, not linguistic "inventions" but manifest themselves in the style of a writer.[11] The opportunity of finding the "treasures" of history (its building blocks) presents itself in the hieroglyphic nature of texts, in the *tropes* of language which etymologically suggests the word *trouver: to find* a meaningful connection. If the hieroglyph was originally a pictogram, then deconstructing the image complex into its various image and imaginative components and reassembling them is to treat the image complex as writing, to rewrite the connections between the individual fragments of images.

Again, let me cite Derrida's fascination with Warburton's research into ancient hieroglyphs, since it was Warburton who recognized the significance of the fusion between ideogram and letter in the later history of writing. For Warburton, maintaining the hieroglyph alongside alphabetic writing meant that certain cultures wanted to preserve "the very treasurehouse of their lore, whose antiquity is thereby demonstrated."[12] In another era, Benjamin will insist that the allegorical nature of writing demonstrates a similar historicity of writing, if not its tropological effects of meaning in language. Derrida, for his part, will answer the question, what is a veiled writing, by saying that it is "a tropical revolution, inside the trope, since the first tropes served to manifest and the second to encrypt. . . . 'The tropical hieroglyph served to divulge, and the tropical symbol to keep hidden.'"[13] Again, it is the metaphysical symbol that obscures the "natural," physical origin of writing and the historical inscription of how people made meaning. Derrida gives an example from Warburton which I quote in order to demonstrate the refinement of tropes into symbols and their reversal in and through an allegorical reading that is close to Benjamin's concerns.

> One is the figure commonly called *Diana multimammia*; the other is a winged globe with a serpent emerging from it. The first, which is in the simplest taste, is a curiological hieroglyph; and the second, by its mysterious assemblage, is an enigmatic symbol. But observe that, in the first figure, universal nature is considered *physically*; and in the latter, *metaphysically*, according to the different genius of the times in which these two riddles were invented.[14]

Echoing the young Nietzsche, Derrida critiques metaphysics by pointing out that we can no longer remember the original things figured: the content of the symbol and all the knowledge that led to the creation of symbols. Here Derrida is pointing to a condition that for Benjamin is profoundly melancholic. *Physis* has lost its connection to a divine spirit. Because symbols have become abstract and enigmatic, we learned by way of "priestly guidance" to turn our attention to the "things signified," the "mental ideas," which in Derrida's (but also Michel Foucault's) opinion are merely arbitrary ploys of power.[15]

The "mysterious treasures of inventions" that Benjamin sees in baroque allegories are derived from an ostensibly sacred and mysterious script in Egyptian and Greek antiquity. Indeed, the hieratic element of their hieroglyphs referred the seventeenth century reader not to a sacred inspiration from above but to a study of the earth below: to finding the secrets immanent in life on earth, or rather *below* the surface of the earth where nature becomes mysterious because it is buried underneath multiple surfaces of history, in the sedimentation of emptied-out signs. "Linguistic nature, like material nature, is a repository of all secrets. The writer brings no power to it, creates no new truth from the spontaneous outpourings of the soul."[16]

Benjamin has shown that the written intention of the baroque *Trauerspiel* may have been to display its hieroglyphic element, because the dramatic words do not need to be voiced in order to produce an effect of transcendence, for transcendence is denounced anyway: "rather does the world of written language remain self-sufficient and intent on the display of its own substance."[17] The writer merely (re)arranges the decaying objects of nature. However a melancholy state of mind is required to read the text as a hieroglyphics of a fragmented nature, because only in the sense of a lost origin of nature does the subject recognize a wisdom inherent in this emblematic image of nature. The possibility of wisdom "is secured by immersion in the life of creaturely things, and hears nothing of the voice of revelation."[18] This is the same wisdom that Benjamin ascribes to the genre of fairy tales that counsel the child to master the demonic forces of nature. Such a wisdom concerns survival, of subordinating oneself to nature rather than fighting it.[19]

Allegorical reading is a lesson in how to survive history as separation from the origin—of the mother—and of how to maintain one's own vitality by contemplating "mother earth" as the matter of one's very being.[20] Such contemplation leads to a creativity that is earthbound, rendering art pragmatic instead of sublime. This idea of a wisdom of survival distinguishes Benjamin from Paul de Man's analysis of allegorical modes of writing. This is ironical given that de Man survived the Second World War while Benjamin did not. Unlike Benjamin, de Man did not consider the transference of the feeling of hope through language. Rather, de Man interprets allegory pessimistically by repeatedly exposing aporias located in the temporality of allegorical representations, aporias that cannot be transcended. Benjamin's understanding of melancholy, however, does not express a resignation in the absence of a synthesis between matter and meaning but the possibility of a historical and materialist agency, something de Man repudiated.

In Judaism, memory is considered an aggressive act and, as Yosef Hayim Yerushalmi reminds us, it is history and not nature that is the realm of divine action.[21] Benjamin's version of the messiah consists in the alertness of humans that could recognize and seize the special moment of a historical intervention. Writing and reading struggles against our human tendency to forget and blindly repeat. Writing forces us to move through an archive, "the science of which," Derrida says, "is not at a standstill." Here Derrida espouses Freud in his thinking about the archive and suggests that we take on, become aware of, and respond to the "force and authority of this transgenerational memory" that caused the establishment of histories of culture and has implicated and will always implicate us in questions of memory.[22] For we cannot dissociate memory from language and the writing of culture. In fact, as Freud says, we "cannot imagine [*vorstellen*] one without the other," imagine an ancestral experience without the archive, its written inscriptions passed on to us.[23]

If the modern writer does not really invent signs, he is nonetheless aware of the existing sign's instability, its incapability to stand on its own for long. And he uses this instability if not its semantic decay for his own creations. Benjamin likens the baroque writers (already modern for him) and their experimentations with allegory to alchemists who use the legacy of antiquity as elements, "item for item," to mix the new whole. This technique applies itself to rhetorical figures and rules. In this sense, Benjamin suggests to call literature an *ars inveniendi*, an art that constructs itself together with the ruins of a past culture.

> The experimentation of the baroque writers resembles the practice of the adepts. The legacy of antiquity constitutes, item for item, the elements from which the new whole is mixed. Or rather: is constructed. For the perfect vision of this new phenomenon was the ruin. The exuberant subjection of antique elements in a structure which, without uniting them in a single whole, would, in destruction, still be superior to the harmonies of antiquity, is the purpose of the technique which applies itself separately, and ostentatiously, to realia, rhetorical figures and rules. Literature ought to be called *ars inveniendi*. The notion of the man of genius, the master of *ars inveniendi*, is that of a man who could manipulate models with sovereign skills. 'Fantasy', the creative faculty as conceived by the moderns, was unknown as the criterion of a spiritual hierarchy.[24]

In writing, the sign decays into an emblematic schema, or figure of words, in which its substance is preserved in the status of a commemorative ruin where it only alludes to a fullness of meaning, to the intuition of the sacred whole, that was once legitimized by a divine logos. In the allegory of the seventeenth century, the authoritative status of writing is exposed; allegory is at the same time "expression of convention" and thus "expression of authority, which is secret in accordance with the dignity of its origin."[25] Suffering the loss of transcendental support, a secularized logos performs in the capacity of motivating and supporting a melancholic disposition of the historian vis-à-vis his object. This affective, melancholic sensitivity will still maintain a connection with the sacred and "secret origin" of writing's authority, however negatively, as the experienced impotence of an authority that is incapable of vouching for the being of what is represented. The historian steps into the place of this sacred authority and his melancholy eye is turned toward the lost meaning as he endows the now indeterminate, archival signifier with subjective significance. No longer grounded in a mythological totality of meaning, the object is now up for grabs, for "transformations of every sort."[26] It is this view of the sacred as no longer viable—of not holding out the promise of an end, the final form of meaning, and of therefore plunging knowledge into "the empty abyss of evil,"[27]—that the historian projects into the fragmented sign and the fragments of convention in order to express the loss of an ultimate and universal meaning, the nonexistence of a transcendental anchor of language. The resulting emblematic schema becomes the object for a knowledge of historical forms as ruins.

Allegory becomes a new mode of signification that represents the past in a new, meaningful way as if to guide us in how we can sensibly live with this "past in ruins."[28] Allegory becomes a sort of mental training, an experiencing of the past. As someone who juxtaposes life and language, Derrida says that "to live is not something one learns. Not from oneself, it is not learned from life, taught by life. Only from the other and by death. In any case of the other from the edge of life. At the internal border of the external border, it is a heterodidactics between life and death."[29] The wisdom of the historian as someone who works on the border between life and death, the present and the past, as someone who deals with the "ghosts" of the past, and the unacknowledged historical truths, is what is called for in a project of writing history and of constructing memory with language. It is, as both Derrida and Benjamin agree, an ethical project, a project of response, of responding to history and of choosing life (survival) over death, a life that finds its sustenance in response.

What the allegorical vision of the historian-writer "finds" is precisely not the transcendental ideas of the symbol but "the life of creaturely things."[30] He sees the fallen state of nature that would be subject to death and forgetting were it not for him to rescue nature in the exposition of a historical truth—as opposed to a material truth in the positivistic sense—by means of fictional language. In his book, *Archive Fever*, Derrida has associated this orginally Freudian distinction between historical and material truth with the difference between the archive and the archontic principle, the nomological *arkhé* that figures in tradition instead of an originary *arkhé*, a lifeless archeological treasure. By "nomological" he means that which can be passed on in language but also that which is not fixed since its origin is both sacred and secret and lost to any kind of revelation. And what is secret has no archive—the historian must become a writer who speculates and deals with specters of the past in his own writing to embody the spirit of past lives that are no longer palpable. But what else is literature if not an imaginative embodiment of what cannot any longer be known in itself?

The sight of nature is death, but the site of life rests with the historian and his reconstructive text. His allegorical (linguistic) vision overlaps with a melancholic (emotive) vision of those meanings that he knows are lost for the present. However, he tries to preserve the mood of transience (or finitude) in passing on to us the residue of former, outdated linguistic essences whose senses he inscribes with new affective meanings. Here, Benjamin's excursus into the history of melancholy demonstrates an interesting lesson of psychoanalytic pathology. There is always loss and repression of pain, but there is always life once you dare to remember the *feeling* of loss. As practice, psychoanalysis attempts to neutralize the pain of loss and separation from a state of nature, but only after the affect has been transferred from the lost or dead object to a new linguistic representation of that painful, unconscious memory. Memory is transformed and translated into remembrance whereby language at once absorbs, binds, and structures the affect in the subject's consciousness.

> And indeed this [creaturely] world [of things] is calling upon it [the loyalty—of the historian]; and every loyal vow or memory surrounds itself with the fragments of the world of things as its very own, not too-demanding objects. Clumsily, indeed unjustifiably, loyality expresses, in its own way, a truth for the sake of which it does of course betray the world. Melancholy betrays the world for the sake of knowledge. But in its tenacious self-absorption it embraces dead objects in their contemplation, in order to redeem them.[31]

The manner in which Benjamin formulates his view of melancholy as a redemptive, cognitive faculty harkens back to his epistemology of ideas expounded in the prologue to his book on *Trauerspiel*. Ideas come into being by fragmentary phenomena that cluster around them. "Just as a mother is seen to begin to live in the fullness of her power only when the circle of her children, inspired by the feeling of her proximity closes around, so do ideas come to life when extremes [extreme representations] are assembled around them."[32] If in the above formulation it is "memory" that is surrounded by "the fragments of the world of things" and if it is Benjamin's purpose in the *Trauerspiel* to salvage the material aspect of historical knowledge, then what Benjamin means by an idea differs from the Kantian idea which, in its association with the divine, predates the historical world. Rather, Benjamin's idea is utterly worldly, and hence historical, because it is the truth of a life on earth conditioned by nature, the world of things, and death. Whereas Kant's ideas bind transcendence, Benjamin's ideas bind finitude, since for Benjamin finitude is the communicative intention of allegory, a sharing of "the-finitude-of-the-world" with others.

The movement of history is a process that discards one sign after the other for an ever new representation of its telos and is arrested in allegory by way of an image that freezes the moment of transition between a sign's life and its death of meaning. In this frozen motion of disappearance, historicity becomes apparent as an idea that presents itself in non-sensical impoverished signs. On a first reading of the text, these non-sensical signs or figures appear as hieroglyphics. However, as enigmatic mega-signs, they call on the imagination of the reader, a mimetic faculty that can transcribe these signs into a conceptual language, image, or *Sprachbild*. Through the possibility of constructing concepts from figures, the hieroglyphs signify how the mind can make sense out of what is inscribed in the text by figural language. By breaking the hieroglyph down into concepts, what emerges in the reader's mind is an idea of his relationship to the past, and in this emerging idea, history is neither the archive nor an event but a historical truth that implicates the reader's subjectivity and hence his fantasy. For what we know to be dead or lost is therefore not gone from our mind. A melancholic mind never lets go of what is absent; rather, it is attached to the dead object in a way that infuses the dead with life again. The other lives on because of a life lent to it by the self. Melancholia, therefore, differs from nostalgia in that it does not aspire to go where the other was. It does not regress to an imaginary place libidinally invested as home or maternal ground. If nostalgia signifies the pain of such a longing for another place and another time, the distance and separation between self and other is nonetheless keenly observed. In contrast, melancholy actively transports this other into the present and relocates it in the symbolic status this object or place may have in the here and now. If the other becomes part of the self, nostalgia remains on the level of the imaginary. Melancholy performs a cognitive act with respect to the past; it exhumes the past's potential for a symbolic sense in the future and for the very concept of a future.

In their reduced status of referring to the past as ruins, signs turn into mere signifiers which present historical phenomena that need to be gathered into a form or rather a formation (*Gebilde*) in order to yield the outline or figure of an idea. But such a configured idea does not present itself to the reader unless certain phenomena in his life also take on the role of special signifiers for his own experiences and which will inform his conceptions and concepts of what he finds in a text. From a biographical perspective on reading, a person's life will have had to be versatile enough, if not rightly traumatic, to recognize a figure—Derrida might say a specter—in the text. From the point of view of reading, it always comes second to experience; it legitimates a person's history from the future, a symbolic future. Historical events carry an index that they will have become signs in repetition. In their symbolic status, these events lose their quality of shock or trauma. The past will have never become the past but will have turned into the present in the moment of reading. Without the specter of the past, the letter indeed has no spirit, no meaning for the reader. But for the specter to settle down in the letter it has to be propelled into the future by an act of repression, and of returning from its exile into the unconscious, of once being known by the reader as his self.

Slavoj Žižek finds in the return of the repressed a symbolic necessity of historical events, the guilt over their noninscription in human memory or, better yet, in tradition.[33] The murder of Caesar did not achieve the historical-political change of reaffirming the Republic; instead, it initiated the acceptance of a new political reality by means of a name become law, in the title caesar, Roman emperor. "The repetition announces the advent of the Law, of the Name-of-the-Father in place of the dead, assassinated father: the event which repeats itself repeats its law retroactively, through repetition."[34] Since the historical meaning of the sign is lost to consciousness (the murder of Caesar to prevent monarchy), and since the past exists only as a fragmented sense embedded in a larger structure of figurative meanings, history cannot be known in itself but only retroactively by means of its figural linguistic displacements: a figurality and fictionality of names, words, or texts.

This textual-fictional dependence of history as sense and memory may explain why Benjamin differentiates between knowledge and truth. Whereas concepts and representations are contingent on the horizon of signification that we engage when dealing with knowledge, in transposing a configuration of signifiers we *feel out* the truth value of language. However, truth is a function of language by which Benjamin does not mean the "profane meanings" of words but what language communicates as the essence of things, their linguistic, communicable, and divisible nature (*mit-teil-bar*).[35] In the German adjectival morpheme *bar* the difference between *physis* and meaning is made visible; the ability to mean "means" that the thing *is* not itself: it exists only as a historical name, a nomological *arkhé*. The belated law (nomos) justifies and inscribes in memory the event as an archival trace. Thus, if concepts and intuitions are imaginative tools used to grasp what is figured in the text, then our understanding of the text—our sense of history that we derive from reading—is what Benjamin calls an "idea." But here the idea points to the truth of loss, of nature no longer being whole, of a totality split asunder, and of our nostalgia for the origin.

> Truth is not an intent which realizes itself in empirical reality; it is the power which determines the essence of this empirical reality. The state of being, beyond all phenomenality, to which alone this power belongs, is that of the name. This determines the manner in which ideas are given. But they are not so much given in primordial language as in a primordial form of perception (*Vernehmen*) [i.e., listening] in which words possess their own nobility as names, unimpaired by cognitive meaning.[36]

Here Benjamin argues for an original, "essential" force of language, which is preserved as collective tradition and support of individual memory.

In his reading of Freud's *Moses and Monotheism*, Derrida demonstrates that memory is a historical truth that, although repressed or suppressed, resists and returns in people's psyches "as the spectral truth of delusion or of hauntedness."[37] The historical thus turns into a psychological phenomenon. In German, the word for essence and for ghost is *Wesen* which, as Heidegger has philosophically elaborated, is derived from *Gewesen*, the past, that which has been and now calls on the present for regaining its lost status of being through a new inscription. Without the *Wesen*, the reminder of an event in the past, language would not have the figurative dimension that helps us imagine what we cannot grasp, and the ruins of history incorporated in our figures of speech could not signify for us the temporality of experience and of our own being.

In language the ruins of history consolidate into hieroglyphs, into figures which are not representations of things. They become linguistic essences which exercise a disfiguring if not destructive power over things. They challenge the concepts and conceptions of the reader by breaking them down and, consequently, forcing us to reassemble their merely representational or prejudgmental elements within a linguistic context. For Benjamin, this seems to be the value of a new strategy of reading the historic (obscure) text allegorically. Since hieroglyphs or word complexes appear as configurations of texts, which resist a representational reading (interpretation), they have the character of a constellation; that is, they represent a micro-model of historical constellations which Benjamin uses to illustrate the fusion of diachrony and synchrony in his idea of a historical cognition.

Benjamin borrows the term *constellation* from astrology where the astrological sign depicts an idea through non-mimetic representation. This idea comes into being by finding correspondences between the constellation of the stars (the formation of a sign) and the course of human events. Applied to the hieroglyphics of writing, the figures that can be read allegorically, in a synthesis of metaphor and metonymy in our old model, resemble the coming into being of ideas "which are to objects as constellations are to stars."[38] The truth of allegory is the *grasping* of an idea in physical or visual terms. On the level of thought, "ideas are not represented in themselves, but solely and exclusively in an arrangement of concrete elements in the concept: as the configuration of these elements."[39] The elements of concepts refer, however, to the historical reality that for the subject are his or her experiences that have been both repressed and preserved in the unconscious. In their haunting reappearance as affect and affective states these unknown experiences gain access to consciousness through the disfigured images of word-representations which help the subject to form a concept of what is experienced through words in the mind, that is, through his creation of a linguistic image (*Sprachbild*). Crucial for the crystallization of experiences into an idea is the creation of a context in which all "elements," all experiences of the past, can be placed and thus redeemed in the greater unity of an idea as figural intuition. The formation of such a redemptive idea (of history and its value) is the ultimate task of the historian who has to keep tradition and the transmission or rather the reconstructability of experience and of meaning alive.

With respect to the question, what is an idea?, we might now say that ideas are historical necessities. Ideas are to language what memories are to the mind. Since an idea is a redeemed linguistic state of experience, it preserves an experiential truth for human history. Yet, the archive of ideas is language, the bound or figural language of texts. As such, ideas are initially outside the psyche and confront the reader as an other, even as an unreadable other or hieroglyph, until the archive commands not only a second or third reading but also commands the reader to remember times past. Such an imperative over memory makes language part of human experience and links the concept of "idea" with what Benjamin might mean by the messianic, the experience of a redemption in a psychological sense, the experience of *anamnesis*. For the Jews the future is remembrance. The experience of a messianic promise lies in the fully conscious experience of the past. Constant reading of the Torah provides the way to such remembrance.

The primordial force of language which Benjamin sees to be in need of restitution rests in the appeal to tradition which the reader is supposed to hear (*vernehmen*), its "messianic" force that commands us to remember. Although Gadamer did not cite Benjamin as a source for his concepts of language and tradition, the coincidence of both their concepts is more than striking. Of course, Benjamin worked up a detailed historical background for his concept of tradition as the accessibility of history through allegory, while Gadamer by way of hermeneutics bound tradition to the language of the text and its historical interpretations.

The idea of history as transience is missing in Gadamer. Instead, what counts for him is a confined dialogue between the text and the historical situation of the reader. Beyond that dialogue—which however does change the self-understanding of the reader but does not change his understanding of history—no ideas that might change the course of history or the social subject are deduced. For Gadamer, this suggests the conclusion that the value of *Bildung* remains in the accumulation of knowledge, in the form of books.

In thematizing the essential power of language, Benjamin must arrive at a different conclusion regarding *Bildung*, since *Bildung* implies the development of imagination into a perception of tradition. Such development requires the experience of reading as much as it does a willingness to change the reading approach to one of allegory in order to revive the lost spirit of language. In the figure of allegory this may mean to re-spirit, with enthusiastic inspiration as it were, the ruins of history in the sign or word. Without such an allegorical sensitivity to language, the world of ideas may indeed be permanently lost to us. Benjamin's definition of the philosopher's tasks may serve to illustrate this type of remembrance:

> It is the task of the philosopher to restore, by representation, the primacy of the symbolic character of the word, in which the idea is given self-consciousness, and that is the opposite of all outwardly-communication. Since philosophy may not presume to speak in the tones of revelation, this can only be achieved by recalling in memory the primordial form of perception. Platonic anamnesis [re-presenting the *eidos* of the symbol] is, perhaps, not far removed from this kind of remembering; except that here it is not a question of the actualization of images in visual terms; but rather, in philosophical contemplation, the idea is released from the heart of reality as the word, reclaiming its name-giving rights.[40]

The philosopher's preoccupation with the word implies a remembrance facilitated by "divine learning."[41] In representation remembrance overcomes the imaginary lure of *being*, the trap of the metaphorical (m)other. In the interest of an allegorical revision of texts, the subject's desire for being must be transformed, not into a desire to know, given that knowledge is always object bound, but into a desire for the logos that names *Wesen*, the being of the past. This logos would not exist absolutely but would gradually emanate from reading.

Benjamin's "name-giving rights" of the word entangle the reader in the debt of reading, of having to read what's written, what has always been written and what is therefore sacred in the secrecy of writing's origin. This is what the word and the idea of the Torah also mean: "study" the law, in infinite re-readings of the text, in returning to what legitimates our experience of the world. Such reading is necessary, as Benjamin concludes from his study of Kafka's text, because the law cannot be intuited (*angeschaut*) or, as knowledge, read into the text. In the Rabbinic tradition, the sacred text is a compilation and superimposition of generations of commentaries. And by analogy, the law has to be found, or, as Benjamin the philosopher of history asserts, construed and invented. As verbal icons, the words in the text cannot produce an (intellectual) intuition of the idea; rather, they configure the scene of that visualization itself, a scene always already inherently allegorical. This allegorical scene *is* the truth of the text's words. Benjamin has concerned himself with this scene or scenario of representation in the

German tragic drama in order to gain insight into the form of truth which he has found in its theatricality: "its theatricality [is] its essential mode of presenting itself as the realm of ideas."[42]

Ideas have their representatives only in the theater, but theater with its colorful backdrops, puppets, and stage properties is first and foremost a sensual realm—it appeals to the senses. Senses and sense impressions surround, like children the mother, the idea (of motherhood). They prop up the significance of those dead signs by relating one to another. The body of woman becomes signified as mother in relation to her children. The haggadah of the Talmud operates through the world of the senses[43] which is a world transmitted and transmittable in language. But the halakhah or the truth of the text has to be (re)found and construed with each generation anew through (allegorical) readings. The emphasis on reading is therefore performative rather than merely representational. Ideas perform to the reading of language. What can be transmitted is a certain subject matter (*Sache*) as history, but the idea as the truth or doctrine of that history has to be gathered retroactively.

Benjamin submits history as mere material to emblematic inscriptions which make up the tradition of texts. Script turns into hieroglyphics when the absolute, or, in Derridian terms, the *arkhé*, resists representation; the script itself takes on the status of an unknowable God. (We may remember Derrida's shrewd remark in *Grammatology*, that the history of writing has not yet been written, and in *Archive Fever*, that an "archiviology," the science of the effects of the archive, that is, tradition, can at best be projected together with a "science" of psychoanalysis.) In the Jewish tradition of history, the dead letter of the sacred text has not been reanimated by divine incarnation; the letter cannot therefore function as (Christian) symbol which "transforms the phenomenon into an idea, the idea into an image"[44] through which God might be imagined; rather, the dead letter has to be animated by the life of humans, their remembered experiences which might lend the text an allegorical eye that looks back from the expressionless skull with a wink toward death itself.

Death is what the subject in the present has in common with all those before her, because she lives in a body that is mortal. The corpse of a life already lived remains enigmatic only in reference to the meaning and circumstances of that (past) life and also with respect to the identity of the person, but, as dead body, it has a natural affinity with the perceiver's life in the present. The dead letter of the script shares its linguisticity with the reader's mental experience, as the dead body does with the reader's sensibilities: "I, too, could be dead; I, too, might not be understood by others." The meaning of the life of that body has to be inferred, carried into it as an

artificial or fictive life that the reader adapts from her own. But this inferred life lives as it were not in the body of the reader but in her mind, as
her historical or sensuous imagination that is fomented and formed
(*gebildet*) by language for a transfer of meaning. If it can be said that experience in its *mnemic* structure of a temporalization constitutes the human
archive in language as our canon of non-mimetic representations or "virtual" archives, then it is this experienced virtuality of life or virtuality of
experience in language with which a joint history of writing and mental
representation (*Vorstellung*) would have to begin. Derrida elaborates
Yerushalmi's reading of Freud into a prime example of a virtual experience
of the archive. By interviewing Freud, in his book *Freud's Moses: Judaism
Terminable and Interminable,* Yerushalmi brings his own experiential
archive to bear on Freud's textual archive. For Derrida the effect of such a
reading or interviewing of Freud's texts is a merger of archives where the
text can no longer be separated from the reader's (Yerushalmi's) experience
of his own past through the experience of the text's (Freud's) fictions.

This virtuality of experience in language names the imperative of a
debt, to be indefinitely paid off in reading, which is to reconstruct the doctrine or the law of what always escapes, life itself. Allegory knows of the
heterology of life and text, it exhibits the dead body for a representation of
the representability of life as such, yet this *ability* is an effect of linguistic
history, the natural history of signification, of symbolizing if not fictional-
izing what was first of all experienced as raw sensations without ideation.
In allegory, the disjointed body parts have taken on symbolic value in expressions of language, in turns of phrases, and ways of saying what cannot
be said directly. Benjamin valorized allegory for an expression of both the
historicity of meaning as "sense" and of what Freud calls historical truth
that determines people's lives.

This link between the history of language and the history of life that
manifests itself in the concept of tradition has been Derrida's object of
speculation, if not his worry that such a link will soon be destroyed by the
"anarchive" of technological memory and the instantaneous reproduction
of the same or its permanent deletion. Given the modern means of speedy
and disposable communication—Derrida mentions e-mail in particular—
the archive is no longer processed or reread at different times; it no longer
has a chance of becoming unconscious and of being redeemed in a future
memory. Indeed, electronic memory, the storing of data, makes remembrance superfluous. Data or images are called up, they are digitally assembled and printed; but they are no longer recollected and filtered by a mind
trained by historical effects of language. The manner of archiving affects
the way we experience the archive, the past, history. "The technical struc-

ture of the *archiving* archive also determines the structure of the *archivable* content even in its very coming into existence and in its relationship to the future."[45] What Derrida means by the "virtual archive" instead is the responsibility of a reader whose literacy—the sense impressions language left on his imagination—will enable him to recast the names of the dead for naming and signing his own experience, his own life and thus share it with others.

The form in which the reader recovers his experience is but a *persona* in language, a mask or dead face which humans can wear when they want to be what the dead were, a figure they may use to imagine and name their feelings and describe themselves to others. There exists then, finally, a dynamic relationship between the living and the dead; the living proceed to lend the dead their voice for an appearance, or rather an apparition, of a spirit that we can recognize as our psychic archive.

Notes

INTRODUCTION

1. David Marc, *Bonfire of the Humanities. Television, Subliteracy, and Long-term Memory Loss* (Syracuse: Syracuse University Press, 1995), 27. Emphasis added.

2. Ibid., 62.

3. Walter Benjamin, "Über den Begriff der Geschichte," in *Illuminationen* (Frankfurt: Suhrkamp, 1980), 261.

CHAPTER 1. TRADITION: SEARCH FOR THE LOST OBJECT

1. "An essential component of this experience of satisfaction is a particular perception (that of nourishment, in our example), the memory image of which remains associated thenceforward with the memory-trace of the excitation produced by the need." Freud, *The Interpretation of Dreams, Standard Edition*, trans. James Strachey, (London: Hogarth Press, 1953–1974), 5:565. (Subsequently, abbreviated as *S.E.*)

2. "*Repression depends on systems of social constraints and sanctions.* Its power to exclude and hence to enclose—which is nothing short of its power to allow cathexes and, hence, the psychic, to take place—depends on a *place* that it does not constitute, but that is already structured by the metapsychic forces and traditions." Samuel Weber, *The Legend of Freud*, 47–48. Weber's emphasis. (Here, Weber gets at the relationship of repression and language which I will come back to below in chapter 3.)

3. Notice his juxtaposition of death and pleasure drives in *Beyond the Pleasure Principle, S.E.*, vol. 18.

4. Consider esp. Novalis and Friedrich Schlegel.

5. In the eighteenth century social-theoretical thinkers and authors like Rousseau, Kant, and Schiller reflected upon the destiny of humans with the result that *Glückseligkeit*, happiness, became an expectation in life. Happiness as a legitimating value for activities was correlated, in the Enlightenment, with the subject's efforts to achieve an autonomous state of being. Striving for happiness or bliss thus justified and elevated all materially bound demands. This open acknowledgment of human desire provided, for instance, the rationale for a new society in the United States. Promoting human happiness was seen as acting in accordance with the "will of nature," i.e., nature and reason were in harmony in this pursuit.

6. Reinhart Koselleck elaborates this semantic shift and hints at the transcendental nature that history, as a category, acquired: "The conditions for experiencing history and the conditions for cognizing history are subsumed under the same term." *Vergangene Zukunft. Zur Semantik geschichtlicher Zeiten* (Frankfurt: Suhrkamp, 1979), 265.

7. Cf. *Der Streit der Fakultäten* and *Idee zu einer allgemeinen Geschichte in weltbürgerlicher Absicht*, cited in Koselleck, ibid.

8. Cf. Koselleck, *Vergangene Zukunft*. Koselleck shows how the projection of a better future was a necessary consequence of Kant's notion of "moral imperative" attendant upon practical reason. This led to the conception of history as a temporalized institution of executing moral power ("eine temporalisierte Vollzugsanstalt der Moral," 268).

9. Cf. Benjamin, "Über den Begriff der Geschichte."

10. "[T]hat is to say, only by the ability to use the past in one's life to turn what has happened again into history [*Geschichte*], does man become a human being." Friedrich Nietzsche, "Vom Nutzen und Nachteil der Historie für das Leben," in *Unzeitgemäße Betrachtungen* (München: Goldmann, 1964), 78.

11. See his theory of shock in the essay "Über einige Motive bei Baudelaire," in *Illuminationen*, 185–229.

12. "'The function of memory,' it says in Reik, 'is the protection of the impressions; recollection aims at its destruction. Memory is essentially conservative, recollection is destructive.' The fundamental sentence of Freud on which these assertions are based, articulates the assumption that 'consciousness comes into being in the place of the memory trace.'" "Über einige Motive bei Baudelaire," 190.

13. Ibid.

14. Cf. Benjamin, "Das Kunstwerk im Zeitalter seiner technischen Reproduzierbarkeit," in *Illuminationen*, 159.

15. Benjamin quotes the example of the press whose aim (and success) it is to separate the reader from the events, instead of making them part of his experience: "The principles of journalistic information (novelty, brevity, understandability and, above all, the disconnectedness of the individual news) contribute to this kind of success just as does the layout and the style." "Über einige Motive bei Baudelaire," 188.

16. This temporal space may also be understood as the cultural space which in modernity became increasingly commodified and thus colonized. If it is true that the effects of culture and the emergence of an unconscious in the individual are interrelated, then the new mediation techniques of an instrumentally and economically controlled mass culture in modernity also infiltrate and colonize the unconscious. The unconscious "Now," accessible through the space of tradition-turned-into-culture, becomes an important political tool for the synchronization and conformity of individual experiences in society. Benjamin's *Kunstwerk* essay demonstrates the manipulation of the unconscious through the media and derives this development from the loss of tradition in experience. This process, in Benjamin's own definition, eliminates experience in the sense of *Erfahrung*, leaving only the aspect of *Erlebnis*, which in mass culture is engineered as collective phenomena. Through the interference of the machine (the representative of modernity) in producing experience, the temporal space of experience and the necessary delay of meaning formation are destroyed. Benjamin formulates this as the loss of "aura." "The definition of aura as 'unique appearance of distance, as near as it may be,' represents nothing more than the formulation of the cult value of the work of art in the categories of a spatial and temporal perception. Distance is the opposite of closeness [*Nähe*]. The *essentially* distant [*das wesentlich Ferne*] is inapproachable [*das Unnahbare*] ..." "Das Kunstwerk," 143. The distance to the work of art has to be both experienced and overcome, by oneself being transported towards it (*erfahren*), if art is to carry any

meaning. The event (or in Benjamin's example, the work of art) can never be appropriated because its essence is distance, but in the experience of this distance it has a significance, a value. Benjamin calls it cult value which, in his terms, is a function of spatial-temporal perception, an awareness of the past in the perception of the present. Also dealing with the appropriaton of the past through texts, Fredric Jameson entitled one of his major works *The Political Unconscious* (Ithaca: Cornell University Press, 1981) in which he uncovers a mutual contingency of ideology and the individual unconscious which he sees as an essential manifestation of history. The nature of history is Jameson's true object in this book.

17. Benjamin, "Über einige Motive bei Baudelaire," 186.

18. At this preliminary point I shall connect the two concepts hidden in the unconscious as adjective and noun. This relates to the notion of an intersubjective sphere of language in which the subject participates without being conscious of its determining qualities. The effects of language on consciousness involve a process constituting a *Bewußtseinseffekt* that as process will never completely become conscious. Yet it is in this unconscious process or unconscious realm that language relates to the world.

19. Weber, *The Legend of Freud* , 33–34.

Chapter 2. The Representation of History

1. Hayden White, "Historical Text as Literary Artifact," in *Tropics of Discourse* (Baltimore: Johns Hopkins University Press, 1978), 91.

2. Ibid., 5.

3. White states the connection between a historical narrative and literature such: "Viewed in a purely formalistic way, a historical narrative is not only a *reproduction* of the events reported in it, but also a *complex of symbols* which gives us directions for finding an *icon* of the structure of those events in our literary tradition." *Tropics of Discourse*, 88. White cites C. S. Peirce in his distinction of sign, symbol and icon, to show how the "historical narrative points in two directions simultaneously: *toward* the events described in the narrative and *toward* the story type or mythos which the historian has chosen to serve as the icon of the structure of the events. The narrative itself is not the icon; what it does is *describe* events in the historical record in such a way as to inform the reader *what to take as an icon* of the events so as to render them 'familiar' to him." Whereas White establishes a direct relationship to literature in terms of plot structures and meanings that are presupposed as familiar, I will go a step backwards and address this relationship on the common basis of language that is itself metaphorical and mediatory in its semiotic function. In the following, I will pursue a relation between the construction of history, its representation, and the meaning mechanism in language itself.

4. James Engell, *Creative Imagination: From Enlightenment to Romanticism* (Cambridge: Harvard University Press, 1981), 207. The second part of my book is devoted to the emergence of imagination as an epistemological power in the course of the eighteenth century. In the guise of the debate over what constitutes genius and *Geist* in relation to artistic representation of experience, the issue of cognition as determined by language has already been broached, though it was only with the Romantic thinkers, first and foremost with Novalis (esp. his *Fichte-Studien*) that a theory of signs was conceived along the lines of imagination, unconscious tradition, and feeling.

5. Ibid.

6. Hayden White, *Metahistory: The Historical Imagination in Nineteenth-century Europe* (Baltimore: Johns Hopkins University Press, 1973), 30. "The important point is that every

history, even the most 'synchronic' or 'structural' of them, will be emplotted in some way." *Metahistory,* 8.

7. Ibid., 30.

8. White's definition of "conceptual" implies that the text is consciously constituted by such linguistic strategies rather than that there is already a figurative mechanism at work at any level of textuality which shapes consciousness and the figures of thought unconsciously.

9. Jacques Lacan, "Agency of the letter in the unconscious," in *Écrits. A Selection,* trans. Alan Sheridan (New York: Norton, 1977), 164.

10. "The full word, in fact, is defined by its identity to that of which it speaks." Lacan cited in Anthony Wilden, *Speech and Language in Psychoanalysis* (Baltimore: Johns Hopkins University Press, 1968), 196.

11. Hans Robert Jauss, *Ästhetische Erfahrung und literarische Hermeneutik.* 2nd ed. (Frankfurt: Suhrkamp, 1984), 662.

12. "The dialectic of question and answer thus always already preempts the dialectic of interpretation. It is what determines understanding as a happening [or event]." Hans Georg Gadamer, *Wahrheit und Methode.* 4th ed. (Tübingen: Mohr, 1975), 447.

13. Because of the intermediary of language and signification, Gadamer's metaphor "the fusion of horizons" [*Horizontverschmelzung*] should be interpreted, and corrected, as a mediation between the other and one's own horizon; cf. also Jauss's critique of Gadamer in *Ästhetische Erfahrung und literarische Hermeneutik,* see esp. 657 ff.

14. Cf. Valentin Volosinov: "One cannot draw any distinct lines between understanding and answer. Every understanding is already a reply, i.e. it translates that which needs to be understood into a new context, into the possible context of an answer."*Marxismus und Sprachphilosophie,* ed. Samuel Weber (Frankfurt: Ullstein, 1975), 124.

15. Cf. White, *Tropics of Discourse.*

16. White, *Tropics of Discourse,* 5.

17. Cf. Gadamer, *Wahrheit und Methode.*

18. Freud, *Moses and Monotheism, S.E.,* 23:97.

19. Lacan makes it clear that the unconscious is different from the conventional conception of the Freudian instinctual Id: "It's wrong to think that the unconscious exists because of the existence of unconscious desire, of some obtuse, heavy, caliban, indeed animalic unconscious desire that rises up from the depths, that is primitive, and has to lift itself to the higher level of consciousness. Quite on the contrary, desire exists because there is unconsciousness, that is to say, *language which escapes the subject in its structure and effects, and because there is always, on the level of language, something which is beyond consciousness and it is there that the function of desire is to be located.*" Lacan, quoted in *Qu'est-ce que le structuralisme?,* ed. J. Wahl (Paris: Seuil, 1968), 252–53. Emphasis added.

20. Freud, *S.E.*, 5:489.

21. Cf. Freud's model of the psyche as formed through a layering of experiences in memory traces. Memory according to Freud is present not once but repeatedly and it is inscribed in various kinds of signs: "I am working from the assumption that our psychical mechanism was formed through a layering [of memories] whereby, from time to time, the existing material of memory traces experiences a re-ordering [*Umordnung*] according to new relations, a transcription [*Umschrift*]. What is essentially new in my theory is the claim that memory is not a singular entity but exists in multiple forms; it is deposited in various kinds of signs." *Aus den Anfängen der Psychoanalyse. Briefe an Wilhelm Fliess, Abhandlungen und Notizen aus den Jahren 1887–1902* (London: Imago, 1950), 185.

22. Rainer Nägele, *Reading after Freud* (Baltimore: Johns Hopkins University Press, 1987), 174. Nägele draws on Jean Laplanche and J.-B. Pontalis, *Vocabulaire de la Psychanalyse*

(Paris: Presses Universitaires de France, 1997), for a synthesis of "Nachträglichkeit" and "Umschrift."

23. Walter Benjamin, *Das Passagenwerk* (Frankfurt: Suhrkamp, 1982), 576–77.

24. Benjamin, "Über den Begriff der Geschichte," 258.

25. Benjamin, *Passagenwerk*, 578.

26. Cf. the very lucid chapter on Benjamin by Rainer Rotter, "Die Bestimmung der Aktualität bei Walter Benjamin," in *Die Gegenwart der Geschichte* (Stuttgart: Metzler, 1990). Rotter interprets Benjamin's expression as designation for actuality, "namely a determination of a past which is subjected to a process of actualization, consequently this past appears as timely and proves that it is [really] not past," 52.

27. Benjamin, "Über das mimetische Vermögen," in *Angelus Novus. Ausgewählte Schriften 2* (Frankfurt: Suhrkamp, 1988), 98–99 ["Alles Mimetische der Sprache kann vielmehr, der Flamme ähnlich, nur an einer Art von Träger in Erscheinung treten. Dieser Träger ist das Semiotische. So ist der Sinnzusammenhang der Wörter oder Sätze der Träger, an dem erst, blitzartig, die Ähnlichkeit in Erscheinung tritt. Denn ihre Erzeugung durch den Menschen ist—ebenso wie ihre Wahrnehmung durch ihn—in vielen und zumal den wichtigen Fällen an ein Aufblitzen gebunden. Sie huscht vorbei."]

28. "The Word *Wolke*—If it is one," in *Benjamin's Ground. New Readings of Walter Benjamin*, ed. Rainer Nägele (Detroit: Wayne State University Press, 1988), 147–76.

29. "Their likeness is never the sensuous likeness of correspondence [to an extratextual reality] but rather a non-sensuous likeness which two different elements maintain in their common relationship to a third element—an element that is never, or if so, only preliminarily, given . . ." *Benjamin's Ground*, 154.

30. Benjamin, *Passagenwerk*, 578.

31. Ibid.

32. "Über das mimetische Vermögen," 97.

33. An instructive chapter of Rainer Koch's dissertation explicates this move on Benjamin's part in his *Theses of History*; cf. *Vom Mythos zum dialektischen Bild. Geschichtskritik und ästhetische Wahrheit bei Adorno/Horkheimer, Peter Weiss und Walter Benjamin* (Ph.D. diss., University of Hannover, 1987/88). I do not agree totally, however, with Koch on identifying "the claim of the past" as merely the desired state of happiness which requires a revolution. Precisely in the *Theses of History*, Benjamin constructs the philosophical *and* psychological constituents of a "historical consciousness" that emerges once we remember instead of repress. Koch's work abandons the psychoanalytical aspect of Benjamin's theory of history in favor of critiquing its sociological and sociocritical potential.

Chapter 3. Repetition and Experience

1. Freud, *Beyond the Pleasure Principle*, S.E., 18: 38 (translation modifed).

2. Ferenczi, cited in Freud, *Beyond the Pleasure Principle*, 41–42 (translation modified).

3. Cf. Freud, ibid., 41.

4. "In the unconscious nothing can be brought to an end, nothing is past or forgotten. This is brought most vividly home to one in studying the neuroses, and especially hysteria. (. . .) A humiliation that was experienced thirty years ago acts exactly like a fresh one throughout the thirty years, as soon as it has obtained access to the unconscious sources of emotion." Freud, *The Interpretation of Dreams*, S.E., 5:577–78.

5. "The way backwards, to complete satisfaction, is as a rule obstructed by the resistances which maintain the repressions. So there is no alternative but to advance in the other direction in which growth is still free—though with no prospect of bringing the process to a conclusion or of being able to reach the goal. The processes involved in the formation of a neurotic phobia, which is nothing else than an attempt at flight from the satisfaction of a drive, present us with a model of how this apparent 'drive towards perfection' comes about." Freud, *Beyond the Pleasure Principle*, S.E., 18: 42 (translation modified). What Freud calls a neurotic phobia resulting from evasion of the past, the satisfaction of desire, impacts on Benjamin's theory of history as it transpires from his treatise on fashion as expression of the, let's say here, "perverted" desire for the ever-new which reflects a historical consciousness that recognizes and values only progress. Intent on progress and fast change, individuals and societies avoid "working through" the past, a work that involves the arresting of time in an experience of recognizing the familiar, the old in the new. It was Benjamin's attempt in the aborted *Passagenwerk* to trace these "old" covered-up desires, the unconscious past in the modernity of the cityscape of Paris. The accomplice of fashion, of the cover-up, Benjamin states allegorically, is death itself, and by that he means the death of history, the end of human experience with an entailing incapacity for suffering life. History figures as corpse: "Fashion's tall and rude salesman, death itself, measures the century by the yard. And, in order to be economical, death itself plays the fashion model and manages the store sale, which in French is called 'revolution.' For fashion was never anything but the parody of the gay corpse, death's provocation through woman, and a sarcastic dialogue with decadence whispered between shrill bouts of affected laughter. This is fashion. That is why it changes so rapidly, teases death, and is already another, new one, whenever death turns around trying to beat it." *Das Passagenwerk*, 111.

6. "The rhythm of the messianic nature is bliss," Benjamin, "Theologisch-politisches Fragment," in *Illuminationen*, 262.

7. "Another striking fact is that the life drives have so much more contact with our internal perception—emerging as breakers of the peace and constantly producing tensions whose release is felt as pleasure—while the death drives seem to virtually work unobtrusively." Freud, *Beyond the Pleasure Principle*, S.E., 8: 63 (translation modified).

8. Benjamin, "Theologisch-politisches Fragment," in *Illuminationen*, 262.

9. Benjamin, in *Gesammelte Schriften*, ed. Rolf Tiedemann and Hermann Schweppenhäuser, vol. I, 3 (Frankfurt: Suhrkamp, 1985), 1243.

10. "It is known that the Jews were forbidden to inquire about the future. The Thora and prayer instructed them, instead, in the practice of remembrance (*Eingedenken*). This demystified the future for them, by which only those were enticed who obtained an inquiry from the truth tellers. For the Jews, the future did not, however, become a homogeneous and empty time, because in it every second was the little door through which the messiah could enter." Benjamin, "Über den Begriff der Geschichte," Appendix B, in *Illuminationen*, 261.

11. Gadamer, *Wahrheit und Methode*, 283.

12. Ibid. Emphasis added.

13. Ibid.

14. Ibid., 289.

15. I choose the word "work" here because it encompasses aspects of both process and efficacy which are contained in the German *Wirkung*, the work of effects that originated in the past.

16. Gadamer, *Wahrheit und Methode*, 285.

17. Ibid., 285–86.

18. For developing an understanding of transference which is not merely reducible to a notion of narcissistic projection, I find the definition given by George Atwood and Robert Stolorow in *Structures of Subjectivity: Explorations in Psychoanalytic Phenomenology* (London: Erlbaum Assoc., 1984) very useful: "The concept of transference may be understood to refer to all the ways in which the patient's experience of the analytic relationship becomes organized according to the configurations of self and object that unconsciously structure his subjective universe. The transference is actually a microcosm of the patient's total psychological life, and the analysis of the transference provides a focal point around which the patterns dominating the patient's existence as a whole can be clarified, understood, and changed," 47.

19. Benjamin, "Über den Begriff der Geschichte," 259.

20. Benjamin, "Paris, die Hauptstadt des XIX. Jahrhunderts," in *Illuminationen*, 184.

21. "The arcades and interiors, the exhibition halls and panoramas stem from this epoch. They are remainders of a dream world. Processing the dream elements upon awakening is the textbook case of dialectical thinking. . . . Every epoch dreams not only the next one but, by dreaming, it urges toward awakening," Benjamin, "Paris," 184.

22. Although the concept of "chronotope" is usually associated with Mikhail Bakhtin, its religious and existential dimensions were already part of the intellectual literary discourse of the 1920s. Erich Auerbach's elaboration of the literary concept of *figura* illuminates the historical experience and the social imaginary behind its rhetorical use in literature. It is against this currency of thinking the historical with the fantastic that Benjamin coins his metaphor of the "dialectical image."

23. Benjamin, *Passagenwerk*, 578.

24. Ibid., 576–77. The present or the past do not serve as perspectives or categories under which to view an experience, rather the cognitive image of the experience is a synthesis of past and present.

25. Ibid., 577–78.

26. Inherent in the fantasy of bliss and the image of the past "there is a secret agreement between the past generations and ours. (. . .) Like every generation which existed before us, ours is given a weak messianic power to which the past has a claim [and which it calls on]." Benjamin, "Über den Begriff der Geschichte," 251–52.

27. Benjamin, "Über einige Motive bei Baudelaire," 222 ["Was die Lust am Schönen unstillbar macht, ist das Bild der Vorwelt, die Baudelaire durch die Tränen des Heimwehs verschleiert nennt. 'Ach, du warst in abgelebten Zeiten / Meine Schwester oder meine Frau'—dies Geständnis ist der Tribut , den das Schöne als solches fordern kann. So weit die Kunst auf das Schöne ausgeht und es, wenn auch noch so schlicht, 'wiedergibt', holt sie es (wie Faust die Helena) aus der Tiefe der Zeit herauf"].

28. Ibid., 221–22 ["Diese [die Phantasie] läßt sich vielleicht als ein Vermögen fassen, Wünsche einer besonderen Art zu tun; solche, denen als Erfüllung 'etwas Schönes' zugedacht werden kann. (. . .) Ein Gemälde würde . . . an einem Augenblick dasjenige wiedergeben, woran sich das Auge nicht sattsehen kann. Womit es den Wunsch erfüllt, der sich in seinen Ursprung projizieren läßt, wäre etwas, was diesen Wunsch unablässig nährt"].

29. Baudelaire, cited in Benjamin, "Über einige Motive bei Baudelaire," 224.

30. "Theologisch-politisches Fragment," 262.

31. Benjamin, *Passagenwerk*, 580.

32. Ibid.

33. Rainer Nägele, *Reading after Freud*, 16.

34. Ibid.

CHAPTER 4. DESIRE AND THE BODY IN KANT

1. Kant, *Kritik der Urteilskraft* (Frankfurt: Suhrkamp, 1981), 85; "als Vermögens, durch seine Vorstellungen Ursache von der Wirklichkeit der Gegenstände dieser Vorstellungen zu sein." (In the following I will abbreviate *Kritik der Urteilskraft* as *K.d.U.*. All translations are mine unless otherwise indicated.)

2. Kant, *Critique of Judgment*, trans. J. H. Bernard (New York: Hafner Press, 1951), 14. (In the following I will refer to this translation of Kant's *Kritik der Urteilskraft* as *Critique*)

3. Cf. Samuel Weber's analytic reading of this passage in "The Foundering of Aesthetics" in *The Comparative Aspect on Literature*, ed. Clayton Koelb and Susan Noakes (Ithaca: Cornell University Press, 1988), 71.

4. Kant, *K.d.U.*, 86. Emphasis added.

5. Kant, "First Version of Introduction," *K.d.U.*, 22.

6. In his book, *A Peculiar Fate. Metaphysics and World History in Kant*, Peter Fenves comes to a similar conclusion by examining Kant's mention of *Triebfedern* (motives) in the *Critique of Pure Reason;* here Kant insists that motives do not have an effect on history in terms of progress. For my purposes of illuminating the cognitive aspects of aesthetic experience I have confined myself to Kant's *Third Critique*.

7. Kant, *K.d.U.*, 85.

8. "Desire is interested not simply in reality or realization but in the capacity of representations to cause reality, to become reality. In this sense, desire contains a reflexive element: it is the representation of the causality of its representations in respect to their objects. It is the 'other side' of reflective judgment, which is also suspended between reality and representation, between the reality of the particular, individual event or object and the effort to grasp it in and as a representation." Weber, "The Foundering of Aesthetics," 71.

9. Rolf Grimminger, *Die Ordnung und das Chaos* (Frankfurt: Suhrkamp, 1986), 144.

CHAPTER 5. THE MATERNAL GROUND OF AESTHETIC EXPERIENCE

1. This does not mean that Kant does not try to think the body. In their book on the repression of the body in Kant, Hartmut Böhme and Gernot Böhme have demonstrated that Kant merely tried to exclude the body from metaphysics, by displacing it into tractati on physics and a theory of matter. In his works on nature, however, Kant turns the body into a means, a sensorium for experiments of the power of reason, "for [there] it is never that body which makes itself felt in urges, which proves to be a source of fear or pleasure, and which the subject experiences as spatial rhythms of tension and tumescence." Böhme and Böhme, *Das Andere der Vernunft* (Frankfurt: Suhrkamp, 1985), 108–9.

2. Kant, *Opus Postumum*, in *Kants Gesammelte Schriften*, ed. Königliche Preußische Akademie der Wissenschaften, vols. 21–22 (Berlin, Leipzig: de Gruyter, 1900–1955), 461.

3. "We can refer all acts of understanding to judgments, in such a way that understanding in general may be represented as the faculty of judging." Kant, *Kritik der reinen Vernunft*, vol. 1 (Frankfurt: Suhrkamp, 1982), 110.

4. Kant, *Kritik der reinen Vernunft*, 69.

5. Ibid.

6. Cf. esp. § 49 and § 59 in *Critique of Judgment*.

7. "Just as the ideality of the objects of sense as phenomena is the only way of explaining the possibility of their forms being susceptible of a priori determination, so the idealism

of purposiveness, in judging the beautiful in nature and art, is the only hypothesis under which critique can explain the possibility of a judgment of taste which demands a priori validity for everyone (without grounding on concepts the purposiveness that is represented in the object)." *Critique*, 196; cf. *K.d.U.*, 294.

8. Kant, *Critique*, 41; cf. *K.d.U.*, 120.

9. "If, now, in this comparison [of the forms of intuitions to concepts] the imagination (as the faculty of a priori intuitions) is placed by means of a given representation undesignedly . . ." *Critique*, 26; cf.*K.d.U.*, 100.

10. "Moreover, real fictionality does not constitute an error from which we must extricate ourselves. Such would be unthinkable—indeed, it would be so in the strictest of terms, for it is impossible for us to think without fictions: 'To language, then—to language alone—it is, that fictitious entities [e.g., faculties, powers of the mind, dispositions] owe their existence; their impossible, yet indispensable, existence.'" Luiz Costa Lima, here citing from Jeremy Bentham's *Theory of Fictions*, in his book *The Control of the Imaginary. Reason and Imagination in Modern Times* (Minneapolis: University of Minnesota Press, 1988), 35–36.

11. Cf. *Kritik der reinen Vernunft*: "[P]ower of judgment, however, is a special talent which cannot be taught but only practiced. Hence, it is also the specific feature of the so-called mother wit whose lack no school can replace. (. . .) Therefore, examples [e.g. fictions, metaphors, etc.] are the wheels for the capacity to judge, and are indispensable to those who lack this natural talent." 184–85.

12. Cf. Jacques Derrida's analysis of Kant's usage of the "parergon" in the *Critique of Judgment*. He analyzes how the work of the frame actually supplants and subtracts from the work of art, the beautiful that he calls "ergon": "They [the examples] can also reverse, become unbalanced, turn natural movement [i.e., the natural talent of mother wit] into a parergonal movement, deflect the energy of the *ergon*, introduce chance and the abyss into the necessity of *Mutterwitz*: not a contrary order, but an aleatory separation . . . Like the wholly other of heteroaffection, in pleasure without *jouissance* and without concept, it [the parergon] elicits *and* delimits the work of mourning, work *in general as* the work of mourning." Jacques Derrida, "The Parergon," trans. Craig Owens, *October*, vol. 9 (1979): 38.

13. For an analysis of Kant's near fantastic representations of the universe that seem to reflect Kant's own unconscious desires and fears of an all-encompassing *matter* or *maternal* universe, see Hartmut and Gernot Böhme's revealing book *Das Andere der Vernunft*.

14. Luce Irigaray, *Speculum of the Other Woman*, trans. Gillian Gill (Ithaca: Cornell University Press, 1985), 210.

CHAPTER 6. THE UNCONSCIOUS HERMENEUTICS OF "WIT"

1. Herder finally distinguished aesthetics from art: aesthetics is not the work of those who feel but the work of philosophers: "Our aesthetics is science [*Wissenschaft*], and nothing less than people of genius and taste; it wants to train [*bilden*] none other than philosophers," Herder cited in Alfred Bäumler, *Kants Kritik der Urteilskraft. Ihre Geschichte und Systematik. (=Das Irrationalitätsproblem in der Ästhetik und Logic des 18. Jahrhunderts bis zur Kritik der Urteilskraft* (Halle: Niemeyer, 1923), 93. In this definition, of course, those philosophers have the same attributes as the artist: genius and taste; in other words, they have the capacity for artistic expression, in Kant's terms.

2. "Kant expresses the nonconceptual with the word sentiment, which arrives at the universal without acting according to universal laws. It does not need the 'digression of the proofs' but stems from the heart. Kant relates the sentiment to 'common sense', which is the faculty to judge right in a concrete case [cf. "Mutterwitz" above]. *That rules are missing in the abstract establishes the pecularity of the judgment, i.e. the critique in contrast to the doctrine. The principles cannot be taught, only practiced. The rules are therefore only empirically deduced and abstracted from experience.*" Bäumler, *Kants Kritik der Urteilskraft*, 281. Emphasis added.

3. Cf. Bäumler, 148–49.

4. Elaborating on the cultural history of mimetic capacity, Benjamin compares language to astrological figurations to show how nonsensical similarities can be produced in imagination: "However, we, too, are in possession of a canon which can help explain what non-mimetic representation [*unsinnliche Ähnlichkeit*] means. And this canon is language." "Über das mimetische Vermögen," in *Angelus Novus* (Frankfurt: Suhrkamp, 1988), 97.

5. Bäumler, *Kants Kritik*, 148.

6. Ibid.

7. Ibid. 148.

8. "A second group of technical methods used in jokes—unification, similarity of sound, multiple use, modification of familiar phrases, allusions to quotations—we can single out as their common characteristic the fact that *in each of them something familiar is rediscovered*, where we might instead have expected something new. This rediscovery of what is familiar is pleasurable, and once more it is not difficult for us to recognize this pleasure as a pleasure in economy and to relate it to economy in psychical expenditure." Freud, *Jokes and their Relation to the Unconscious* in *S.E.*, trans. and ed. James Strachey, vol. 8 (London: Hogarth Press, 1960), 120; cf. *Der Witz und seine Beziehung zum Unbewussten*, in *Gesammelte Werke*, vol. 6 (London: Imago, 1940), 135. Emphasis added.

9. "But the subjective element in a representation, which cannot be an ingredient of cognition, is the pleasure or pain which is bound up with it. . . . The purposiveness, therefore, which precedes the cognition of an object and which, even without our wishing to use the representation of it for cognition, is at the same time immediately bound up with it, is that subjective [element] which cannot be an ingredient in cognition. Hence the object is only called purposive when its representation is immediately combined with the feeling of pleasure, and this very representation is an aesthetical representation of purposiveness." Kant, *Critique*, 26; cf. *K.d.U.*, 99–100.

10. "Pleasure is [according to Wolff] . . . an intuition of perfection. . . . To recognize something intuitively means to recognize it immediately, without the mediation of signs. To contemplate a perfection is to become conscious of it immediately. What we are only immediatly conscious of are the acts of our own consciousness." Bäumler, 108.

11. "To discover perfection in an object is not enough, we also have to find it with our senses." Wolff cited in Bäumler, *Kants Kritik*, 108.

12. Cf. Dietmar Kamper, *Zur Soziologie der Imagination* (München: Hanser, 1984).

13. "Now between the faculties of cognition and desire there is the feeling of pleasure, just as the judgment mediates between the understanding and reason. We may therefore suppose provisionally that the judgment likewise contains in itself an *a priori* principle. And as pleasure or pain is necessarily linked with the faculty of desire . . . we may also suppose that judgment will bring about a transition from the pure faculty of cognition, i.e. the realm of concepts of nature, to the realm of the concept of freedom, just as in its logical use, judgment makes possible the transition from understanding to reason." Kant, *Critique*, 15; translation adapted; cf. *K.d.U.*, 87.

CHAPTER 7. INTUITION VERSUS REPRESENTATION

1. Kant, *Critique*, 38; cf. *K.d.U.*,115–16.

2. Kant, *Critique*, 26; cf. *K.d.U.*, 99.

3. I owe the term "syntagmatic" to Paul de Man's analysis of Kant's theory of the sublime, in which he compares the two acts of imagination, apprehension and comprehension, to the act of reading along the syntagmatic and paradigmatic axes of a text. Cf. "Phenomenality and Materiality in Kant," in Gary Shapiro and Alan Sica, eds., *Hermeneutics* (Amherst: University of Massachusetts Press, 1984).

4. Kant, *Critique*, 90; cf. *K.d.U.*, 173–74.

5. "If pleasure is bound up with the *mere apprehension* (apprehensio) of the form of an object of intuition, without reference to a concept for a definite cognition, then the representation is thereby not referred to the object, but simply to the subject and the pleasure can express nothing else than its harmony with the cognitive faculties which come into play in the reflective judgment, . . . If, now, in this comparison [of the forms of intuition to concepts], the *imagination (as the faculty of a priori intuitions)* is placed by means of a given representation undesignedly." Kant, *Critique*, 26; cf. *K.d.U.*, 100. Emphasis added.

6. Kant, *Critique*, 157; cf. *K.d.U.*, 249–50.

7. "The figurative writing of the dream does not operate with simple, straightforward images. What Freud calls the 'perceptual identity' is formed from the material of perception, but the material does not function by virtue of what it represents. For its representational, or ideational content—its *Vorstellungsinhalt*—functions only as a sign of something radically different, something that is unrepresentable as such, since it consists of a change in tension, a quantitative, differential alteration in the distribution of energy, producing a qualitative effect: the transition from pain to pleasure . . . The identity [of perception] involved is the result of a repetition in which the qualitative content functions simply as a formal support for the unrepresentable experience of satisfaction it is meant to conjure." Weber, *The Legend of Freud*, 36.

8. "It will be seen that the chief characteristics of these processes is that the whole stress is laid upon making the cathecting energy mobile and capable of discharge; the content and the proper meaning of the psychic elements to which the cathexes are attached are treated as being of little consequence." Freud, *The Interpretation of Dreams*, in *S.E.*, 5: 597.

CHAPTER 8. THE "GENIUS" OF TRADITION

1. Kant, *Critique*, 200–201; cf. *K.d.U.*, 299–300.

2. Kant, *Critique*, 160; translation modified; cf. *K.d.U.*, 253.

3. Kant calls these productions aesthetical "ideas", "because they at least strive after something which lies beyond the bounds of experience [empirical reality] and so they seek to approximate to a presentation of concepts of reason (intellectual ideas), thus giving the latter the appearance of objective reality, but especially because no concept can be fully adequate to them as *internal intuitions*." *Critique*, 157; cf. *K.d.U.*, 250. Emphasis added.

4. Kant, *Critique*, 159; cf. *K.d.U.*, 252.

5. Kant, *Critique*, 197–98; cf. *K.d.U.*, 296.

6. Kant, *Critique*, 189; cf. *K.d.U.*, 286.

7. "For, while the relationship of the present to the past is merely temporal, the relationship of what-has-been to the Now is dialectical: it is not of a temporal nature but has the quality of an image. Only dialectical images are really historical, that is, they are not archaic images." Benjamin, *Das Passagenwerk*, 578.

8. The beautiful has the character of an appeal. Cf. Benjamin: "In its *historical* existence, the beautiful is an appeal to us to join those who have admired it before. To be ravished by the beautiful means to go to the many (ad plures ire)." "Über einige Motive bei Baudelaire," in *Illuminationen*, 215.

9. "The imagination (as a productive faculty of cognition) is very powerful in creating another nature, as it were, out of the material that actual nature gives it. We entertain ourselves with it when experience becomes too commonplace, and by it we remold experience, always in accordance with analogical laws." Kant, *Critique*, 157; cf. *K.d.U.*, 250.

10. Kant, *K.d.U.*, 255.

11. Kant, *Critique*, 189; cf. *K.d.U.*, 286.

12. "It can only be that in the subject which is nature and cannot be brought under rules of concepts, i.e. the supersensible substrate of all his faculties (to which no concept of the understanding extends), and consequently that with respect to which it is the final purpose given by the intelligible [part] of our nature to harmonize all our cognitive faculties," Kant, *Critique*, 189.

13. François Lyotard, *Der Enthusiasmus: Kants Kritik der Geschichte*, ed. Peter Engelmann (Wien: Passagen Verlag, 1988), 95.

14. "But although the judgment upon the sublime in nature needs culture (more than the judgment upon the beautiful), it is not therefore primarily produced by culture and introduced in a merely conventional way into society. Rather it has its root in human nature." *Critique*, 105; *K.d.U.*, 190.

15. "Culture is, above all, the development of a capability in a reasonable being to whatever purpose (therefore in its freedom)." *K.d.U.*, 390.

16. Cf. *Kant. On History*, ed. and trans. Lewis White Beck (New York: Macmillan, 1963), 11–27; German: *Idee zu einer allgemeinen Geschichte in weltbürgerlicher Absicht* in *Schriften zur Anthropologie, Geschichtsphilosophie, Politik und Pädagogik* (Frankfurt: Suhrkamp, 1977).

17. *Idee zu einer allgemeinen Geschichte*, 47.

18. Kant, *K.d.U.*, 392.

19. Lyotard, *Der Enthusiasmus*, 74.

20. Citing the beginning of Kant's *Idea for a Universal History*, Lyotard emphasizes Kant's view of necessity (i.e., nature's genius) for a Newton and Kepler to emerge and rewrite the history of mankind: "But if the idea of a universal history is an idea of the imagination, then Kepler and Newton, who on account of this idea fabricate a fiction of the universal history, would have to be geniuses. They would not 'explicate' this idea but demonstrate it without referring it back to a concept." *Der Enthusiasmus*, 94.

21. "Namely, that it is in the power of an author of the world to ensure that man should always conform to the moral laws. But this presupposes a conception of freedom and of nature—of which latter alone we can think an external author—that implies an insight into the supersensible substrate of nature and its identity with what is rendered possible in the world by causality through freedom, but such insight far exceeds that of our reason." Kant, *K.d.U.*, 411.

CHAPTER 9. TRADITION: A MATTER OF *BILDUNG* IN NOVALIS

1. Novalis, fragment 2722, in "Fragmente der letzten Jahre,1799-1800," *Gesammelte Werke*, ed. Carl Seelig, vol. 4 (Heerliberg-Zürich: Bühl, 1946), 231. (Hereafter, I refer to this edition with the abbreviation *GW*).

2. Hans-Georg Gadamer, *Wahrheit und Methode* (Tübingen: Mohr, 1975), 9.

3. Novalis, fragment 2392, "Fragmente der letzten Jahre," *GW*, 4: 163.

4. Gadamer, *Wahrheit und Methode*, 9.

5. Fragment 1600, "Allgemeines Brouillon," *GW*, 3: 244.

6. Fragment 2093, "Allgemeines Brouillon," *GW*, 4: 57. "Man muß die Wahrheit über-all vergegenwärtigen—überall *repraesentieren* (im tätigen, produzierenden Sinn) können." [One has to be able to make the truth present everywhere—to be able to *represent* it everywhere (in the active, productive sense).]

7. Novalis, fragment 2416, ibid., 167.

8. "The creative spark of the metaphor does not spring from the presentation of two images, that is, of two signifiers equally actualized. It flashes between two signifiers one of which has taken the place of the other in the signifying chain, the occulted signifier remaining present through its (metonymic) connexion with the rest of the chain." Jacques Lacan, "Agency of the Letter in the Unconscious," in *Ecrits. A Selection*, trans. Alan Sheridan (New York: Norton, 1977), 157.

9. See Gadamer on Hegel in *Wahrheit und Methode*, 10 ff.

10. "To recognize properties of the self in the alien, to feel at home in it, is the basic move of the spirit whose being is nothing but a return to itself from having been other [*aus dem Anderssein*]." Gadamer, *Wahrheit und Methode*, 11.

11. Fragment 1684, "Das allgemeine Brouillon ," *GW*, 3: 259.

12. Fragment 1900, "Das allgemeine Brouillon," *GW*, 4: 9.

13. Fragment 1600, ibid., 3: 244.

14. Fragment 1776, ibid., 284.

15. Fragment 1601, ibid., 244-45.

16. Fragment 2069, ibid., 4: 51.

17. Fragment 908, "Fragmente des Jahres 1798," *GW*, 3: 53.

18. Fragment 1836, "Das allgemeine Brouillon," *GW*, 3: 304.

19. Fragment 73, "Blütenstaub," *GW*, 2: 25-26.

20. Fragment 1894, "Das allgemeine Brouillon," *GW*, 3: 320.

21. A careful study of the language of Novalis' fragments will reveal the numerous, nearly verbatim borrowings that Benjamin employed in his own ideas and writings.

22. Walter Benjamin, *The Origin of German Tragic Drama*, trans. John Osborne (London: NLB, 1977), 229.

23. Fragment 319, "Philosophische Studien," *GW*, 2: 153.

24. "Rede über die Mythologie," in *Friedrich Schlegel, Kritische Ausgabe seiner Werke*, ed. Ernst Behler, vol. 2 (München: Schöningh, 1958), 312 f.

CHAPTER 10. THE HIEROGLYPHIC NATURE OF TRADITION

1. Philippe Lacoue-Labarthe and Jean-Luc Nancy, *The Literary Absolute. The Theory of Literature in German Romanticism*, trans. Philip Barnard and Cheryl Lester (Albany: State University of New York Press, 1988), 15.

2. "Romantic poetry sets out to penetrate the essence of poiesy, in which the literary thing produces the truth of production in itself, and thus . . . the truth of the production *of itself,* of autopoiesy." Ibid., 12.

3. These references to Novalis I owe to Alice Kuzniar's article "Reassessing Romantic Reflexivity," *The Germanic Review* 63, no. 2 (1988). Kuzniar traces a similar but very brief argument of the self being split in language. However, I do not share her implied post-structuralist view that the self as subjectivity does not exist prior to language. Such a view is blind to the cognitive ground of the body and feeling. She is mistaken in her assumption that "the subject as split and mutable" cannot "endure" (84) in his/her subjectivity. Novalis's notion of the subjective "sphere" imports the unconscious mind for the production of sense; the unconscious does not change, it renders the affective permanence of subjectivity. The subject may not become fully conscious of his/her self, but s/he can become conscious of his/her feelings and ground them in remembrance. Kuzniar's approach to Novalis limits her explanations. It does not go beyond a close reading of the text to a theory of meaning or experience that involves the human psyche. Her work is barely informed by psychoanalytic insights into the historical structure of the mind.

4. Novalis, "Monolog," in *Schriften,* ed. Richard Samuel, et al., vol. 2 (Stuttgart: Kohlhammer, 1981), 672–73.

5. Novalis, fragment 1093, "Fragmente des Jahres 1798," *GW,* 3: 101.

6. *Hymnen an die Nacht* (Athenaeum-Version), in *Gedichte. Die Lehrlinge zu Sais,* ed. Johannes Mahr (Stuttgart: Reclam, 1984), 156.

7. Given the hermeneutic situation required for animating the hieroglyph, I differ essentially from Azade Seyhan's interpretation of Novalis's "hieroglyphistics" as "second order semiology" which she adapted from Roland Barthes's analysis of myth; see esp. pp. 40–41 of her book *Representation and Its Discontents. The Critical Legacy of German Romanticism* (Los Angeles: California UP, 1992). Myth can precisely not be the vehicle to explain the hieroglyph because Novalis, and subsequently Benjamin, associate it with allegory, the breaker of the totality of myth. Hieroglyphs are fragmentary remnants of a historic cultural context which is lost, and, in avoidance of a new myth, the poet-historian is to use them to create a "chaotic" image (Benjamin's "dialectical image") of one's historical experience. Seyhan posits the hieroglyph as parallel to language which, in fact, it is not; as signifier it only facilitates the construction of a new, that is, poetic language. If Barthes claims that myth is based on a preexisting system of signification, then hieroglyphics is not based on such a system; hence, in a presumed second order it cannot function as a "new signifier or image in the symbolic realm of myth." Instead, hieroglyphistics, refers to the subject's retroactive (*nachträglich*), imaginative construction of sense, based on an emotional projection. Although the title of Seyhan's book suggests a Freudian slant on the topic, Seyhan never makes reference to Freud nor uses psychoanalytic theory to illuminate the concepts of representation and the self. Yet, Seyhan makes a strong case for the temporality of sense and being; she leaves off where I start with the necessity of tradition for recreating the sense of being.

8. Novalis, fragment 290, "Philosophische Studien," *GW,* 2: 129.

9. Ibid., 122, fragment 270.

10. Ibid., 121, fragment 263.

11. Ibid., 137, fragment 297.

12. Gezá von Molnár, *Romantic Vision, Ethical Context. Novalis and Artistic Autonomy* (Minneapolis: Minnesota University Press, 1987), 51.

13. Ibid.

14. Cf. Jochen Hörisch, *Die fröhliche Wissenschaft der Poesie* (Frankfurt: Suhrkamp, 1976), 185–87.

15. Hörisch works off of Novalis's *Fichte-Studien*, which I, for the most part, neglect here, since it is the theoretical specimen of Novalis that has received the most attention from scholars. Hörisch emphasizes the "ordo inversus" of feeling and reflection in Novalis's theory of subjectivity; subjectivity as opposed to the subject implies the formation and dissolution of images that reflect the Ego's reality of feeling. In the intuition, the analytical Ego changes places between image and being (feeling). The Ego can only posit itself through an image because as pure feeling it cannot posit its being. Hence the object serves the analytical Ego as stimulus for the formation of an image not of the object at hand, but of the feeling of the Ego's being. The object is here only a medium. Cf. Hörisch, *Die fröhliche Wissenschaft*, 70–88.

16. Novalis as cited in von Molnár, *Romantic Vision*, 53. Von Molnár translates "wollen" with "willing", which dissimulates the meaning with respect to the complexity of the mind by giving it a metaphysical connotation of free will. By contrast, Novalis acknowledges an interdependence of body and mind numerous times in citing, esp. in the *Fichte-Studien*, the notion of drive, "der Trieb Ich zu Seyn;" cf. fragments 326, 330, 336, "Philosophische Studien," *GW*, 2: 161, 164, 167; and, "Trieb ist Tätigkeit auf eine bestimmte Art;" [drive is an activity of a special kind] ibid., 95, fragment 195. The Ego can only be recognized by its actions and by its lack: "Ich bedeutet jenes negativ zu erkennende Absolute, das nach aller Abstraktion übrig bleibt. Was nur durch Handeln erkannt werden kann und was sich durch ewigen Mangel realisiert." [Ego means to recognize the absolute as negative which remains after all abstraction. What can only be recognized by acting on it and what realizes itself through an eternal lack.] ibid., 173, fragment 342.

17. Ibid., 158, fragment 270.

18. Ibid., 159, fragment 325.

19. Fragment 989, "Fragmente des Jahres 1798," *GW*, 3: 72.

20. Fragment 2002, "Das allgemeine Brouillon,"*GW*, 4: 39.

21. Fragment 2683, "Fragmente der letzten Jahre,1799–1800," *GW*, 4: 220.

22. Ibid., fragment 2685.

23. "If the object becomes allegorical under the gaze of melancholy, if melancholy causes life to flow out of it . . . then it is exposed to the allegorist, it is unconditionally in his power. That is to say it is now quite incapable of emanating any meaning or significance of its own. (. . .) In his hands, the object becomes something different; . . . and for him, it becomes a key to the realm of hidden knowledge; and he reveres it as the emblem of this." Benjamin, *The Origin of German Tragic Drama*, 183–84.

24. Ibid., 166; translation modified.

25. Fragment 316, "Philosophische Studien," *GW*, 2:151.

26. Winfried Menninghaus, "Die frühromantische Theorie von Zeichen und Metapher," *German Quarterly* 62, no. 1 (1989): 52.

27. Ibid.

28. Ibid.

29. Fragment 878, "Fragmente des Jahres 1798," *GW*, 3: 38.

30. Fragment 326, "Philosophische Studien," *GW*, 2: 161.

31. Fragment 2069, "Das allgemeine Brouillon,"*GW*, 4: 51.

32. Novalis, fragment 341, "Philosophische Studien,"*GW*, 2: 170.

33. Winfried Menninghaus, *Walter Benjamins Theorie der Sprachmagie* (Frankfurt: Suhrkamp, 1980), 94. Emphasis mine. In this book, Menninghaus lists many correspondences between Benjamin's philosophy of language and the reflections of Novalis on representation and translation. The translatability of all languages is originally Novalis's idea, not Benjamin's. To date, Menninghaus is the only author that uncovers the roots of Benjamin's

thought in the philosophical fragments of early German Romanticism. Yet, his work suffers from the limitations of a purely intertextual approach rather than an interdisciplinary study that could further the debates over culture or historical agency in the humanities. The occasional references to contemporary theories of the sign do not make up for Menninghaus's tendency toward a neopositivist presentation of his research.

34. Novalis, fragments 2722 & 2724, "Fragmente der letzten Jahre, 1799–1800," *GW*, 4: 231–32.

35. Novalis, fragment 34, "Blütenstaub," *GW*, 2: 18.

36. Fragment 930, "Fragmente des Jahres 1798," *GW*, 3: 57.

37. Fragment 1615, "Das allgemeine Brouillon," *GW*, 3: 247.

38. Novalis, fragment 811, "Fragmente des Jahres 1798," *GW*, 3: 24.

39. Novalis, fragment 813, ibid.

40. Ibid., 55, fragment 914.

41. Novalis, fragment 530, "Philosophische Studien," *GW*, 2: 231.

42. Fragment 2715, "Das allgemeine Brouillon," *GW*, 4: 230.

43. Novalis, *Schriften*, ed. Richard Samuel, et al., vol. 3 (Stuttgart: Kohlhammer, 1960), 123–24.

44. Fragment 883, "Fragmente des Jahres 1798, *GW*, 3: 39.

45. Benjamin, "Über das mimetische Vermögen," in *Angelus Novus*, 96–97.

Chapter 11. Building the Memory from Signs

1. According to Jacques Lacan, the split between *being* and *language* is the basis and cause of the desire for the original physical experience of being whole. This experience of the "real," he says, can never be represented in language, it does not exist in representation.

2. Gadamer, *Wahrheit und Methode*, 279.

3. "The carrier of tradition is not that manuscript as a piece of times past but the continuity of memory. Through this continuity, tradition becomes part of one's own world and thus that which tradition communicates can come to language immediately." Ibid., 368.

4. Ibid., 340.

5. Cf. Lacan, "The Unconscious and Repetition," in *The Four Fundamentals of Psychoanalysis* (New York, London: Norton, 1981), 32: "Ontically, then, the unconscious is the elusive—but we are beginning to circumscribe it in a structure, a temporal structure, which, it can be said, has never been articulated." What is articulated, though, is the desire as other that is expressed in the repetition of meaning formation, or in perceptions of endless false identities, mis-takes, that are conditioned by the metonymic nature of language, hence the "rhythmic structure" of temporary arrests of desire in perception and the compulsion to abandon the perceived sign in a frustration of the expected congruence of self and other. From this point of view, of the thwarted illusion of a being (whole) in language, Lacan expanded on the Freudian concept of desire in terms of a "manque-à-être, a want-to-be."

6. Cf. Lacan: "If I speak of being and the letter, if I distinguish the other and the Other, it is because Freud shows me that they are the terms to which must be referred the effects of resistance and transference against which . . . I have done equal battle. (. . .) If the symptom is a metaphor, it is not a metaphor to say so, any more than to say that man's desire is a metonymy. For the symptom *is* a metaphor . . . as desire *is* a metonymy." "The Agency of the letter in the unconscious or reason since Freud," in *Écrits*, 175.

7. "If we try to understand a historical phenomenon from the historical distance which determines our hermeneutical situation we are always already subjected to the effects of operative history (*Wirkungsgeschichte*). It predetermines what shows itself to us as worthy of questioning and as an object of investigation." Gadamer, *Wahrheit und Methode*, 284.

8. By comparison, Gadamer's use of the symbol implies that it can represent the individual past of the language user for whom a sign, besides referring to something else that is not present, can become a symbol. The symbol has a double function. As a sign it refers to an object but is at the same time a signifier for the subject's past which determines the signified. This approaches Lacan's theory of language that is based on a double function of signs with the addition that the signified can also act as a signifier in the unconscious. This suggests that by symbol Gadamer does not mean what Ernst Cassirer has theorized as the expression of all forms of life, given the premise that there exists a natural and not merely a conventional connection between the symbol and its object: "First and foremost meaning must be explained in terms of being; for being, or substance, is the most universal category which links and binds together truth and reality. A word could not 'mean' a thing if there were not at least a partial identity between the two." Cassirer, *An Essay on Man* (1944; New Haven: Yale University Press, 1979), 112. This definition of meaning is radically different from one based on a theory of displacement that tries to account for historical finality and change.

9. Cf. W. R. Bion, *Second Thoughts. Selected Papers on Psychoanalysis.* (Northvale, NJ: (Jason Aronson, 1967); see "A Theory of Thinking," 110–19.

10. Serge Leclaire, *Écrits pour la psychanalyse*, vol. 1 (Paris: Arcanes, 1996), 146.

11. Lacan points to the Surrealist school that has shown us "that any conjunction of two signifiers would be equally sufficient to constitute a metaphor, except for the additional requirement of the greatest possible disparity of the images signified, needed for the poetic spark, or in other words for metaphoric creation to take place." "The Agency of the letter," *Écrits*, 156.

12. "Here the motion of determining [the sense of the sentence] is not tied to the firm basis of the subject 'in which it runs to an fro.' The subject is not determined as this as well as that, in one respect such and in other respect such. That would be the manner of representational thought, not of the manner of conception (*des Begriffes*). In conceptual thinking, the natural move of determination to reach beyond the subject of the sentence is inhibited and the movement of representation suffers a reverse blow. Starting with the subject as if it stayed in its base position [thus grounding the sentence] (*zum Grunde liegen bliebe*), the determining move rather finds it transformed in the predicate and thus unfounded [sublated] because the predicate is more likely the substance [of the sentence]." *Wahrheit und Methode*, 442; Gadamer is citing Hegel here to use his refutation of specular philosophy that treats the sentence as judgment, as well as to demonstrate the difference between referential-representational thinking and constructive-conceptual thinking in understanding: "The form of the sentence thus destroys itself in that the speculative sentence does not make a statement about something but in that it causes the unity [of God in Gadamer's example] to represent itself in its conception." Gadamer, *Wahrheit und Methode*, 442.

13. Ibid., 439.

14. Ibid.

15. Ibid.

16. "Explain" and "plane" are joined in the same etymological ground of Latin "planare," to flatten out.

17. Gadamer, *Wahrheit und Methode*, 382.

18. Ibid., 389.

19. Ibid., 381.

20. Ibid., 323.

21. Cf. Lacan, "The Agency of the letter in the unconscious," *Écrits*, 161.

22. Lacan, "The subversion of the subject and the dialectic of desire in the Freudian unconscious," *Écrits*, 309.

23. Lacan, "The signification of the phallus," *Écrits*, 286.

24. Cf. Lacan, "The mirror stage as formative of the function of the I," *Écrits.*

25. Lacan, "The subversion of the subject and the dialectic of desire," *Écrits*, 312.

26. Lacan, "Subversion of the subject," 312.

27. Ibid., 316.

28. Ibid.

29. The relation of the subject to the signifier in articulation is one that prevents a representation of being because it "kills" the I of articulation: "Being of non-being, that is how *I* as subject comes on the scene, conjugated with the double aporia of a true survival that is abolished by knowledge of itself, and by a discourse in which it is death that sustains existence." Ibid., 300.

30. Ibid., 312.

31. Lacan, "The signification of the phallus," *Écrits*, 284.

Chapter 12. Woman as the Allegory of Modernity

1. Benjamin, "Das Kunstwerk im Zeitalter seiner technischen Reproduzierbarkeit," in *Illuminationen* (Frankfurt: Suhrkamp, 1980), 148.

2. See, for example, Luce Irigaray as quoted by Alice Jardine, "Theories of the Feminine: Kristeva," *Enclitic*, 4: no. 2 (Fall 1980): 5–15.

3. Cf. Benjamin's chapter on "Allegorie und Trauerspiel, " in *Ursprung des deutschen Trauerspiels*, 138–67; or his work on allegory as commodity in the nineteenth century, *Charles Baudelaire* (Frankfurt: Suhrkamp, 1974).

4. Benjamin, *Das Passagenwerk* (Frankfurt: Suhrkamp, 1983), 612.

5. Ibid., 613.

6. "Due to the new production techniques that produce imitations, *appearance* [i.e., illusions] now adheres to the commodities." Benjamin, *Charles Baudelaire*, 164.

7. "Whereas in the symbol destruction is idealized, and the transfigured face of nature is fleetingly revealed in the light of redemption, in allegory the observer is confronted with the *facies hippocratica* of history as a petrified, primordial landscape." Benjamin, *The Origin of German Tragic Drama*, trans. John Osborne (London: NLB, 1977), 166.

8. Ibid.

9. Benjamin, *Passagenwerk*, 130.

10. Ibid.

11. Cited in Craig Owens, "The Discourse of Others: Feminists and Postmodernism," in *The Anti-Aesthetic: Essays on Postmodern Culture*, ed. Hal Foster (Port Townsend: Bay Press, 1983), 70.

12. Freud assumed "a primal repression [*Urverdrängung*], an initial phase of repression which consists in denying mental representation [*Vorstellungs-Repräsentanz*] access to consciousness. This is accompanied by a fixation; from this moment on, the representation concerned remains unchanged together with the drive that is attached to it." *Standard Edition*, trans. James Strachey (London: Hogarth Press, 1957), 14 : 140.

13. *Passagenwerk*, 131.

14. *Origin of the German Tragic Drama*, 176.

15. *Charles Baudelaire*, 162.

16. Ibid., 167.

17. Ibid., 163.

CHAPTER 13. BENJAMIN'S HIEROGLYPHS

1. Cf. Paul de Man, "The Rhetoric of Temporality, " in *Blindness and Insight*. (Minneapolis: University of Minnesota Press, 1983).

2. Cf. his article "The Structure of Allegorical Desire," in *October* 12 (1980).

3. "[W]ith its poeticality defined as structure superintended upon metonymy, allegory initiates and continually revivifies its own desire, a desire born of its own structuring. Every metaphor is always a little metonymic because in order to have a metaphor, there must be a structure and where there is a structure, there is already piety and nostalgia for the lost origin through which the structure is thought. Every metaphor is a metonymy of its own origin, its structure thrust into time by its very structurality. (...) In terms of literary response, the structuring of the text holds out the promise of a meaning that it will also perpetually defer, an image of hermeneutic totality martyred and consecrated by and as the poetical." Fineman, "The Structure of Allegorical Desire," 59.

4. Hans-Georg Gadamer, *Wahrheit und Methode*. 4th ed. (Tübingen: Mohr, 1975), 293.

5. A note to Jacques Derrida's critique of writing might be of illustrative value here because what he, in essence, inscribed in his *Of Grammatology* (Baltimore: Johns Hopkins University Press, 1974), is that the age of the sign is theological. This view aligns him with the Benjaminian view of history, encompassing 5000 years of *Jetztzeit*, which implies that the past is always present in the signifying effect of a sign.

6. Jean Laplanche and Serge Leclaire, "The Unconscious: A Psychoanalytic Study," *Yale French Studies* 48 (1973): 118–75.

7. Ibid., 150.

8. Ibid., 167.

9. Werner Hamacher, "The Word *Wolke* —If it Is One," in *Benjamin's Ground. New Readings of Walter Benjamin*, ed. Rainer Nägele (Detroit: Wayne State University Press, 1988), 155.

10. My translation of language as canon of nonsensuous similarities.

11. Cf. Nägele's introduction: "The subject [in Benjamin's texts] appears not as creator, but as *Kreatur*, as creature; not as beautiful *Gestalt* of the ego ideal, but as the fragile tortured body." Nägele foregrounds a different concept of history, one that is congruous with Jewish theology, and refers to both as models that "structure the political unconscious that Benjamin's thoughts attempt to outline," clarifying them psychoanalytically as castration, "its symbolic representation as circumcision in the constitution of the subject and of the social community." *Benjamin's Ground*, 13.

12. In Benjamin's text, the books' insides are compared to the womb where colors were "turning into a violet that seemed to stem from the interior of an animal for slaughter." Benjamin, cited in Hamacher, "The Word *Wolke*," 148.

13. Susan Buck-Morss, "Aesthetics and Anaesthetics: Walter Benjamin's Artwork Essay Reconsidered," *October* 62 (Fall 1992): 5.

14. Ibid., 13.

15. "If it is however true that the mimetic genius was a life determining power of the ancients, then it is not hard to imagine that the newborn was conceived of as in full possession of this gift, and especially, as perfectly assimilated to the cosmic form of being." "Über das mimetische Vermögen," in *Illuminationen,* 97.

16. Ibid., 98–99.

17. Lacan, "Agency of the letter," 167; this passage is interesting not for what it says but for how Lacan says it. By using a signified, a reference—the Bible—as a metaphorical signifier for signifying the meaning of desire—to return home—he demonstrates the necessity of a history that through the New Testament and its interpretation established a tradition of linguistic reference in the allegories of Christianity.

18. Benjamin, *The Origin of German Tragic Drama,* 69.

CHAPTER 14. THE MELANCHOLIA OF IDEAS

1. Jacques Derrida,"White Mythology: Metaphor in the Text of Philosophy," in *Margins of Philosophy* (Chicago: Chicago University Press, 1982), 269.

2. Derrida, "White Mythology," 244.

3. Benjamin claims the congruence of natural history with the history of signification in various places; but for signification he stresses in particular the death of nature which is what allegory represents in the "facies hippocratica" of history; cf.: "That worldly, historical breadth which Görres and Creuzer ascribe to allegorical intention is, as natural history, as the earliest history of signifying or intention, dialectical in character." *Origin of German Tragic Drama,* 166. In this same passage Benjamin goes on to make the connection between man's subjection to nature, that is, to mortality and the significance of the individual's biographical historicity.

4. Derrida, "Scribble (writing power)," *Yale French Studies* 58 (1979): 121.

5. Ibid., 123.

6. "Even the story of the life of Christ supported *the movement from history to nature which is the basis of allegory.*" *Origin of German Tragic Drama,* 182. Emphasis added.

7. "From the simplest of stages onward the pictogram is scribbled by an entire rhetoric. Things that had no bodily shape were represented by 'other significant character': an-Indian-kneeling-before-a-priest signified 'I confess,' three-heads-crowned stood for Trinity." Derrida, "Scribble," 124.

8. Ibid., 126.

9. Benjamin, "Über den Begriff der Geschichte," in *Illuminationen,* 252; the German word *Verabredung* is actually closer to the meaning of meeting, date, or appointment than to "agreement" as Harry Zohn translates it in *Illuminations,* ed. Hannah Arendt (New York: Schocken, 1969); but the main verb *reden* in the lexical composite *Verabredung* does refer to speech and discussion.

10. Ibid.

11. Cf. Lacan: "It is among the figures of style, or tropes—from which the verb 'to find' (*trouver*) comes to us—that this name [the name of the 'properly signifying function of language depicted in language'] is found. The name is *metonymy.*" "The Agency of the letter," 156. Although Lacan, not being overly concerned with the concept of history for a theory of meaning does not address allegory, his analysis of metonymy as the displacement of the signifier and the subject structurally supports the textual arrangement in the readability of allegory.

12. Derrida, "Scribble," 130.

13. Ibid., 133.

14. Ibid., 134.

15. Ibid., 136.

16. Benjamin, *Origin of German Tragic Drama*, 179.

17. Ibid., 201.

18. Ibid., 52.

19. Benjamin appreciated Brecht's didactic plays for an embodiment of figures of wisdom, a wisdom that teaches one's survival of death: "Thus, if you want to overcome death, you will overcome it once you know death and are in accord with it." *Baadener Lehrstück vom Einverständnis*, cited in Rainer Nägele, *Theater, Theory, Speculation. Walter Benjamin and the Scenes of Modernity* (Baltimore: Johns Hopkins University Press, 1991), 61; I owe this parallel of Brecht and Benjamin to Nägele.

20. Benjamin affirmatively cites the influence of the tradition of esoteric meaning on baroque allegory, because it refocuses the realm of ideas on the material world and the body. *Eso-teric* means inside the earth as opposed to *exo-teric* referring to an outside of the world and body. But esoteric meanings only present themselves to a melancholic speculation, the longing for being connected with an other, the mother or lost natural state: "Everything saturnine points down into the depths of the earth. . . . For the melancholic the inspirations of mother earth dawn from the night of contemplation like treasures from the interior of the earth; the lightning-flash of intuition is unknown to him. The earth, previously important only as the cold, dry element acquires the full wealth of its esoteric meaning in a scientific reflection of Ficinus [the Renaissance scholar on melancholy]." *Origin of German Tragic Drama*, 152–53.

21. Cf. Yosef Hayim Yerushalmi, *Zakhor: Jewish History and Jewish Memory*. (New York: Schocken, 1982).

22. Jacques Derrida, *Archive Fever. A Freudian Impression*, trans. Eric Prenowitz (Chicago: Chicago University Press, 1996), 35.

23. Freud cited in Derrida, *Archive Fever*, 35.

24. Benjamin, *Origin*, 179.

25. Ibid., 175.

26. Ibid., 229. The allegorist's knowledge is not firmly grounded in things; to his melancholy eye the things "lie before it as enigmatic allegorical references," and as things "they continue to be dust."

27. The idea behind knowledge as evil is the separation of spirituality from materiality after the fall into history. Without a link to the sacred, spirituality means nothing and arbitrarily attaches itself again to materiality, "but here soulless materiality," because "consciousness is their illusory synthesis, in which the genuine synthesis, that of life, is imitated," *Origin*, 230. Lacan expressed the same "satanic" realm of psychological knowledge with the concept of the Ego's "méconnaissance" as it mistakes its representation for its self.

28. "In his [the writer's] hand the object [the sign] becomes something quite different; through it he speaks of something quite different and for him it becomes a key to the realm of hidden knowledge [the knowledge of history]; and he reveres it as the emblem of this. This is what determines the character of allegory as a form of writing. It is a schema; and as a schema it is an object of knowledge, but it is not securely possessed until it becomes a fixed schema: at one and the same time a fixed image and a fixing sign [i.e., the sign of history]." Benjamin, *Origin*, 184.

29. Jacques Derrida, *Specters of Marx*, trans. Peggy Kamuf (New York: Routledge, 1994), xviii.

30. Cf. Benjamin: "For all the wisdom of the melancholic is subject to the nether world; it is secured by immersion in the life of creaturely things, and it hears nothing of the voice of revelation." *Origin*, 152.

31. Ibid., 157.

32. Ibid., 35.

33. Slavoj Žižek, *The Sublime Object of Ideology* (London: Verso, 1989).

34. Ibid., 61–62.

35. "*Jede Sprache teilt sich selbst mit.* (...) was an einem geistigen Wesen mitteilbar ist, *ist* seine Sprache. Auf diesem 'ist' (gleich 'ist unmittelbar') beruht alles.—Nicht, was an einem geistigen Wesen mitteilbar ist, *erscheint* am klarsten in seiner Sprache . . . , sondern dieses Mitteil*bare* ist unmittelbar die Sprache selbst. Oder: die Sprache eines geistiges Wesens ist unmittelbar dasjenige, was an ihm mitteilbar ist." [*Each language communicates itself.* (...) What can be communicated of a mental essence *is* its language. Everything depends on the 'is' (i.e., the immediacy of the word 'is'). What is communicable of a mental essence does not [just] *appear* most clearly in its language . . . , but the communic*ability* as such is the immediacy of language itself. Or, the language of a mental essence is immediately that which is communicable about it], "Über die Sprache überhaupt und über die Sprache des Menschen," in *Angelus Novus*, 11 (Benjamin's emphasis).

36. Benjamin, "Epistemo-Critical Prologue," in *Origin*, 36.

37. *Archive Fever*, 87.

38. Benjamin, *Origin*, 34.

39. Ibid.

40. Ibid., 36–37.

41. "In the field of allegorical intuition the image is a fragment, a ruin. Its beauty as a symbol evaporates when the light of divine learning falls upon it. The false appearance of totality is extinguished. For the eidos disappears, the simile ceases to exist, and the cosmos it contained shrivels up. The dry rebuses which remain contain an insight, which is still available to the confused investigator." *Origin*, 176.

42. Nägele, *Theater, Theory, Speculation*, 132.

43. "Every elemental utterance of the creature acquires significance from its allegorical existence, and everything allegorical acquires emphasis *from the elemental aspect of the world of the senses.*" Benjamin, *Origin*, 228. Emphasis added.

44. Nägele, *Theater, Theory, Speculation*, 130; Nägele cites Goethe here in his critique of the concept of *Anschauung* which he deliberately leaves in the German so that it does not absorb the unconscious perceptions in imagination that are at stake in the English translation of Kant's concept of "intuition." Goethe serves Nägele for a distinction between symbol and allegory. *Anschauung*, which I would translate here as "visualization," belongs to the realm of the symbol and suggests a conscious sense of the body as a whole. *Anschauung* supports the conception of the aesthetic realm as reconciliation of the senses and split spheres of human existence, because, in the beautiful, the subject knows herself as one in the symbolic unity with God. Nägele's point is to demonstrate Benjamin's critical and philosophical resistance to such a view, and use, of art in modernity. Excavating allegory from the sixteenth and seventeenth centuries as an art form, with the dead and dismembered human body as its subject matter, enabled Benjamin to insist on the physical immanence of history and sense.

45. Derrida, *Archive Fever*, 17.

Bibliography

Adorno, Theodor. *Negative Dialectics.* Translated by E. B. Ashton. New York: Continuum, 1973.

———. *Ästhetische Theorie.* In *Gesammelte Schriften.* Vol. 7. Frankfurt: Suhrkamp, 1970.

Atwood, George, and Robert Stolorow. *Structures of Subjectivity: Explorations in Psychoanalytic Phenomenology.* London: Erlbaum Associates, 1984.

Bakhtin, Mikhail. "Forms of Time and of the Chronotope in the Novel: Notes towards a Historical Poetics." In *The Dialogic Imagination.* Austin: University of Texas Press, 1981.

Bäumler, Alfred. *Kants Kritik der Urteilkraft. Ihre Geschichte und Systematik. (=Das Irrationalitätsproblem in der Ästhetik und Logik des 18. Jahrhunderts bis zur Kritik der Urteilskraft*). Halle: Niemeyer, 1923.

Benjamin, Walter. *Angelus Novus. Ausgewählte Schriften 2.* Frankfurt: Suhrkamp, 1988.

———. *Das Passagenwerk.* Frankfurt: Suhrkamp, 1983.

———. *Ursprung des deutschen Trauerspiels.* Edited by Rolf Tiedemann. Frankfurt: Suhrkamp, 1982.

———. *Illuminationen.* Frankfurt: Suhrkamp, 1980.

———. *Reflections.* Edited by Peter Demetz, translated by Edmund Jephcott. New York: Harcourt, 1978.

———. *The Origin of German Tragic Drama.* Translated by John Osborne. London: New Left Books, 1977.

———. *Charles Baudelaire.* Frankfurt: Suhrkamp, 1974.

———. *Gesammelte Schriften.* Edited by Rolf Tiedemann and Hermann Schweppenhäuser. Frankfurt: Suhrkamp, 1972.

Bion, W.R. *Second Thoughts. Selected Papers on Psycho-Analysis.* Northvale, N. J., London: Jason Aronson, 1967.

Böhme, Hartmut, and Gernot Böhme. *Das Andere der Vernunft.* Frankfurt: Suhrkamp, 1985.

Buck-Morss, Susan. "Aesthetics and Anaesthetics: Walter Benjamin's Artwork Essay Reconsidered." *October* 62 (Fall 1992): 3–41.

Cassirer, Ernst. *An Essay on Man.* 1944. New Haven: Yale University Press, 1979.

Costa Lima, Luiz. *Control of the Imaginary. Reason and Imagination in Modern Times.* Translated by Ronald Sousa. Minneapolis: University of Minnesota Press, 1988.

De Man, Paul. "Walter Benjamin's *The Task of the Translator*." In *The Resistance to Theory.* Minneapolis: University of Minnesota Press, 1986.

———. "Phenomenality and Materiality in Kant." In *Hermeneutics.* Edited by Gary Shapiro and Alan Sica. Amherst: University of Massachusetts Press, 1984.

———. *Blindness and Insight.* Minneapolis: University of Minnesota Press, 1983.

Derrida, Jacques. *Archive Fever. A Freudian Impression.* Translated by Eric Prenowitz. Chicago: University of Chicago Press, 1996.

———. *Specters of Marx.* Translated by Peggy Kamuf. New York: Routledge, 1994.

———. *The Postcard.* Translated by Alan Bass. Chicago: University of Chicago Press, 1987.

———. "White Mythology: Metaphor in the Text of Philosophy." In *Margins of Philosophy.* Translated by Alan Bass. Chicago: University of Chicago Press, 1982.

———. "Scribble." *Yale French Studies* 58 (1979): 117–47.

———. "The Parergon." *October* 9 (1978): 3–40.

———. *Of Grammatology.* Translated by Gayatri Spivak. Baltimore: Johns Hopkins University Press, 1974.

Engell, James. *Creative Imagination: From Enlightenment to Romanticism.* Cambridge: Harvard University Press, 1981.

Fineman, Joel. "The Structure of Allegorical Desire." *October* 12 (1980): 47–86.

Fenves, Peter. *A Peculiar Fate. Metaphysics and World History in Kant.* Ithaca: Cornell University Press, 1991.

Frank, Manfred. *Der kommende Gott.* Frankfurt: Suhrkamp, 1982.

Freud, Sigmund. *Standard Edition.* London: Hogarth Press, 1953–1974.

———. *Aus den Anfängen der Psychoanalyse. Briefe and Wilhelm Fliess, Abhandlungen und Notizen aus den Jahren 188 –1902.* London: Imago Press, 1950.

———. *Gesammelte Werke.* London: Imago Press, 1948.

Gadamer, Hans-Georg. *Wahrheit und Methode.* 4th ed. Tübingen: Mohr, 1975.

Grimminger, Rolf. *Die Ordnung, das Chaos und die Kunst.* Frankfurt: Suhrkamp, 1986.

Habermas, Jürgen. *Der philosophische Diskurs der Moderne.* Frankfurt: Suhrkamp, 1985.

Hamacher, Werner. "The Word *Wolke*—If It Is One." In *Benjamin's Ground. New Readings of Walter Benjamin.* Edited by Rainer Nägele. Detroit: Wayne State University Press, 1988.

Heidegger, Martin. *Sein und Zeit.* Tübingen: Klostermann, 1962.

———. "Zeit und Sein." In *Zur Sache des Denkens.* Tübingen: Niemeyer, 1962.

Jardine, Alice. "Theories of the Feminine: Kristeva." *Enclitic,* 4, no. 2 (Fall 1980): 5–15.

Irigaray, Luce. *Speculum of the Other Woman.* Translated by Gillian Gill. Ithaca: Cornell University Press, 1985.

Jameson, Frederic. *The Political Unconscious.* Ithaca: Cornell University Press, 1981.

Jauss, Hans-Robert. *Ästhetische Erfahrung und literarische Hermeneutik.* 2d ed. Frankfurt: Suhrkamp, 1984.

Kamper, Dietmar. *Zur Soziologie der Imagination.* München: Hanser, 1984.

Kant, Immanuel. *Kritik der reinen Vernunft.* Edited by Wilhelm Weischedel. Vol. 1. Frankfurt: Suhrkamp,1982.

———. *Kritik der Urteilskraft.* Edited by Wilhelm Weischedel. Frankfurt: Suhrkamp, 1981.

———. *Allgemeine Naturgeschichte und Theorie des Himmels*. In *Vorkritische Schriften bis 1768*. Edited by Wilhelm Weischedel. Vol. 1. Frankfurt: Suhrkamp, 1977.

———. *Idee zu einer allgemeinen Geschichte in weltbürgerlicher Absicht*. In *Schriften zur Anthropologie, Geschichtsphilosophie, Politik und Pädagogik*. Edited by Wilhelm Weischedel. Frankfurt: Suhrkamp, 1977.

———. *Idea for a Universal History from a Cosmopolitan Point of View*. In *Kant. On History*. Edited and Translated by Lewis White Beck. New York: Macmillan, 1963.

———. *Critique of Judgment*. Translated by J. H. Bernard. New York: Hafner Press, 1951.

———. *Opus Postumum*. In *Kants Gesammelte Schriften*. Edited by Königliche Preußische Akademie der Wissenschaften. Vols. 21–22. Berlin, Leipzig: de Gruyter, 1900–1955.

Koch, Rainer. "Vom Mythos zum dialektischen Bild. Geschichtskritik und ästhetische Wahrheit bei Adorno/Horkheimer, Peter Weiss und Walter Benjamin." Ph.D. diss., University of Hannover, 1987/88.

Koselleck, Reinhart. *Vergangene Zukunft. Zur Semantik geschichtlicher Zeiten*. Frankfurt: Suhrkamp, 1979.

Kristeva, Julia. *New Maladies of the Soul*. Translated by Ross Guberman. New York: Columbia University Press, 1995.

———. *Black Sun. Depression and Melancholia*. Translated by Leon Roudiez. New York. Columbia University Press, 1989.

———. *Revolution in Poetic Language*. Translated by Leon Roudiez. New York: Columbia University Press, 1984.

Kuzniar, Alice. "Reassessing Romantic Reflexivity—The Case of Novalis." *The Germanic Review* 63, no. 2 (1988): 77–86.

Lacan, Jacques. *The Four Fundamentals of Psycho-analysis*. Translated by Alan Sheridan. New York: Norton, 1981.

———. *Écrits. A Selection*. Translated by Alan Sheridan. New York: Norton, 1977.

———. *Qu'est-ce que le structuralisme?* Paris: Seuil, 1968.

Lacoue-Labarthe, Philippe and Jean-Luc Nancy. *The Literary Absolute. The Theory of Literature in German Romanticism*. Translated by Philip Barnard and Cheryl Lester. Albany: State University of New York Press, 1988.

Laplanche, Jean, and Serge Leclaire. "The Unconscious: A Psychoanalytic Study." *Yale French Studies*, 48 (1973):118–75.

Leclaire, Serge. *Écrits pour la psychanalyse*. Vol. 1. Paris: Arcanes, 1996.

Lyotard, Jean-François. *Der Enthusiasmus: Kants Kritik der Geschichte*. Edited by Peter Engelmann. Wien: Passagen, 1988.

———. "The *Différend*, the Referent, and the Proper Name." *Diacritics* (Fall 1984): 4–14.

Marc, David. *Bonfire of the Humanities. Television, Subliteracy, and Long-term Memory Loss*. Syracuse: Syracuse University Press, 1995.

Menninghaus, Winfried. "Die frühromantische Theorie von Zeichen und Metapher." *German Quarterly* 62, no.1 (1989): 48–58.

———. *Walter Benjamins Theorie der Sprachmagie*. Frankfurt: Suhrkamp, 1980.

Molnár, Géza von. *Romantic Vision, Ethical Context. Novalis and Artistic Autonomy*. Minneapolis: University of Minnesota Press, 1987.

Nägele, Rainer. *Theater, Theory, Speculation. Walter Benjamin and the Scenes of Modernity*. Baltimore: Johns Hopkins University Press, 1991.

————, ed. *Benjamin's Ground. New Readings of Walter Benjamin.* Detroit: Wayne State University Press, 1988.

————. *Reading after Freud.* Baltimore: Johns Hopkins University Press, 1987.

Nancy, Jean-Luc. *The Inoperative Community.* Translated by Peter Connor, et al. Minneapolis: University of Minnesota Press, 1991.

Nietzsche, Friedrich. *Unzeitgemäße Betrachtungen.* München: Goldmann, 1964.

Novalis. *Schriften.* Edited by Richard Samuel, et al. 4 Vols. Stuttgart: Kohlhammer, 1960–1981.

————. *Gesammelte Werke.* Edited by Carl Seelig. Vols. 2–4. Herrliberg-Zürich: Bühl Verlag, 1946.

Peirce, Charles Sanders. *Collected Papers.* 8 Vols. Cambridge: Harvard University Press, 1931–1958.

Rauch, Angelika. "The I and the (M)other. Why the Ego's Narcissism Can be Exploited by the Media." *Literature and Psychology* 23, nos. 3/4 (1987): 27–37.

Rotter, Rainer. "Die Bestimmung der Aktualität bei Walter Benjamin." In *Die Gegenwart der Geschichte.* Stuttgart: Metzler, 1990.

Seyhan, Azade. *Representation and its Discontents. The Critical Legacy of German Romanticism.* Berkeley: University of California Press, 1992.

Skura, Meredith Ann. *The Literary Use of the Psychoanalytic Process.* New Haven: Yale University Press, 1981.

Taylor, Charles. *The Ethics of Authenticity.* Cambridge: Harvard University Press, 1992.

Volosinov, Valentin. *Marxismus und Sprachphilosophie.* Edited by Samuel Weber. Frankfurt: Ullstein, 1975.

Weber, Samuel. "The Foundering of Aesthetics." In *The Comparative Aspect on Literature.* Edited by Clayton Koelb and Susan Noakes. Ithaca: Cornell University Press, 1988.

————. *The Legend of Freud.* Minneapolis: University of Minnesota Press, 1982.

White, Hayden. *Tropics of Discourse.* Baltimore: Johns Hopkins University Press, 1978.

————. *Metahistory: The Historical Imagination in Nineteenth-Century Europe.* Baltimore: Johns Hopkins University Press, 1973.

Wilden, Anthony. *Speech and Language in Psychoanalysis.* Baltimore: Johns Hopkins University Press, 1968.

Yerushalmi, Yosef Hayim. *Freud's Moses: Judaism Terminable and Interminable.* New Haven: Yale University Press, 1991.

————. *Zakhor: Jewish History and Jewish Memory.* New York: Schocken, 1989.

Žižek, Slavoj. *The Sublime Object of Ideology.* London, New York: Verso, 1989.

Index